David Swift is an academic and writer based in London. His research interests span a range of issues relating to twentieth-century history and contemporary politics. He has written for several traditional and digital media such as *The Times*, the *Independent*, *Standpoint*, the *Spectator*, *The Jewish Chronicle* and *UnHerd*, as well as socialist blogs such as *LabourList*, the *Fabian Review*, and *Progress Online*.

The Identity Myth

Why We Need to Embrace Our Differences to Beat Inequality

David Swift

CONSTABLE

CONSTABLE

First published in Great Britain in 2022 by Constable
This paperback edition published in 2023 by Constable

1 3 5 7 9 10 8 6 4 2

A CIP catalogue record for this book
is available from the British Library.

ISBN: 978-0-34913-534-2

Typeset in Minion Pro by Hewer Text UK Ltd, Edinburgh
Printed and bound in Great Britain by Clays Ltd, Elcograf, S.p.A.

Papers used by Constable are from well-managed forests and other responsible sources.

Constable
An imprint of
Little, Brown Book Group
Carmelite House
50 Victoria Embankment
London EC4Y 0DZ

An Hachette UK Company

www.hachette.co.uk

www.littlebrown.co.uk

This book is dedicated to my grandparents,
Betty and John Suffield and Ann and Stanley Swift.

Contents

Preface

Around the world, culture wars waged on the margins of our society have come to divide populations and poison discourse. What is usually called the culture war is fought largely on the periphery by professional activists, career demagogues and opportunist charlatans. Many totemic 'culture war' issues are not particularly contested, and have either broad consensus or are of little concern to most people. And yet these culture warriors have a disproportionate influence on our politics and national discourse.

In particular, issues around 'identity' allow extremists and bad faith actors – on both the Left and Right – to rise to prominence, power and financial success on the backs of people they don't really understand and often despise. In many cases these identities have become powerful signifiers in their own right, detached from any material realities and instrumentalised, idealised and imitated. Their boundaries are policed and their significance exploited, so that the identities themselves matter more than the lives of the individuals concerned.

These powerful identities can be used for various purposes, from the commercial to the aesthetic to the political. This trend has accelerated in recent years, with increasing precarity and evermore obvious inequality fuelling popular anger, and the internet acting as a perfect mechanism for the construction of identity myths.

In his *Contribution to the Critique of Political Economy* (1859), Karl Marx outlined the idea of a material 'base' and politico-cultural 'superstructure'. According to this formula, a material reality – wealth, income, occupation – determined your politics, leisure habits, tastes, and how you made sense of the world.

Today, the importance of material deprivation, in terms of threats to life, health and prosperity, are as acute as ever. But the identities apparently generated by these realities are increasingly detached from material circumstances. At the same time, different identities are needlessly conflated through a process of reeling off a list of -isms and -phobias, as when someone says they are fighting against classism, racism, sexism, ableism, homophobia, transphobia, Islamophobia, etc., or when 'people of colour, women, LGBTQIA+ folks, disabled folks, the neurodiverse', etc. are lumped together, as though these groups all somehow have something in common with one another. This process is not just inappropriate but obscures the specific nature of problems being faced by particular people, and makes political victories for such people even harder to achieve.

As this book will show, politics and solidarity are complicated and convoluted *within* specific identity groups, never mind between different ones, and this 'Roll Call' of -isms and -phobias, this conflation of vastly disparate and distinct groups, is unhelpful and needs to end.

This book covers the four different kinds of identity most susceptible to these trends. Firstly, class. Debates around class have been given fresh intensity by the changing economy and apparent political realignment in many developed nations. Increasingly, conservative journalists and politicians invoke the language of class – specifically, that of the working class – to validate their agendas. At the same time, many on the Left decry outdated notions of class and claim our definitions need to be recalibrated. Part I discusses exactly who or what we should consider to be 'working class' in the twenty-first century, and what types of politics and culture could best be said to characterise this group.

With 'race', calls to address racial inequality at a national and global level and examine the histories that have led to it have received greater prominence in recent years. These are countered by voices heralding the decline of anti-racist attitudes in white-majority societies, and the existence of an increasingly diverse political and business class. Part II considers national difference, ethnic and religious inequalities within multi-racial countries, and the political and cultural misuses of 'race'.

Part III is concerned with sex: how the idea of manhood or masculinity can be misused, whether to argue that apparently 'male' traits are inevitable, or that 'toxic masculinity' can be to blame for many of the problems pursuant to men. As with masculinity, issues around womanhood are also contested, with right-wing and even ethnonationalist politicians donning the mantle of feminism, while other feminists debate whether their solidarity should extend to trans women. This leads to a debate about who should even be counted as a woman and whether some women don't count, either due to their politics or their biology. LGBT identity is likewise contested, with some positing a moral obligation to reject 'heteronormative' conformities as well as conservative politics.

The final section, Part IV, moves on to consider another 'misused' and contested identity. The idea of 'youth' itself and whole generations of young people are either held up as a cautionary tale, an example to criticise progressive ideas and policies, or else assumed to be the future saviours of such politics. Apparent 'youthful' attitudes on politics, the internet, social media and celebrity are misused in the politics and punditry of others from diverse perspectives and for various reasons.

This book considers how the boundaries of different identities are policed, and how different versions of the same identity can be deployed to different ends. Ultimately, the argument is not just that 'identities are more complex' than they appear, but rather that there are more important commonalities, specifically around poverty, inequality, lack of resources and lack of opportunities. The identity myths are a cultural trend resulting from globalisation, neoliberalism and the mediation of cynical actors such as corporations and mass media. This book calls for an end to the obsession with identity, hierarchies of victimhood and quick emotional responses in favour of structural analysis and an appreciation of complexity.

Part I

Class

The word disabled, Diogenes held, ought to be applied not to the deaf or blind, but to those who have no wallet.

Diogenes Laertius, *Lives of the Eminent Philosophers*

When it comes to class, there is little identity myth-making around 'middle-classness'. While plenty of people like to disparage middle-classness, it currently lacks the cultural cachet and political potency of 'working class'. That's why this section is concerned with the latter; if I were writing this in the 1990s, there would be a lot to say about the shifting definitions and political appropriations of the term 'middle class', but from the perspective of the 2020s this seems an irrelevance – the political developments of recent years have been based on loud and often angry contestations over exactly who, or what, is 'working class'.

In the wake of 2016, with the Brexit referendum and the election of Donald Trump, the political Right discovered a newfound interest in class, and in class snobbery. Suddenly left-wing academics, journalists and politicians found their every action and intervention met by accusations that they were motivated by hatred of 'the working class' or of 'working-class values'. Across the world, conservatives, nationalists and authoritarians have made hay by posing as champions of 'the working class' against a caricatured 'metropolitan liberal elite'. Although the

1

picture varies between nations, this constructed working class is habitually patriotic, hostile to immigrants, resistant to change, and generally suspicious of anything redolent of book-learning, latte-sipping, big-city folk. This working class is likely male, in middle age or older, and predominantly based in small towns or rural areas. Some of these newly enthused class warriors, attempting to undermine efforts at securing social justice for women, BAME and LGBT people, pit the struggles of these groups against those of a homogenised 'working class'. Some go as far as to say that class snobbery is a sort of more respectable racism.

In fairness, there are some on the Left who – through accident or design – create a dichotomy between representation and redistribution, and caricature the 'white working class' as innately hostile to gays and foreigners. And there is a prominent strain among many middle-class white leftists of a kind of handwringing, apologetic insecurity that can lead to a snobbishness and class resentment. For evidence of this, look no further than the sculpture of a beer-bellied, bald-headed white man in a string vest that was placed on the plinth of the toppled statue of slave trader Edward Colston in Bristol in 2020. But this does not mean that the newfound interest of conservatives in the working class is somehow genuine; not least because they do not show much interest in policies to help working-class people in a meaningful way. It is also pretty disingenuous for right-wingers to claim that some working-class people might have their sensibilities hurt by comments on social media, after years of branding those who claim the same about other groups as 'snowflakes'.

Irrespective of the cynicism of conservatives reaping the electoral benefits of the social, economic and cultural disenfranchisement caused in no little part by their own historic and present policies, this class stereotype is as false as it is calculated. Whichever way you're inclined to define the term working class – by income, occupation, wealth, accent or any other variable – you will be left with a group that is multi-racial, multi-generational and has a varied range of views on political issues, including various culture war totems. And yet, the likes of Trump and Johnson and Netanyahu and Erdoğan and Putin and Bolsonaro must be on to something: around the world, in diverse economies, societies and polities, these kinds of authoritarian populists owe much of their success to voters who stand to benefit little from their economic policies.

The apparent support of working-class voters for parties of the Right has led some on the Left to redefine that term in ways that are equally dubious, and sometimes similarly cynical. According to this school of thought, the 'traditional' working class is no longer fit to be described as such, having lost their right to the title due to their age, homeownership and political views. According to this school of thought, the 'real' working class are young, metropolitan, private renters who remain overwhelmingly supportive of the Labour or Democratic parties – conveniently abnegating those parties of the need to worry about losing the working-class vote. The first thing to say about this argument is that it is a little too convenient; you don't have to be the most sceptical person in the world to suspect that it would not be advanced if the class-political alignment of a few decades ago still prevailed.

Nonetheless, leaving politics and culture to one side for a moment, it is worth focusing purely on economics to ascertain exactly who we should define as working class, and for what reasons. A key problem with this aim is that the term is impossibly broad, and with poorly defined borders. The term 'working class' could include people in the most desperate circumstances, sleeping on the streets or in emergency accommodation, going hungry in between visits to foodbanks, and also people far removed from such acute distress, with a good job and disposable income – who might nonetheless feel hopeless, dispirited and disenfranchised.

Chapter 1

What Is the Working Class?

One of the many contradictory things about the designation 'working class' in modern Britain is how it is both coveted and evaded. Despite the 'demonisation' of the working class by right-wingers until the Brexit referendum, supposed aspects of working-class culture have long been appropriated, from football to tracksuits to the word 'mate'. *The Times* columnist Deborah Ross describes queueing to enter Waitrose during the middle of the COVID-19 pandemic, when 'everyone greets the security guard who manages the queue with a "cheers, mate" or "ta, mate" and also "all right, mate?"' She recalls the fear when:

> on one occasion the guard tried to strike up a conversation with the shopper first in line, at which point you could see the panic behind that shopper's eyes – 'oh my God, I don't know any more of this non-middle-class speak!'; 'what if I'm asked about *Mrs Brown's Boys*!' – and that shopper had to shuffle from foot to foot and shrug until finally being allowed inside to find safety.[1]

Most people, when asked, say they do not belong to a class – and this has not changed since the 1960s – but when forced to choose, roughly 60 per cent self-describe as working class, and 40 per cent as middle class – a ratio unchanged since 1983.[2]

A problem stemming from the breadth of the term is that it can be used by people from widely different backgrounds to claim the same kudos and recognition. I was recently having a conversation with a friend of mine, raised like me in suburban south Liverpool, his then-girlfriend's family live in a working-class area more redolent of the type of imagery normally associated with Liverpool. My friend told me that he couldn't really understand how the two areas could be in the same city; that the divides within Liverpool were much greater than he had ever assumed growing up; and how sometimes he felt like a bit of a fraud claiming the identity of a Scouser, and all of the positive and negative associations that came with it.

In many ways the designation 'working class', like other designations in this book – black, white, Asian, gay, trans, etc. – has more utility when used by other people, such as politicians, journalists and academics, than it does for the group to which it ostensibly refers. When Tony Blair learned that Alan Johnson MP – a former postman and trade union official who went on to hold five different ministerial positions – had fathered three children by the time he was twenty, he is said to have exclaimed: 'Gosh, you really are working class, aren't you?' Many have interpreted this as a patronising aside but, in fairness to Blair, after three years at Oxford and decades in Labour activism and politics, he would have heard more pointedly dropped aitches than the casting director of *My Fair Lady*, and become so used to the parents-were-from-working-class-backgrounds-but-became-teachers-or-social-workers that make up so much of the activist base of the Left that it must have been a genuine shock to meet someone who actually walked the walk.

According to the British Social Attitudes Survey, almost half (47 per cent) of Britons in middle-class professional and managerial jobs identify as working class. This is not always due to their parents' backgrounds: one quarter of those people whose parents had professional occupations also identify as working class.[3] One recent academic paper found that of seventy-five actors, architects, accountants and television professionals investigated, thirty-six of those from middle-class backgrounds identified as working class.[4] The researchers attributed this to the need for an 'origin story', attributing their rise to meritocratic advancement and hard work. One of the academics involved, Sam Friedman, told the *Guardian* that 'such misidentification was higher among the actors and television professionals we spoke to. This is not coincidental; there is arguably a particular market for downplaying privilege in these professions.'[5]

The desire of people in objectively middle-class occupations, with middle-class incomes and tastes, to appropriate the 'authenticity' they feel comes with the working-class designation has a mirror image in the status anxiety of many people from underprivileged occupations, and this has important intersections with race: the Jamaican-born cultural theorist Stuart Hall used to tell an anecdote of how, when he first moved to the UK to study at Oxford, his mother would anxiously enquire: 'I do hope they don't think you're an immigrant over there?' Hall was from a prominent middle-class family, and the thought of white Britons assuming he was just another West Indian migrant worker caused a great deal of upset for Mrs Hall.[6]

As Mrs Hall well knew, location and environment can affect how someone's class is perceived. Every September, thousands of students from northern cities descend on elite universities in the south and, surrounded by people from the Home Counties, have a similar experience to Stuart Hall; they have gone from being a bog-standard middle-class eighteen-year-old to being 'the northern one'. Many of the black students at these institutions undergo the same process: although from perfectly ordinary middle-class backgrounds, they are now the 'black' one in an overwhelmingly white environment. The *New Statesman* journalist and Oxford graduate Stephen Bush recounts how he 'became black at university. Not because I experienced any racism worth talking about but simply because for the first time in my life, anyone describing me could mostly get away with "black".[7]

As with race, class can be 'played' and manipulated in some circumstances to the advantage of someone perceived as 'working class'. James Baldwin wrote that he knew all too well 'what Americans saw when they looked at me and this allowed me to play endless and sinister variations on the role which they had assigned me'.[8] Speaking of the character Tyree in Richard Wright's novel *The Long Dream* (1958), who likewise manipulates the white southerners who fear and revere him, Paul Gilroy writes that 'the scope he enjoys to master [the white people] cannot match the power of the institutional order they control, but it is certainly significant'.[9] For some this will be a discombobulating and unpleasant experience; for others it is exhilarating. Likewise, in *Poverty Safari*, his recent memoir of growing up poor in Pollack, a deprived part of Glasgow, the rapper Darren McGarvey recalls the reaction of a group of 'posh' kids to his presence in a fancy part of Glasgow's West End. Used to fearing for himself in most surroundings, he realised that these kids actually feared *him*, and 'experienced a mix of pride at being feared and resentment at feeling misunderstood'.[10]

This is an important element of the current 'kudos' attached to being working class, and to being 'black'; it does not come with great structural or material advantage, and may serve to perpetuate inequalities; but nonetheless has power and importance in our culture.

In July 2015, during the second night of the Durham Miners' Gala, I was smoking outside the County Hotel and talking with an old trade union organiser about the changing nature of Labour activists (essentially that there were fewer people like him and more people like me). I mentioned that the recently retired John Cummings, formerly the MP for Easington, had worked for years as a miner before entering politics, and how unusual it would be for someone from his background to become an MP today. At this the old geezer said dryly, 'Well, John was a pit electrician, he never worked at the coal face.' This reminded me of being told that former workers on the Liverpool docks used to get quite snooty when Len McCluskey, for several years leader of the UK's largest trade union, was referred to as a former docker, as he had been a ship's planner – a white-collar job. These two incidents drummed home to me one inescapable truth: there is always someone prolier than thou. Just as two people I always assumed to be emblematic of northern working-class labourers had people who felt they were basically middle-class aesthetes, so there is no one you can find that someone else doesn't think is a bit posh.

US Congresswoman Alexandria Ocasio-Cortez is a child of immigrants who through education, ability and hard graft ascended to the House of Representatives at the tender age of twenty-nine. Yet her claims to working-class status chiefly come from her previous stints as a waitress and bartender; in virtually all of her speeches and media she alluded to her parents' immigrant background, and in many of them she emphasised that she can empathise with the working class, as she used to 'wait tables'. The problem is, so has nearly everybody. Apart from those who came from an upper-middle-class background or grander, virtually everyone has had at least one temporary job where they worked in a shop or behind a bar or in a restaurant. The key word is temporary. Doing something to pay your way through university, or to support yourself in the short term, is clearly not the same as someone doing that job for life, with no option to do anything else.

Lots of young people today who thought they might be in certain jobs temporarily are discovering that the career they have studied for won't be an option – and yet they still have to pay off their student loans. Nonetheless, people with large amounts of social, cultural and sometimes financial (albeit held by their parents) capital, who are best placed to thrive in the future economy, are not in the same position as those who have lost their careers, or never had the opportunity to aspire to have one, and are forced to eke out the rest of their days in unsecure, unfulfilling work. At the same time, we cannot blame people, or suggest they are inauthentic, for not doing the jobs their parents did, not least because those jobs may not exist any more. Furthermore, very often their parents worked hard so that their kids would not have to do the same jobs.

This contributes to an argument that has gained traction recently on the Left: since incomes have shrunk in real terms across developed economies in recent decades (and particularly since the 2008 financial crisis), increasing lifespans, rising property prices and mounting debt have resulted in a disparity in wealth, if not necessarily income, between different groups of people who might be called working class, and this is most evident in the wealth disparities between generations. In the UK, people aged between sixty-five and seventy-four now hold more wealth than everyone under forty-five, even though the latter group is twice the size of the former.[11] Most of this wealth, especially among poorer pensioners, comes in the form of property, specifically their home.

If you own your home, you not only have security of tenure but, with mortgage rates at historic lows, it is likely to be much more affordable than renting privately. Furthermore, your property not only provides you with a valuable asset to borrow against in times of need or to fund possible opportunities, but is an appreciating asset for your familial wealth, which will transfer to your children, either through inheritance or through assistance in buying their own home. Many other indicators of hardship, such as vulnerability to violence, also correlate with homeownership: children aged between ten and fifteen who live in social housing are 37 per cent more likely to be a victim of violence than children of owner-occupiers.[12] Contrastingly, for private renters, insecurity of tenure and ever-increasing rents

– for many constituting over half of their income – are coupled with myriad indignities and obstacles imposed by landlords and rental agencies.

Nonetheless, there are several important reasons why income, rather than wealth or homeownership, should be the primary economic criterion for discerning class. There are clear correlations between income and location and life expectancy, mental and physical health, vulnerability to violence, propensity to alcohol and drug abuse, life opportunities, and optimism about the future. As Kerry Hudson writes in *Lowborn*, her memoir of growing up in poverty: 'Income affects everything, from your likelihood of mental illness or substance abuse to domestic violence, low educational attainment, even the number of metal fillings in your teeth.'[13] The British parliamentary constituency worst affected in the first wave of COVID-19 was the post-industrial area Penistone and Stocksbridge, with a deathrate of 129.5 per 100,000; this was eight times higher than London, which had a lower death rate per capita even at the peak of the virus.[14]

According to Claire Ainsley – until recently director of the anti-poverty organisation the Joseph Rowntree Foundation – mental health issues feature more strongly in lower income groups, and those with poor mental health are more likely than those with physical ailments alone to be trapped in precarious and low-paid work. Furthermore, adults in the lowest-income households, where income is less than £10,000 per year, are more than 50 per cent more likely than the average person to be a victim of violence, robbery or theft.[15] Where you live, what you earn and how you earn it affects your safety, day-to-day lifestyle and mental state with far greater regularity and predictability than housing tenure.

If we use occupation, income and location as metrics to decide who is or isn't working class, this leaves us with a very diverse group. As Ainsley puts it, 'if there ever was a "typical" working-class person, there certainly isn't now'.[16] This new working class is 'multi-ethnic, comprised of people living off low to middle incomes, and likely to be occupied in service sector jobs like catering, social care or retail'.[17] Ainsley's book uses research conducted by Mike Savage's team at the London School of Economics, which was published as *The Great British Class Survey* in 2013. In Savage's study, 14 per cent of the population are in what he calls the 'traditional working class'. This group has an average age of sixty-six, is 91 per cent white, and has an average household income of £13,000 per year; well below the national median, which reached £29,600 in 2019.[18] However, they hold more accumulated wealth than the three groups Savage calls the 'new afflu-ent', 'emerging service workers' and 'precariat'. The traditional work-ing class are likely to enjoy a reasonable level of 'highbrow' cultural capital, such as museums and galleries, but are more limited in the number of people they know outside of their own class compared to other groups.

Savage puts 19 per cent of the population into the 'emerging service workers' category, who have an average age of thirty-two, are 21 per cent minority ethnic, have the highest levels of cultural capital and considerable social networks, and are, in Ainsley's words, 'much more likely than other groups to use social media, enjoy contemporary culture and take part in sport and fitness'. Finally, 15 per cent are clas-sified as 'precariat', who are lacking in income, economic and cultural capital, 'but they are culturally engaged with social networks in their community'.[19] This gives a total of 48 per cent of the British popula-tion categorised as 'working class' according to Savage's formula. The other half of the population is broken down to the 'elite', who consti-tute 6 per cent; the 'established middle class' at 25 per cent; the 'tech-nical middle class', also at 6 per cent; and 'new affluent workers', who make up 15 per cent.

One's perception of class often depends on how far you are exposed to people from other social groups. This is one important way in which gender difference affects what it means to be working class: although there are exceptions, overwhelmingly the bulk of caring, whether for children or elderly or disabled relatives, is done by women, and through their roles as carers they come into frequent contact with the state. As such, they are often on the sharp end of prejudice, class hatred or the cold, officious indifference of bureaucracy.

The sociologist Lisa McKenzie has conducted an extensive analysis of class on the St Ann's estate in Nottingham, where she lives. St Ann's is a traditional working-class neighbourhood, and is notably ethnically diverse, with 16 per cent Asian, 14 per cent black and 10 per cent of mixed ethnicity according to the 2011 census. One of the women McKenzie spoke to only became aware of how her estate was depicted after she was told by social workers that her children would be safer in another area.[20]

In contrast, most men in St Ann's have very little contact with anyone from outside the neighbourhood, especially with the benefits system and social services.[21] In order to avoid the shame and loss of face associated with being poor, men can turn their back on the world of bourgeois values, and take refuge in other systems that provide respect and validity; men can earn money through the informal economy, or even through crime. These are options usually not open to women stereotyped as bad mothers. Another of McKenzie's interviewees, who has an autistic son, spoke of her being the focus of so much unwanted negative attention. This is something also faced by middle-class women, but they do not face the judgement of being representative of an entire class.[22]

Despite suggestions that overeducated and underemployed graduates are 'the new working class', there are clear correlations between poor educational outcomes and poverty. For example, only 4 per cent of the precariat have a degree, compared to 56 per cent of the elite and 40 per cent of the established middle class.[23] For the new working class, as Ainsley says, work tends to be 'non-graduate, less well paid, difficult to progress in, and a number will be not working due to health or caring'.[24] Even today, a 'university degree is generally a signifier of upward mobility' and, nationwide, degree holding is still a rarity: in only 99 out of 346 council wards do more than one-third of people hold degrees.[25] Unfortunately, for children born into the poorest households, as they get older the educational disparities between them and their middle-class contemporaries increase. There is a big deterioration in attainment by the poorest children between junior school, where the difference between the richest and poorest neighbourhoods is less stark, and senior school, when it becomes a chasm.[26]

At the 2017 general election, Labour promised to abolish student tuition fees, but made no pledge to reverse Conservative welfare cuts. This proved to be good politics and secured the votes of many students – and the parents of current and probable future students. At the same time, the Tories were robbed of a useful line of attack against the party as being soft on 'welfare scroungers', while Jeremy Corbyn's socialist credentials meant that many assumed that Labour *had* promised to repeal the cuts. Nonetheless this could be seen as a shift in focus for the party away from 'the working class' – however construed – and towards graduates. Whatever the electoral considerations behind this move, it would be a betrayal of the party's founding aims; underemployed graduates are not the new working class, however convenient it might be to pretend otherwise.

Anger, often directed at the powerful and sometimes focused elsewhere, is a driving theme of McKenzie's analysis of the people of St Ann's, alongside a feeling that they had been abandoned by politicians of all stripes who were only interested in lining their own pockets. This sentiment is understandable, given the decline in interest exhibited by the UK's political parties in talking about class. In their book *The New Politics of Class*, Geoffrey Evans and James Tilley reveal that the election manifestos of both main parties have seen a decline in references to the working class over the past forty years. Political scientists argue that the decline in working-class MPs has affected support for the Labour Party among the working class, and that working-class voters are less likely to trust the wealthy or find them approachable.[27] Those who see themselves as working class, regardless of their material status, are 'significantly' more likely to distrust MPs on the whole than those who do not self-describe as working class.[28]

Back in 1964, fully 90 per cent of voters described the Conservatives as a middle-class party, and 85 per cent said Labour were a working-class party. By 2015, 88 per cent said the same of the Tories, but only 38 per cent identified Labour as a working-class party. In fact, almost half of people surveyed described Labour as for the middle classes.[29] This may be an electoral problem for Labour, as while 'people in working-class occupations that see Labour as a working-class party are always more likely to support Labour' – thus suggesting that residual loyalty can win votes for Labour if they are still perceived as representing the working class – increasingly few people do see them as such.[30]

In the 1980s there was a 5 per cent difference in turnout between middle- and working-class people; by 2017 this had risen to almost 30 per cent.[31] Rather than attribute the decline of the class-based voting that was dominant in twentieth-century Britain on the decline of class as a relevant issue, Evans and Tilley blame the politicians: 'classes, and particularly the working class', have not 'lost their social cohesion and distinctiveness ... Neither the objective realities of class, nor the political attitudes that these objective realities produce have changed greatly.' Although people's policy views have not changed, 'the policy choices the parties offer have'.[32]

It is for this reason that the working class, whoever they are, should be central to politics, particularly left-wing politics. The French author Édouard Louis argues that 'politics is what separates some populations, whose lives are supported, nurtured, protected, from other populations, who are exposed to death, to persecution, to murder'.[33] Although it might be convenient to pretend otherwise, graduates living in big cities and paying sky-high rents are not the new working class. As Evans and Tilley conclude, class differences today are in terms of 'resources, risks, opportunities, and educational achievement'.[34] Although their position doesn't look great at the moment, people with academic qualifications and high levels of cultural capital are the best placed to succeed in the economy of the twenty-first century. Being on low wages at any given time is not necessarily a long-term problem as 'for lots of people it will be temporary, and many on low pay will be living in a household with a higher earner' or have parents in that category.[35]

As Ainsley says, 'from education to immigration to housing, it is clear that the interests of each person have not been given equal consideration'.[36] And yet at the same time 'the working class' has never been more politically potent as a term, among politicians of all stripes, but also on social media, in academia and in the popular imagination. Why, despite the overt appeal of both Conservative and Labour, Democrat and Republican, have the interests of the working class not been advanced with the same force that politicians have seized the mantle of tribunes of the working class?

Enter the Atomists: downwardly mobile postgraduates and the 'new working class'

The currently out-of-fashion libertarian trend within conservatism believes in a future economy in which people would be atomised economic units, hiring themselves out hither and thither as freelancers in the knowledge economy. The insecurity this would entail would be mitigated by the fact that people could just move to wherever skills were in demand.[37] On the Right, this tendency is best exemplified by Conservative MP Liz Truss, who exalts the 'Airbnb-ing, Deliveroo-eating, Uber-riding' gig economy as the future, and urges the rest of us to get with the programme. Yet this vision of atomised utopia, an economy of gig workers juggling several jobs, working as and when they please, and living wherever they can find work, is not confined to right-wingers. Some commentators on the Left implicitly echo Truss's views, and roll their eyes at those who talk of the importance of continuity, stability and community, depicting the latter as fundamentally naive and possibly sinister. This vision of the future is one built around and for city-living, train-riding, highly mobile graduates. These Atomistic leftists would argue that the key difference between their version and that of Truss – for they seem pretty similar at first glance – is that their world involves labour rights, robust welfare provision and an economically interventionist state, but it is hard to imagine how the political will for such a communitarian economy can be reconciled with such an atomised and mobile society.

Many have pointed out that those characterised as 'anywhere' (people with liberal, internationalist values, who are often highly mobile and do not usually value stability and continuity) are often highly public spirited and community minded. There is something in that argument, but it is worth reading the following from Malakaï Sargeant about the impact of gentrification on his part of Hackney:

I won't lie and suggest that there is no longer a sense of community in Hackney, because there definitely is – among the white middle class who have infiltrated and colonised all of the places I grew to love . . . Places where people have spent their entire lives living and working are rapidly losing their identity, and are becoming replicas of other bougie-fied areas where the white middle class have Christopher Columbus-ed entire neighbourhoods by claiming them as cool, telling all their mates to come and forming their own communities within them, rather than engaging with the existing community who, more often than not, lose out economically and become displaced once their area begins to be infiltrated by self-interested 'young professionals'.[38]

Here Sargeant makes a forceful case that 'anywhere' can indeed be community-minded, but the type of community they wish to create often comes at the expense of the existing community, with negative implications for the diversity and cultural and political cohesion of the area.

Assumptions about the atomised, highly mobile economy of the future are closely tied to attempts to rebrand private renters, post-graduates and freelancers with portfolio careers as the *real* working class, a mantle its traditional bearers are no longer fit to wear due to their homeownership and, implicitly, their political views. The academic Joe Kennedy argues that we need to recalibrate how we see class 'in an employment ecology of low-paid clerical work and precarious or zero-hour contracts . . . with so few opportunities opening in journalism "proper" for those who don't have a nepotistic way in, and with permanent academic work hard to find . . . a new category of young, pissed-off intellectuals is emerging'.[39]

This is misguided for several reasons. Firstly, it does not reflect socio-economic realities; secondly, it is politically cynical, an all-too-convenient attempt to seize the moral affirmation of the label 'working class' for people who already vote Labour and have the right cultural politics; and practically, such a constituency is too geographically concentrated to deliver majorities under a first-past-the-post electoral system. As the political scientists Robert Ford and Maria Sobolewska note, graduates live mainly around other graduates (and non-graduates tend to live around fellow non-graduates), and there is a particularly stark divide in educational levels in the UK, compared to the US where for some time it has been common for working-class school leavers to go on to at least one or two years of college.[40] If elections were to pitch younger, graduate, private renters against older homeowning non-graduates, then there can only be one winner.

Furthermore, there is no guarantee that the present economic disadvantage of many young people will persist in perpetuity. They are, after all, best placed to benefit from the likely economy of the twenty-first century. Rising prosperity, the coming digital economy, a sizable increase in housing supply – or, more likely, reforms to private renting to make it as attractive as owner-occupation – may rob these 'pissed-off intellectuals' of their redistributive instincts and see them become more economically conservative as they age, just like every single other generation in human history. Then, a Conservative or Liberal party with all the right cultural politics might steal their political allegiance.

None of this is to downplay the many struggles facing young graduates across a whole range of issues, from housing to jobs. They are especially acute for young people living in certain big cities, and in specific sectors such as the media and academia. Clearly, academia is vastly underfunded, and there are far too many PhD students competing for too few academic posts: a 2010 Royal Society report found that of every two hundred people completing a PhD, only seven will get a permanent academic post, and only one will become a professor – and I would assume the situation has become worse since then. These two issues are related, as cash-hungry universities greatly expanded their numbers of postgraduates in order to secure valuable fees and cheap teaching assistants, without thought for their future employment.[41] While there are many problems with our universities that could be solved, or at least ameliorated, with more cash, nonetheless there are also too many people completing PhDs.

This is not to endorse the proud philistinism that increasingly characterises conservatism in Britain and the United States, but there is a tendency among left-leaning people in academia and the media to associate conservatism with stupidity and the pursuit of wealth with conservatism. However, a large number of highly intelligent, well-read and erudite people who might have had successful academic careers (if intellectual capability were the only criterion for success) deliberately and wisely choose to pursue private sector careers. During the height of the COVID-19 pandemic, one disappointed PhD holder lamented on his blog that he was 'qualified to do exactly two jobs [university teaching and writing], and I have every reason to suspect that within a few months' time these jobs will for all intents and purposes no longer exist'. Of course, that is exactly wrong. He is qualified to do several jobs, or could easily achieve qualification for them with a little retraining, including in secondary education, the charity sector, social work, law, the civil service and all kinds of sales-recruitment-administrative work.

What the blogger meant to say was that they were the only two jobs he *wanted* to do, and he had been working towards for several years. In this respect, he has a point. A portion of the blame must be levelled at universities who have churned out PhDs and journalism postgraduates knowing full well how dire the prospects were. Having said that, many of them do indeed attempt to make it plain at the outset to their students how few of them are likely to secure a permanent job in their chosen industry, and yet plenty of those students, being fully aware of the odds, nonetheless believed they would be one of those who defied probability and who made it. In this sense they share something with the tech pioneers of Silicon Valley, which indicates how far the neoliberal, entrepreneurial spirit of the tech tycoons has permeated the broader culture and been absorbed by many millennials, despite their socialistic facade.

This is not the only way. *The Times* columnist Robert Crampton – an Oxford graduate, as is his wife Nicola Almond – felt compelled to write a column defending the decision of his son to leave school at sixteen and train as a chef. He pointed out that cooking had always been a passion for his lad, it was a valuable skill to have, being 'useful, portable, satisfying', and – given the persistence of human desire for well-cooked food and the difficulty of designing an AI system to replicate the invention and subtlety of a human chef – 'enduring'. Nonetheless, when they told their friends (middle-class London professional types) about their son's vocation, they reacted 'as though we've announced our son has decided to join a fundamentalist cult in Texas and we're trying to put a brave face on it'. One person even asked whether it was 'fair to "write him off" at such an early age', while others pulled patronising, sympathetic faces.[42]

Lest this be mistaken for a Norman Tebbit-style get-on-your-bike bromide (although ironically this should be appreciated by the Atomists, given their usual love of cycling and economic migration), I am not blaming the lack of jobs in certain sectors on the people trying to find work in those industries. Nor am I saying that people trying to find these jobs should just give up, not least because those most likely to benefit from that are those with familial wealth and connections to fall back on. However, I am saying that we need to stop taking the experience of specific young people in expensive cities and competitive industries as representative of an entire generation.

If there genuinely were no jobs and no future prospects of steady employment for young graduates; if mass homeownership was fundamental to a good life, rather than an innovation of the past century that found its greatest advocate in no less a socialist hero than Margaret Thatcher; if childless freelance writers and temporary lecturers genuinely were in the same position as immigrants of the same age with several kids forced to drive an Uber or ride a Deliveroo bike every waking hour, or middle-aged Brits with no qualifications and no prospect of ever leaving the Amazon warehouse, then I'd be singing a different tune. But this is not the case – and downwardly mobile graduates are not 'the new working class'.

*   *   *

A common complaint from the Atomist school is that only certain types of people seem to qualify as 'working class'. Or at least, only certain types of working-class people are considered by politicians and the media to have opinions that matter. Specifically, they allege that white people in post-industrial towns are held up as the personification of 'working class', while black and brown people in big cities are excluded from this definition, and their opinions not coveted in the same manner. There is some truth in this, but a key reason for the focus on white people in post-industrial communities is that their political allegiances are in flux, with dramatic consequences for the politics of Western democracies. If – and in fact it might be when – black people in big cities start to vote Conservative and Republican in big numbers, you can guarantee there will be an avalanche of think pieces, documentaries and book deals devoted to the phenomenon; I hope to be well-positioned to get at least one book out of it myself.

For now, 'traditional Labour and Democrat voters continue to vote Labour and Democratic' is not a story, hence the lack of vox pops asking black people in Lewisham or Detroit how they will be voting. But 'traditional Labour and Democratic voters are shifting to the Conservative and Republican parties for the first time, with profound consequences' *is* a story, hence the media, academic and political focus on a certain type of working-class person over the past few years. Liberals and leftists should be animated by trying to understand why this is happening and how to stop it, rather than pointing out that plenty of historically right-wing constituencies are still right-wing. At the same time, as we will see in Part II, the opinions of many Nigerians in Plaistow or Poles in Ealing – on race, gender, LGBT issues and, perhaps surprisingly, immigration – would make Barry the Brexit voter from Bolsover seem like Judith Butler.

Aside from political factors, there are many social, economic and cultural reasons why the working class of post-industrial areas are more disadvantaged than those in big cities. Having spent most of the past thirty-three years living in Liverpool and inner London, I am under no illusions that the streets of big cities are paved with gold – yet there are several structural advantages benefitting even the poorest and most disadvantaged big-city inhabitants. This is perhaps most notable in education: in inner London, 45 per cent of those eligible for free school meals at age fifteen are in university by age nineteen – barely lower than the 53 per cent of kids not on free school meals who go to university.[43] And nor is this confined to London: growing up close to a university has a direct correlation with attending one. According to the University of Oxford, there's a 1 per cent drop in higher education attendance for every 6 km you live from a university. This could be one reason why most BAME Britons are actually overrepresented at elite universities, as they tend to live in large conurbations near higher education institutions.[44] This is not the case for kids from northern towns, who are often some distance from unis, so a British Pakistani boy from Burnley or Batley is more disadvantaged in this respect than one from Birmingham or Barking.[45]

Shortage of nurses and doctors is particularly acute for non-metropolitan healthcare providers, and one report found that people in medium-sized towns need to travel twice as far as those in cities to reach their nearest hospital, and people in small towns and villages three or four times as far. Although these disparities are not as pronounced in terms of access to GPs, dentists and pharmacies, the further you move away from cities the longer it takes to access these services, and this will only become more challenging given the aging populations of towns.[46] Likewise, while banks, pubs and high-street shops have been closing across the country, the effect of this is mitigated in cities and exaggerated in towns and villages. Similarly, given the vast disparities in arts and culture funding – the Arts Council spends £7 in Islington for every £1 it spends in former coalfield areas[47] – poor people in big cities tend to have free access to museums, art galleries and libraries, which their fellow citizens in post-industrial areas might not.[48] (Although it is debatable whether or not the poorer citizens of big cities get to actually enjoy these facilities; I remember my shock at reading a few years ago that the rapper Dizzee Rascal first saw the tower housing Big Ben when he went into central London at age eighteen to sign a record deal – despite living a few miles away in Bow his entire life.)

Apart from these structural disadvantages, possibly even more significant are the intangible problems of non-metropolitan Britain. One of the most important reasons even relatively disadvantaged people are better off in cities is the much higher age profile of towns and rural areas: young people leave, and often don't come back. Older people living outside big conurbations are more likely to live apart from their family, whereas people in big cities are likely to see their family more often.[49] People in towns – irrespective of their wealth or ethnicity – are also less likely to feel that their communities are noticed and important. The Centre for Towns found that 53 per cent of people in cities say 'politicians don't care about my area' compared to 67 per cent for people in towns. When it comes to the future, fully 71 per cent of people in towns say that their area will be less central to British society, compared to 53 per cent for people in cities. Only 32 per cent of city dwellers think that their area will be financially worse off in the future, compared to 51 per cent for towns.

Professor Will Jennings notes that people living in towns are 'more likely to believe they or people like them are worse off than other people – both in the past, present, and future'.[50] Therefore, possibly the greatest difference is one of hope: people in big cities might still believe that their area is significant to broader society and have hope for the future; this is much less likely in towns and villages. For the 'Red Wall' voters interviewed by pollster Deborah Mattinson as part of her focus groups, the biggest worry was what the future held for their kids: 'there's thousands of kids here with no work and no hope' was a typical complaint.[51]

So, who or what is 'working class'? Even though they suffer from the same economic ill winds as the rest of the population, underemployed graduates are still relatively privileged compared to those who are really suffering: unable to acquire jobs commensurate with their qualifications and trapped in private renting, yes, but usually not surviving on foodbanks, living in hostels or being beaten up or killed because of who they are. They are well-educated, usually technologically adept, mobile, and relatively well-positioned to benefit from the future economy of the twenty-first century; certainly much more so than the biggest losers from the last decades of the twentieth century. As Ford and Sobolewska note, those with lower levels of formal education are less mobile: 47 per cent of those with GCSEs as their highest qualification live within fifteen minutes of their mother, compared to 22 per cent of graduates.[52] Given how important mobility is to today's economy, and the likely economy of the future, this is a strong indication that those who do have an undergraduate degree are likely to be far better equipped to deal with the future economy than those without. Whether or not it is in the interests of the Labour Party to persevere in winning back the votes of traditional supporters is another question, but this electoral realignment is no reason to entirely reinvent our conception of class.

Chapter 2

Authentocrats and Exonerators

If we accept that the designation working class should be determined by income, education and location rather than homeownership, there is still a tightly fought contest between various identity
mythmakers over exactly what this working class is like, and what it
believes.

As mentioned earlier, class-based identity myths on the Right
brand this group as homogenous, instinctively conservative and
irrevocably anti-immigration. This is overly and deliberately simplistic, flattening the massive variety and heterogeneity of working-class
life into cartoon stereotypes for their own mean causes. It is also cynical and disingenuous – if you seriously believe that people go into
conservative politics to uplift the most disadvantaged then, frankly,
you'll believe anything. Ben Bradley MP, whose 2017 victory in
Mansfield provided a foretaste of the 2019 collapse of the Red Wall (it
was the first time the constituency had been won by a Conservative),
nonetheless opposed the extension of free school meals for poorer
children during the summer of 2020 for giving '£20 cash direct to a
crack den and brothel'.

Yet there are clearly some truths in their characterisation of working-class culture and politics as fundamentally small-c conservative;
if not, then how can you explain the capture of so much of that
constituency by the parties of the Right in recent years? I doubt it is

due to a genuine belief that they will offer transformative economic change; to the extent that economic motivations play a role it is probably out of desperation: they have voted for parties of the Left for years and feel that little has changed, so what harm can it do to give the other side a chance? Although politicians such as Boris Johnson, Donald Trump and Marine Le Pen have promised the return of jobs and industry and infrastructure investment in order to capture traditionally left-voting working-class constituencies, they have offered this as a side order to their main dish of immigration restrictions and attacks on 'metropolitan liberalism'.

Despite their bold promises about infrastructure investment, they are far less willing to commit to making the kind of funding commitments working-class communities urgently need: to healthcare, education, retraining, justice reform and so on. These infrastructure commitments come alongside the same 'pull yourself up by your bootstraps' platitudes deployed by conservatives since the advent of modern democracy. Bradley continued that 'at one school in Mansfield 75% of kids have a social worker, 25% of parents are illiterate. Their estate is the centre of the area's crime. One kid lives in a crack den, another in a brothel', and so money intended for their kids' meals would not be spent on such. Notwithstanding the fact that such platitudes have always found a receptive audience among a section of the working class, we can see that right-wing invocation of 'white working-class boys' is useful for culture war nonsense but does not translate into a desire to ensure they are well fed. Nonetheless I would bet money that Bradley is re-elected at the next election, probably with an enhanced majority. Thus, there must be some cultural factors at play in motivating poor and working-class people to vote for conservative politicians.

Because I expect the Right to instrumentally use people for their own gain, and because their understanding of the small-c conservatism of most working-class people on non-economic issues is fundamentally correct, this chapter is mainly focused on the claims of working-class culture and politics put forward by the Left, and a particular section of the Left which I term the Exonerators. Unlike the Atomists, who reject that these people even are working class, the Exonerators accept the traditional definition of the term but argue that suggesting this working class is culturally or politically conservative is an outrageous slur, indicative of class hatred. This is because they view such attitudes (that nation states have a right to regulate immigration, or that violent criminals should suffer long jail sentences) as inherently immoral, if not fascistic, and wish to 'exonerate' an idealised working class from having such abhorrent beliefs.

Of Chavs and Fegs

Paisley is a former industrial town of around seventy thousand people in the west of Scotland. In Paisley, the word 'feg' is a ubiquitous working-class insult, analogous to the English 'chav'. Historically it was used to describe the residents of Ferguslie Park, a particularly deprived area that is separated from Paisley by railway lines – literally on the wrong side of the tracks. The historian Valerie Wright – herself a Paisley native – has studied the area and the complex hierarchies of class and respectability among the people of Ferguslie Park. She recalls that when her father – a former shipbuilder and trade union activist – heard about her research, he responded with bewilderment: 'But why? Those people are scum.' According to Wright, there is a further hierarchy within Ferguslie Park itself, with the Ardmore Oval – a neighbourhood with a particularly negative reputation – known locally as 'The Jungle'. This area segregated so-called 'problem families' from the rest of the neighbourhood, something that unsurprisingly did not lead to improvements in their wellbeing, but instead resulted in their alienation from the wider community. In the words of Wright, 'even the people in Ferguslie Park looked down on the people who lived in the separation area'.[1]

When I heard of Wright's research, it brought home to me the variety and pervasiveness of these kinds of words among working-class communities in the UK. Growing up in Liverpool, the condign word was 'scally'. Originally common across Lancashire, today it serves the same purpose as feg in Paisley, as an intra-working-class designator of acceptability. Just because the word scally can be and is used by middle-class people – I'm using it now – this does not mean that it is a term of class hatred, and it would be ridiculous to claim otherwise. So too with the word chav. Just because it was adopted by middle-class people as a term of hate does not obliviate its origins as an autochthonous working-class word for scally in the north-east of England; nor does the fact that it is still used in that sense by millions of working-class people every day. (Interestingly, there has been a notable decline in the use of this kind of language in right-wing media in recent years, possibly down to the ongoing political realignment and the cynical repositioning of conservatives as supporters of the working class.) These words cannot be understood in terms of 'class' hatred, or at least not without appreciating that intra-class hierarchies are far more complex than a simple working/middle-class binary.

In his book *44 Years with the Same Bird*, Brian Reade – a long-time columnist at the left-wing *Daily Mirror* – recalls some of the less salubrious assignments he was sent on as a young reporter, which included a 'family of chain-smoking slobs showing me a damp patch on their council house wall' and 'a trip to Newbury magistrates to see the latest batch of inbreds up on cider-related assaults'.[2] Reade doesn't restrict this kind of language to the description of unfortunate Brits; in one of his columns he wrote of 'southern US states that produced George Bush, the Ku Klux Klan, country and western, the world's largest concentration of self-inflicted obesity, Death Row, bigoted rednecks and bent evangelist preachers', and hazarded that the destruction of hundreds of Texas homes by wildfires might be a sign 'their God is trying to tell them something'.[3]

My point here is not to criticise Reade, who is a solid socialist and Liverpudlian legend, but rather to show that even an avowed left-winger, who uses his media platform to attack social and economic inequalities and speak up for the working class, employs this kind of language as a matter of course. And his readership understand that language, appreciate what he's trying to do, and find it funny; his book concerns his travels and travails as a Liverpool supporter, and its target audience is working-class Scousers: there will be a great many of his readers living in council houses, and quite possibly some who had damp stains growing on their walls, who nonetheless laughed uproariously at the above.

In her book *Lowborn*, Hudson combines memories of her impoverished and itinerant childhood with descriptions of her interactions with people on returning to some of the towns and villages in which she grew up. One of the places she visits is the seaside resort of Great Yarmouth, and she returns to the tiny flat she shared with her mother, speaking to the woman currently occupying the residence. Noting how she wakes up at 3 a.m. each day to clean caravans at the local Haven Holiday Park, Hudson adds that 'she'd had her first [of three kids] when she was nineteen. Like me, they'd all gone to Caister High School, so as not to spend time with the estate kids.'[4] Here we have a woman, in dire circumstances, who nonetheless uses the snobbish, one might even say bigoted, language of fear and class hatred.

The radio presenter Stuart Maconie – a self-described Marxist from Wigan – wrote of a trip to Plymouth where he saw 'rural chavs – pimply youths in Burberry caps and Henri Lloyd jackets', and 'weasel-faced youths' in Huyton, Merseyside, dressed in trackies, 'pallid from a lack of vitamin C and generally looking for something to urinate on or set fire to' and describes Greggs's 'difficult reputation as caterer in chief to Chav Britain, the staple diet of the hoodie hordes'. Maconie actually argues that it is his Marxist analysis that causes him to 'bemoan the fact that the working class has become enfeebled in this way'.

Elsewhere he writes of his fury at a London taxi driver assuming he was poor due to his accent, after he had just interviewed Stephen Poliakoff: 'The cabbie would never see this interview as he would doubtless be watching *You've Been Framed* on ITV3, perhaps in a string vest, and probably thought Stephen Poliakoff was a midfielder Chelsea were after.'[5] This is a nice demonstration of how people from working-class backgrounds who are well read and enjoy 'highbrow' culture can react with fury and deploy the language of class hatred when people from a similar background don't recognise this.

Even in historically close-knit working-class communities, class solidarity did not extend to people suspected of not pulling their weight. After Britain introduced conscription during the First World War, men deemed to have genuine political or religious objections to fighting were permitted to appeal for exemption from military service. In order to judge applications for exemption, the government set up hundreds of conscription tribunals across the country, which then received unsolicited letters from people accusing their neighbours of shirking and cowardice, and demanding that they be conscripted.[6] A few years later, during a strike by coal miners, the municipal authorities in the town of Wigan advanced loans to the families of miners, who were suffering from the loss of income during the strike; according to historian Trevor Griffiths, the authorities then received a 'number of anonymous letters naming recipients of relief who were thought to be undeserving'.[7]

The historian Jon Lawrence describes his own mother as a ten-year-old growing up in Bristol during the 1930s who was nonetheless 'fully conscious of micro-differences in communal expectations and norms'. During the Second World War his mother refused to use the communal air-raid shelter during bombing raids because 'so many of the families that did so were dirty and uncouth'.[8] Here we have a woman who was so sensitive to social hierarchy that she would rather risk her life than spend a few hours in close proximity to the 'wrong sort'. And yet, although Lawrence writes that for his mother the language of class was 'a valuable cultural resource to bolster her sense of personal dignity', she nonetheless declared herself 'proud to be a "working-class woman"'.[9]

Lawrence later writes of a Labour councillor and joiner in Wallsend in the 1960s complaining that he had 'to work with men you wouldn't touch with a barge pole socially'.[10] Two decades later on the Isle of Sheppey a man named Stan Cummings, 'who lived in an area of high unemployment and relied on benefits himself, sneered that "half of them round here wouldn't want a job if it was offered to them"'.[11] One of Cummings's neighbours, whose husband had been out of work for over three years, attacked the 'yobs' and 'bums' who used the Job Centre, who had 'never done a day's work – never wanted to go to work – lived off the State all their lives'.[12] There was also no little hypocrisy on this issue among left-wing academics, in the past as today. One of the researchers – a self-identified socialist – whose notes form the source base for Lawrence's book, condemned the 'irrelevant, snobby asides' of one woman, yet agreed that the estate was 'pretty rough', and wrote that he would 'tremble for my car's safety whenever I have to park it on this estate' after his parking light was stolen.[13]

As Mattinson notes, 'in every constituency I visited voters complained about substance abuse ... or the "professional poor"', and people were eager to see more money clawed back from 'scroungers'.[14] (A sad reminder that your likelihood of seeing through tabloid lies about welfare frauds is inversely related to your distance from welfare dependency.) Another woman described in Lawrence's book, who was living with her parents and until recently on benefits, asked the researchers if anyone was to blame for the fact that people are poor, and gave her opinion that 'I think it's themselves', before adding 'that wasn't the right thing to say was it?' This demonstrates not only that people who are themselves struggling to make ends meet are often the biggest supporters of the deserving/undeserving dichotomy, but also that they know that they are not supposed to think as they do. Admittedly, this woman later asked if she could 'retract what I said before' and conceded that 'it's not actually anyone's fault'.[15] This retraction is interesting; it could be because of a concern that she did not want to be seen to be heartless, cruel or right-wing. But my own theory is that she spoke out of anger, and that her retraction better represented her genuine thoughts.

That those near the bottom direct so much of their hatred and anger at the people just below and above them has undermined left-wing politics for over a hundred years, and continues to do so today. An essential first step in somehow ameliorating this is acknowledging that it happens in the first place, rather than brushing it under the carpet. We need to ask *why* terms such as chavs and scallies and fegs are endemic to working-class vocabulary; exactly what forces cause poor people to turn their ire on the likewise disposed, rather than the real frauds (the amount of money lost to overpayment of welfare is minuscule compared to the amount lost to tax evasion). When the disingenuous or the moronic ask 'if black people can say the N-word then why can't we [white people]?' the appropriate response – if it even deserves a response – is patiently to explain to them exactly why black people reclaimed this word, and why that doesn't mean that white people can use it. Nobody says: 'No they don't say that themselves. How dare you!' because that would patently be absurd.

So instead of trying to deny the use of words such as chav, scally and feg by working-class people, we should instead explain why they are used and how they came about, and interrogate what this means for the prospects of redistributive and economically transformative political projects. Unfortunately, there is not much of a market for think pieces about that, much less entire books. There is a huge constituency of well-educated, middle-class people who desperately want to hear that the working class are in reality exactly like them

– from their political views to their penchant for avocados – and given the centrality of these people to the economics of publishing and broadsheet journalism, there are book deals and even national newspaper columns to be had for those willing to say it. It is this desire that sustains the Exonerator's worldview, despite it being obviously and demonstrable false.

There is a related trend that implies or baldly states that 'moral panics' and a preoccupation with crime are essentially middle-class issues, while the working class are generally quite sanguine about criminality. In an article for the *New Statesman*, Megan Nolan – who herself grew up in grim circumstances on an Irish council estate – writes of 'the blatant class hatred which permeate[s] media coverage' of horrific crimes such as the murder of James Bulger.[16] While this is doubtless true, a focus on the deleterious caricaturing of poor and working-class people in right-wing media does not help us understand why such caricatures find a paying audience among poor and working-class people, and it can provide ammunition for the electorally suicidal notion that crime reduction is really a middle-class issue. For those that might be susceptible to this notion, I would urge you to go to YouTube and look at the footage of the crowds at Robert Thompson and Jon Venables's trial for the murder of James Bulger, trying to get into the prison van conveying them to and from the court. They are not middle-class people. In *Lowborn*, Hudson recalls a social sciences lesson after the murder, when her teacher told the class to stand up and then 'asked us to sit down if we thought Jamie Bulger's murderers deserved to receive the death sentence. I was the only one left standing.'[17] Much as many of us would like it to be the case, as convenient as it would be, the people who attack paedophiles or support restoring the death penalty are by and large not the suburban curtain twitchers who serve as folk devils to the Left, but the traditional working class who (used to?) serve as their heroes.

Exonerators Assemble!

Joe Kennedy, an academic at the University of Sussex, puts forward one of the most sophisticated and interesting contributions to the Exonerator school. Kennedy's argument focuses on what he calls 'authentocracy', the cynical use of supposedly authentic working-class tropes and stereotypes to advance centrist or neoliberal political positions. Kennedy fixes on the apparent surprise of Owen Smith – a centrist Labour politician who challenged the socialist Jeremy Corbyn for leadership of the party in 2016 – to be served a cappuccino in a café in his constituency of Pontypridd.

It was a remarkable and bizarre episode, and I cannot understand why Smith thought anyone would believe that he was unfamiliar with cappuccinos, much less why such a pretence would endear him to working-class Labour voters. Nonetheless, Kennedy uses this embarrassing incident as a jumping-off point for a broader, unsustainable and potentially politically disastrous argument: that because many people in former industrial areas enjoy cappuccinos (and hummus and kale and quinoa and so on), political and cultural differences between working-class people in those places and the liberal middle-classes of the great metropolises are exaggerated or even fabricated by ignorant or cynical politicians, journalists and academics.

Early on in his book *Authentocrats*, he analyses 'The Reeve's Tale' from Geoffrey Chaucer's *Canterbury Tales*. In the Reeve's Tale, the character Symkyn is a conniving miller who consistently cheats his customers, only to come up against two students from Cambridge University, John and Aleyn, who are able to outsmart the miller, and make off with his grain and his horse, but not before raping his wife and daughter. Kennedy argues that 'in Symkyn's reasoning, not only are John and Aleyn incapable of outfoxing his "thrift" with their book-learning, they are effectively the *deserving* dupes of his premed-itated con as a consequence of it'. While I assume that Kennedy is criticising this attitude, it would be difficult to argue that this disdain of book learning is not a common feature of many working-class people. Thousands, possibly hundreds of thousands, of people around the world who were the first in their family to go to university will be intimately and inescapably aware of the attitude that no amount of book learning can make up for hard graft, experience and wisdom acquired over time. In many parts of the world, getting a job, getting married, settling down, having kids, are all vaunted above educational attainment. In fact, many people actively despise book learning, and feel it not only a waste of time but a drain on resources.

And why shouldn't they? We can't expect people who have been excluded from access to further or higher education for generations, who have had it drummed into them for decades that the most important thing in life is to learn a trade or find steady work as soon as possible, to embrace learning for its own sake within a generation or two. In fact, given the increasingly poor returns for investment in a university degree, it might be pretty sensible to be sceptical about the benefits of education for education's sake. The hostility of many working-class people towards academia is not an inherent cultural phenomenon but the result of long-standing structural factors. And nor is this true for all working-class people; for some immigrant groups, excluded from trades by racist employers, trade unions or fellow workers, book learning and education were the most sure-fire way for their children to have a better life than themselves, and so they emphasised this instead. But this was usually on the understanding they would study a subject with a guaranteed job at the end of it. Ilyas Nagdee recalls his parents repeating the mantra: 'You have to study, you have to do something with your life, [and of course] you have to become a doctor.'[18] Many working-class Brits from an ethnic minority background will recall their parents' obsessive focus on academia – and their horror when they said they wanted to study philosophy.

There has always been something of a paradoxical attitude when it comes to working-class culture and academia. On the one hand, it is openly despised, but on the other there is a sort of reverence and even sometimes a sense of insecurity. In the words of one 1960s Wallsend shipbuilder: 'I can't think of the words to say what I want. That's where the likes of us always get fucked.' These men often described themselves as 'thick' when talking to the researchers, and one said he was a miner because he was not clever enough to be a fitter.[19] Similarly, as Mattinson argues, for many Red Wallers being 'working class' meant not being a graduate, and 'many challenged the notion that university is a guaranteed route to a successful career for youngsters and were concerned about young people being encouraged to take on massive debt to obtain what they saw as "worthless" degrees'. Yet at the same time 'nothing made the people I met more proud than their own children going to uni – usually being the first member of their family ever to do so.' One of Mattinson's focus group attendees, Yvonne from Darlington, believes that 'if you're an educated person you're part of that socialist tribe and to me it feels tribal'.[20] Many others complained that their own children can be 'intellectually superior' and annoy them.[21] This puts me in mind of a brilliant scene from *The Sopranos*, where Carmella accuses her daughter Meadow of lazing by the pool all summer, rather than doing any work:

> MEADOW: I read, Mom, out by that pool. Probably half the canon.
>
> CARMELLA: 'The canon.' Okay, what is that now?
>
> MEADOW: Now? The great books? Western literature? Dead white males? Who even in their reductionism have quite interesting things to say about death and loss. More interesting than what you have to say.
>
> CARMELLA: Is Mary Higgins Clark part of that group? Because that's what I saw you reading every time I passed by the pool.
>
> ('No Show', Episode 2, Season 4)

The nature of this exchange will be familiar to many parents of first-generation university students: the arrogant, glib invocation of the recently acquired language of the seminar room to silence and humiliate, despite their actual reading extending no further than the trashy airport novels they used to read.

Elsewhere, Kennedy criticises the tendency to behave as though working-class people 'are all Gillian Duffy', referring to the Rochdale woman who cornered Gordon Brown on the campaign trail for the 2010 election, and complained, among other things, about immigration. Brown, caught on a hot mic, later branded her a 'bigoted woman'. Unfortunately, there are millions of Duffys all across the world, and while they come from various races and classes, there is an unmistakable link between class, education and opinions on immigration.[22] Ford and Sobolewska note that education levels and ethnocentric attitudes are more important than income, age or social class in determining attitudes to immigration and 'a white working-class school leaver is no more likely to support UKIP than a white middle-class school leaver' – but age, income and class all affect education level, and while this means that there are plenty of middle-class people opposed to immigration, it does not undermine arguments as to the widespread anti-immigration sentiment among the working class.[23]

Kennedy consistently makes an error central to the Exonerators' thinking, by confusing personal anecdote with evidence. At one point he recalls his mum cutting up an avocado in the kitchen before he started primary school, but simply because *his* family ate avocados in the 1980s does not mean this was unexceptional.[24] Although Marks & Spencer claim to have introduced the avocado to the UK in 1968, it was not popular, and caused all sorts of complaints from people who had cooked, served or eaten them inappropriately.[25] Avocados only became widespread in the UK after 2013, and their increase in popularity is put down to the actor Gwyneth Paltrow. Mrs Kennedy can take heart in knowing she was a culinary innovator and ahead of the time, but we can't extrapolate anything from this about the broader Darlington population, much less the wider British working class.

Likewise, some online Exonerators sneer at anyone who would note the existence of people who eat at Pret and people who eat at McDonald's, and argue that this has political implications. But these distinctions in food are commonly cited by working-class people encountering middle-class culture. Darren McGarvey notes that 'Scottish working-class cuisine is, essentially, a children's menu, but served in adult portions.'[26] Describing the culture shocks of going from working-class suburbia to interning at the Tavistock Institute in central London, the writer Nicholas Preston recalls a colleague going out to get 'snacks': 'I was expecting chocolate or cookies of some sort, and I was mildly disgusted when she returned with grilled artichokes.'[27] Similarly, Malakaï Sargeant notes that there is 'little crossover' between the people who frequent the Dalston McDonald's and the nearby Arcola Theatre, and that 'to generalise, those who visit the Arcola regularly would much rather buy smashed avocado on crusty sourdough for £6 than buy a cheeseburger and fries from McDonald's'. Later he describes 'cafés that cater to the palates of the avocado-devouring, latte-sipping elite'. Having said this, he appreciates that he is 'in flux':

If I'm offered a smashed avocado with a poached egg on sourdough it's very unlikely that I'll say no. If I'm at a meeting in a ridiculously pricey coffee shop, and the barista with the bad haircut and 'LOOK AT ME, I'M A WHITE FEMINIST™' armpit hair asks what I'd like to drink, it's now more likely that I'd say an organic pressed elder-flower juice than a Coke. Fam, I drink coffee now. I still don't know if I even like the taste, or what the difference between a cappuccino and a macchiato is, but I drink it now.[28]

Sargeant is not a flat-cap-wearing, whippet-owning former miner in the north of England. He is a black millennial from Hackney and has the kind of haircut that would make me – if I hadn't read his essay – mark him down as the kind of hipster he so despises. And yet he still knows that there is a difference between the kind of people who prefer McDonald's and the kind who prefer avocados and fancy coffee – even if there is some crossover between the two, and even if it's possible for people to cross fully from one camp to the other. He knows this is real and has economic and political implications.

In *Lowborn*, Hudson writes of her deadbeat stepdad Richie, 'he loved Laurel and Hardy, classical music, crosswords, chess and cards. He wanted to be a writer and was often found with his tree-trunk legs splayed around a charity-shop typewriter, typing with two huge index fingers with bitten-down nails. I think he wrote my mum poetry.'[29] Thereby demonstrating the complexities and nuances inherent to every human, not to mention entire communities. But these diverse interests and hobbies did not stop him from having political opinions and cultural attitudes that Kennedy would presumably find abhorrent. Later in the book, Hudson recalls how a woman her mother sometimes cleaned for bought them a fancy cheese knife and cutting board, 'as though we regularly bought a wheel of Brie for after dinner. We took it on all our moves (after trying and failing to sell it) and sliced our big blocks of sweating mild Cheddar with it for years after.'[30]

In his essay 'Why it is important for young black men to floss (not their teeth)', Suli Breaks describes the meticulous rituals of working-class black men, preparing their clothes and fixing their appearance before a night out. The flossing in the title refers to deployment of a toothbrush to clean and whiten trainers for a box-fresh look. 'People from the outside looking in may not appreciate the gravity of a young black man's emphasis on personal appearance,' writes Breaks, 'but within our community how we looked, and what we wore, was every-thing that defined us. Many times, for us, it has felt like the difference between life and death.' For young black working-class men, 'high-end, branded clothes meant wealth and success. Imitations and knock-offs indicated struggle and disadvantage.' Although it might seem counterintuitive that poorer, sometimes deprived people struggling to make ends meet should spend so much of their income on aesthetics, in fact 'the concept is really simple if you think about it; in an environ-ment where everybody pretty much owned nothing, you prioritised gestures or practices that explicitly show you had something.'[31]

The importance of appearance – of dress, fashion, grooming and aesthetics – is almost entirely missing from pronouncements on working-class culture from both cynical conservatives and left-wing Exonerators. Perhaps this is unsurprising given that both tend to look like the backend of a bus; think of the thrown-together-from-a-jumble-sale look of Dominic Cummings, or the long-hair-and-snag-gle-tooth look that is almost a uniform for a certain kind of male socialist. In contrast, for most working-class people, and perhaps people of colour in particular, their appearance is of the utmost importance. 'I had uncles who were cleaners and security guards,' reflects Breaks, 'but would be dressed like politicians and government delegates on Sundays. In the same manner, aunties would be dressed in hand-tailored traditional clothing of the highest standard', for 'brand new cars or clothes meant that you were someone of value, or you at least valued your personal status enough to understand the response it commanded'.[32]

A glance at footage of football terraces from the period after the Second World War reveals crowds dressed uniformly in suits and ties. Off the terraces, in the dancehalls and coffee shops of the post-war period, fashion remained tremendously important for the working class. A *Sunday Times* feature from 1950s quoted Billy, a seventeen-year-old from the Potteries, who said that if he won money on the football pools, the first thing he would do is 'buy about two-dozen shirts, all different colours and about a dozen pairs of jeans'.[33] A decade later, the American writer Tom Wolfe described one Larry Lynch, an attendee at a mod club in London, as a 'working-class boy . . . he left school at 15 [and] has been having his suits custom-made since he was 12'.[34] This was not restricted to young people: as Keith Gildart notes, 'wearing of a suit for weekends in the pub remained a feature of working-class dress' well into the 1960s.[35] In the 1970s, as fans embraced European labels encountered while following their teams on the Continent, terrace fashion shifted to expensive leisurewear brands, and the suits and ties were left behind. Nonetheless, fashion continued to matter to the working class, as it does today.

On all sorts of issues – from music to food to visual art – it appears that there is a correlation between class and taste. Mattinson describes people's anger directed at the new entrance to the Arndale shopping centre in Accrington, due to a combination of its postmodern art and the lack of consultation with local people.[36] During one focus group in a pleasant suburb of Leeds, Mattinson asked the participants to bring something that symbolised their 'middle classness'. Five out of eight people produced cafetieres; another, who did not drink coffee, brought Earl Grey teabags.

For almost forty years, Mattinson asked focus groups what the Labour Party would be like if it was a person at a party. In the 1980s it was always a traditional male worker with a cloth cap, eating a pie and drinking a pint, a *Mirror*-reading trade unionist living in the north of England. Today, a typical response is: 'He would spend ages sorting through the CDs to avoid talking to the other guests . . . he's a bit socially awkward, listening politely but not really taking it in.' In terms of what food and drink they would bring, it would be 'sausage *en croute*' and craft ale from a micro-brewery. In 2015, when asked who would have benefitted if Labour had won, people suggested it would be a homeless person, a woman in a wheelchair, a scrounger.

Sadly, as Mattinson notes, 'the voters making these choices were ordinary people: hairdressers, carers, electricians, retired delivery drivers and receptionists.' Yet by 2018, 'it was someone "posh" living in a rather grand house in London and eating fancy food: quinoa was the most frequent suggestion.'[37] Labour was the party of 'losers and scroungers', but also 'naïve and idealistic middle-class students'.[38]

This popular culture translates into political culture. Although Kennedy takes aim at 'the covert sententiousness by which some people *just are* idiots, and "bellends" and "wankers"', this banal, common-sensical understanding of the parameters of acceptable behaviour is community in action; you'd be hard-pressed to find a community anywhere that didn't have outcasts and folk devils.[39] It happens in Liverpool, on London estates, and even in Darlington. In fact, there's an argument that it is impossible to have redistributive politics without a sense of belonging and not-belonging.

Kennedy often demonstrates an ignorance of labour and socialist history. At one point he claims that 'it would be much less likely . . . to see someone like [Labour MP Graham Jones] talking about a (supposedly) working-class commitment to "defence" and "nationalism" were it not for the hugely increased visibility of the military in public life that has been a complex consequence of Blair-era foreign policy', thus demonstrating a real obliviousness to the long history of working-class nationalism and the centrality of patriotism to the British labour movement for virtually all of its existence. Another aside about 'the centrality of anti-imperialist thinking to any socialism worthy of the name' suggests that polities as diverse as the 1945–51 Attlee government and Stalin's USSR are unworthy of the designation 'socialist'.[40] A year after *Authentocrats* was published, the Tory appeal to Brexit, anti-immigration sentiment and working-class culture, combined with the Labour Party under Corbyn's active rejection of the latter meant that the Conservatives won Kennedy's home-town seat of Darlington for the first time in thirty-six years – despite a decade of austerity and despite the existence of coffee shops and alternative stores.

More than any other issue, immigration has totemic significance for the Exonerators. Because they instinctively feel any attempt to regulate immigration is inherently racist – despite the fact that it is supported by most people of colour, in the UK and around the world – it is essential that they exonerate the working class of supporting such an abhorrent policy, and they are willing to invoke all kinds of sophistry to do so. The idea that hostility to immigration must be caused by some external factor – be it capitalism, the retreat from Keynesian economics and the undermining of the welfare state, media such as Fox News or British tabloids, or demagogic politicians such as Donald Trump or Nigel Farage – is central to the Exonerator worldview. And yet there is evidence of hostility to strangers and newcomers in virtually every society that has ever existed – indeed, along with complaints that children no longer respect their elders, criticism of foreigners seems to be fairly universal across historical periods and different societies. A law passed in 1596 during the reign of Elizabeth I complained:

> there are lately divers blackamoores brought into the realm, of which kind of people there are already here too manie considering how God hath blessed this lande with great increase of people of our ownie nation as anie countrie in the world, whereof manie for want of service and meanse to sett them in work fall in idleness and to great extremytie . . . that those kinde of people shall be sent forth of the lande.[41]

Apart from the use of an explicitly racist slur, and the olde-timey language, this could have been written yesterday so universal are the themes: there are too many of them here already; they are taking jobs away from our people; we cannot afford to have any more of them – and yet it was written before the transatlantic slave trade, British imperialism or industrial capitalism.

Some historical research on migrants to the UK before the '*Windrush* Generation' stresses cases of 'tolerance, co-operation and dialogue' and emphasises that immigrants had their own sense of agency and economic autonomy – but we shouldn't downplay the extent of racism in British society before 1945.[42] In fact, much the same arguments were advanced by opponents of the 1965 and 1968 Race Relations Acts who stressed the friendly, open nature of the average Brit, which did not require government intervention or heavy-handed legislation to ensure that they extended a warm welcome to strangers. These opponents, who included publicans, hoteliers, factory owners, journalists and politicians, drew attention to examples of inter-marriage and episodes of black and Asian immigrants being warmly received by the local community as evidence that racism was uncommon and confined to a few bad apples.

The reality of the racism faced by South Asian immigrants into Britain is documented in *Finding a Voice*, Amrit Wilson's acclaimed 1978 book based on interviews conducted with Pakistani and Indian women living in Britain during the 1970s. Wilson, herself of mixed British and Pakistani parentage, revealed the often-hidden suffering of women from these communities, who faced not only physical attacks, but the crushing psychological damage of witnessing their husbands and children fall victim to the racist violence and abuse meted out by their neighbours and co-workers. The horrifying accounts recounted by Wilson include a Bengali mother whose son was followed home from school and assaulted in front of her by a gang of his classmates, and another woman who was disturbed one evening by a commotion outside her door and found a group of white teenagers beating her husband. One particularly vicious attack on a widow and her three young children living in Shadwell, just around the corner from Cable Street, scene of the famous street fight involving Oswald Mosley's fascists in 1936, was reported in the *Guardian* at the time:

Last Saturday night they were watching television. They had just had the windows repaired from the last volley of stones. Fists started hammering on their windows. They turned the lights out and sat in fear. They heard sounds in the kitchen; breaking glass . . . Peeking around the kitchen door, they saw rubbish being emptied from dustbins into their home . . . The widow gathered her children and ran out of the front door seeking protection from another Bengali family thirty yards across the court. There were about thirty people waiting for them as they left their home. The bruises on the neck and face and legs of the widow and her children were still livid on the brown skin as they recounted how they had run a gauntlet of fists and kicks and curses of their neighbours.[43]

Wilson's book gives a definitive sense of the terror of feeling that the world outside your door was implacably hostile. One of her interviewees, Arshad, spoke of her time at a Tate & Lyle sugar factory, where one of the Englishwomen on the production line alongside her, after yelling 'Smelly!' at her several times, took a can of air freshener and began spraying it at her: 'All of the other women on the machine – about eight of them – joined her in following me and mocking me.'[44]

In *Natives: Race and Class in the Ruins of Empire*, the rapper Akala blends fiery polemic with a frank account of his own experiences growing up as a mixed-race child in 1980s Britain. Refreshingly, he has no truck with the Exonerators' school. 'It's easy for people just slightly younger than myself', he writes, 'to forget just how recently basic public decency towards black folks was won.' But Akala remembers only too well: 'I grew up routinely watching some of England's greatest ever football players' suffer racist abuse and humiliation, and 'in front of tens of thousands of people, who for the most part seemed to find it entirely acceptable, funny even'.[45]

The widespread racist abuse at the hands of almost uniformly working-class crowds is an obvious visual and audio riposte to the argument of the Exonerators, yet it does not cause them a moment's pause; instead, the argument goes that the *real* racists were those in the boardrooms and corridors of power. But the black and brown migrants who came to rebuild post-war Britain were met not only with a government reluctant to legislate against racial discrimination, but also with 'de facto segregation, verbal abuse, violent attacks and even murder', carried out by the people they lived among and worked alongside.[46] Irrespective of the complex structural precursors of racism, the sharp end of racism – the faeces through the door, the graffiti, the violence – was executed overwhelmingly by working-class men. As Akala says, his 'father's and uncles' bodies are tattooed with scars from fighting the National Front, Teddy Boys and Skinheads', not from encounters with public schoolboys and Conservative MPs.[47]

In the anthology *Safe*, edited by Derek Owusu, various young black British writers talk about their formative experiences. In the chapter 'Treddin' on Thin Ice', Jess Bernard states matter-of-factly that 'living in close proximity to the white working-class sometimes gets you called a "n****r" every now and then'. Recalling his upbringing, he notes that 'in '90s working-class Britain the *hard* racism jumped out'.[48] Similarly, in 'The Sticks', the writer Aniefiok Ekpoudom uses explicitly class-based language to describe the trajectory of the kids in school who racially abused him 'from blue blazers to labouring jobs and building sites'.[49]

Later in his book, Akala writes about the tragic but hate-filled figure of his white maternal grandfather, 'an uneducated alcoholic with few serious accomplishments to speak of' who could nonetheless say, "well at least I am not a n****r" frequently, with argument-concluding certainty. 'What did my grandfather understand about whiteness that so many pretend they cannot?' Akala asks. Such remarks should not be news to anyone: in the 1988 Oscar-winning film *Mississippi Burning*, the father of Gene Hackman's character says almost the exact same thing after killing his black neighbour's mule; these sorts of sentiments – at least I'm not black, at least I'm not gay, at least I'm not a woman – have sustained white working-class masculinity in Britain and America for at least two hundred years, and it is bizarre and perverse to now pretend as though such bigotry was the exception, rather than the rule.

There were obviously very many exceptions indeed – men (and women) who, despite the often-desperate hardship of their own lives, had the strength to refuse the prejudices and hatreds of the world into which they were born. One of the great moral failings of the Exonerator school, in addition to its intellectual dishonesty, is that it occludes and diminishes the bravery of these people. Those who stood up to the pervasive racism of the time, in the workplace, on the football terraces and in the schoolyards, deserve tremendous praise and recognition for their actions and words, something denied them by the false history of the Exonerators.

Perhaps the most telling incident of working-class hostility towards black and Asian migrants is the reaction to Enoch Powell's infamous Wolverhampton speech. After 'Rivers of Blood' in 1968, around one-third of the registered workforce of the London docks – between six and seven thousand men – went out on strike in support of Powell. A much smaller number marched on Parliament – around five to eight hundred assembled at the start of the march, and about three to four hundred arrived at Westminster – where they abused Ian Mikardo, the left-wing Labour MP for Poplar, and cheered the right-wing shire Tory Gerald Nabarro, who had supported Powell.[50]

Forty years after 'Rivers of Blood', the historian Amy Whipple pored over the vast correspondence Powell received in response to his speech – almost all of it positive – and made many depressing findings. An oft-recurring theme was that Powell, unlike the Labour representatives, was standing up for the working classes, and saying what the Labour MPs would not. 'Someone becomes an MP, gets a head full of liberal ideas, and is no longer "one of us"', read one. Powell, a hard-right Tory MP whose entire record in public service had been to the detriment of the workers, was able to secure an outpouring of working-class support because of his racist articulations. The overall theme was clear: Powell's correspondents believed Labour had betrayed its traditional supporters by protecting immigrants at the expense of the working class. 'You have the working man behind you', as many of the letters averred.[51] It is to the enormous credit of Edward Heath and the Conservative opposition that they did not attempt to play the immigration issue to their advantage.

In the early 1960s, almost 90 per cent of Britons supported strong restrictions on Commonwealth or 'coloured' immigration, and 70 per cent supported the Commonwealth Immigration Act of 1962, which limited the rights of citizens of the British Empire or Commonwealth to freely enter the UK. Two-thirds of voters said Heath was wrong to sack Powell from the shadow cabinet, and over 75 per cent agreed with his views on immigration.[52] Between the years 1968 and 1978, between 42 and 64 per cent of Britons supported the repatriation of black and Asian immigrants, and even as late as 1993 43 per cent supported 'helping migrants . . . return to their country of origin' if they had already decided to leave.[53]

In an essay on the history of race and immigration in Cardiff, the sociologists Glenn Jordan and Chris Weedon point attention to a plaque in the Tiger Bay area – a dockside district known for its rich history of migration and settlement, as well as being a historically deprived area – which refers to the neighbourhood as 'the safest place in Britain for men of colour'. The plaque continues by claiming that 'Our Celtic mothers fought in this battle too and preserved a harmonious multi-racial way of life which forms one of the most endearing aspects of community life in the history of South Wales'. Aside from ignoring the historical episodes when Tiger Bay rejected inter-racial harmony, such as the riots of 1919 which witnessed violent attacks against black people in the area, this simplistic history has the inadvertent effect, as Jordan and Weedon argue, of depicting racism as 'something foreign to Tiger Bay but fundamental to the wider Cardiff'.[54]

Kerry Hudson writes how the 'two Middle Eastern men lodged with Grandma and whenever I visited they'd give me a box of chocolates and once for Christmas a Barbie ballerina that spun around on a little stand'.[55] There are all kinds of incidents and vignettes like this from the lives of millions of people, providing a stark warning of the limits of generalisation. However, no number of such incidents could invalidate the argument that working-class people have historically been hostile to immigration. Earlier on in the book, Hudson recalls the shock and fear of seeing her estranged uncle's post on her Facebook wall, 'linking me to a man whose last post had been a meme about illegal immigrants claiming £29,000 of benefits and how it was "bloody disgusting"'.[56] This is a revealing incident, as it reflects both Hudson's association with her past and the people from her past with anti-immigrant sentiment, and her concern that her middle-class London friends, who would never dream of judging her because of her uncle's poverty, might nonetheless judge her for his racism.

As McGarvey describes of working in several communities across Glasgow, all with high migrant populations: 'In these communities, [the fallout from Brexit] was just another week. Here, violence is present every day – it doesn't "spike". Here, racism is a horrible fact of life – it isn't "unleashed".[57] At a school on a council estate in Glasgow for pupils with additional needs, he asks them what annoys them about the city. One says 'immigrants', and then: 'within two minutes, these normally mute, unresponsive, passive-aggressive boys suddenly spring to life and reveal to me an issue they are not only passionate about but clearly believe themselves to be knowledgeable on. It's just a shame that they are racist.'[58]

In case readers might misread my intention here as attacking the historical working class or belittling the suffering of those subjected to these attitudes – far from it. We should not condemn people in the past who held beliefs common to virtually everyone in their milieu at the time, and naturally there were a great many tremendous things about the very same people, who could also be kind, selfless, hard-working and generous; but all of these things could easily go hand in hand with a sort of 'common sense' racial bigotry from which we would now recoil. Indeed, there is an argument that the kind of communitarian welfare state and Keynesian economic policy present in Britain in the decades after 1945 would only have been possible with a distinct and exclusionary sense of group identity. We should not condemn these people any more than we would the medieval gawpers at ritual burnings or executions. Nonetheless, it is intellectually dishonest and counter-productive to pro-immigration arguments to play down the extent of historic working-class racism.

An Exonerator tendency that has excited a great deal of passion recently is the attempt to paint the result of the Brexit referendum – in which the UK voted 52 per cent to 48 per cent to leave the European Union – as a fundamentally middle-class project that was erroneously and libellously blamed on the working class. As Simon Kuper writes in the *Financial Times*, the conversation about populism revolves entirely around the figure of 'the impoverished former factory worker. Pundits are forever explaining why poor Sunderland voted for Brexit, but rarely why wealthy Bournemouth did'. In reality, says Kuper, Brexit represents a middle-class civil war.[59] Kuper bases this argument on the fact that, in pure numerical terms, more middle-class people than working-class people voted for Brexit. But this ignores the fact that (determined objectively, rather than by self-description) there are more middle-class than working-class people in the UK.

In reality, by whichever metric you might choose to use, large majorities of working-class people voted Leave, ranging from 59 per cent according to the National Centre for Social Research, to 63 per cent according to Ipsos MORI.[60] Kuper also argues that more people in the south voted for Brexit than people in the north, conveniently omitting to mention that the population of the south is much larger. If we look at the proportion of votes compared to the registered electorate in these regions, then 39 per cent of people in the north voted for Brexit compared to 36 per cent in the south. There is also evidence that the majority of social and council house tenants voted Leave.[61] Here we can see the whataboutery central to the Exonerators: just because plenty of middle-class shire Tories and 'Joe the Plumber' types voted for Brexit and for Donald Trump, we can ignore the crucial votes of people who until recently were stalwarts of the Labour and Democratic parties.

Kuper poses an interesting question when he wonders why 'well-off people vote against the system' that sustains them, but they were not voting against the prevailing socio-economic system. Instead, they voted, as Kuper acknowledges, against 'positive discrimination for women or people of colour', high taxes and 'handouts'– that is to say, things that are usually *not* part of the system, but which are being advanced by left-liberals. It is no surprise that traditional conservatives do not support these policies, but it is worth wondering why so many of the traditional working class, and recent supporters of left-wing parties in particular, do oppose them. Especially since it is unlikely that the former will ever be brought round to support these policies, but the latter might be yet. As mentioned earlier, it is no surprise that middle-class Tories vote for conservative parties and policies. What is more of a surprise, and what is transforming our politics, is the transference of working-class support to parties of the Right. Liberals and leftists should be animated by trying to understand why this is happening and how to stop it, rather than pointing out that plenty of historically right-wing constituencies are still right-wing. Kuper also argues that 'most journalists and academics still overlook the provincial middle class [while] the socialist-realist figure of the laid-off factory worker remains more compelling'.[62] This is probably because the laid-off factory worker is the personification of the economic changes of the past forty years. It may be that years from now the indebted student or the thirty-something in a flat share becomes a more compelling image, but we are not there yet.

Incidentally, the attempt to rebrand the Brexit vote as essentially a middle-class, Home Counties project does not convince many working-class people. McGarvey writes of how:

The morning of Brexit, multiple crises were announced simultaneously by middle class liberals, progressives and radicals, who were suddenly confronted with the vulgar and divided country the rest of us had been living in for decades. A country filled with violence and racism ... It was infuriating to witness one hyperventilating *Guardian* subscriber after the other, lamenting how a once-great nation had gone to the dogs. Of course, by 'dogs', they meant the working class.[63]

There is always a need to qualify any generalisations. The political scientists Robert Ford and Maria Sobolewska note that there is a 'substantial minority' of white people with few formal qualifications who 'reject ethnocentric conceptions of the nation, and a substantial minority of graduates and ethnic minorities who express at least some support for them'. As an example of the latter, 26 per cent of ethnic minorities and 40 per cent of white graduates think that 'those who do not share British customs and traditions can never be fully

British'.[64] Likewise, language matters, albeit not in the way the Exonerators think: Ford and Sobolewska note that support for firing employees guilty of racist discrimination decreases if this action is framed in terms of 'political correctness'.[65] They also argue that 'younger generations of identity conservatives are much more comfortable with diversity than their parents or grandparents' and 'they often resent accusations of racism and xenophobia from their identity liberal peers, as they feel they have moved away from the prejudices of their parents, but this inclusive shift is not acknowledged by identity liberal voters whose attitudes have moved further and faster'.[66]

At the same time, people can know of and use vogueish terms and yet nonetheless express racist sentiments. Mattinson quotes Julie, a part-time cleaner from Darlington, who was furious that her son had been twice rejected from the police: 'It annoys me that he missed out on the opportunity just because he wasn't a person of colour.'[67] Another of Mattinson's interviewees, a small business owner in Accrington, in the context of complaining that other businesses got off more lightly in terms of council inspections and regulations, insisted that the 'bloke with corner shop [has] mice running over the counters, but they don't dare go to him in case he plays the race card'.[68] The same woman, who was originally distraught and angry with the government after it appeared that she would not be eligible to receive support during the COVID-19 pandemic, later told Mattinson that she was eventually awarded £2000. She added that 'the council didn't notify me ... I found out from the guy in the corner shop – the foreign guy. This lot know every loophole that's going.'[69]

Hostility to 'outsiders' is a near-universal trait across all cultures and time periods. Lawrence highlights one woman from Bethnal Green in the East End of London complaining about the influx of outsiders into the area during the 1940s, even though they were white British people from elsewhere in the East End.[70] Likewise, yesterday's immigrants are today's anti-immigrant voters, and today's immi-grants are tomorrow's anti-immigrant voters. As Ford and Sobolewska argue, UKIP, Nigel Farage and the Brexit campaign did not create nationalistic and anti-immigrant views, but instead activated 'long-standing but previously latent ethnocentric sentiment' which 'had been there all along'.[71]

My theory is that since Exonerators see restricting immigration as illegitimate – not something they oppose, in the way they might oppose cutting taxes or welfare spending, but as something which should not even be considered in polite society, yet at the same time do not feel able to criticise 'the working class' – they will go to any length to deny the extent of working-class anti-immigration senti-ment. Apart from leading them to defend palpably false positions, there is no reason to believe that any kind of immigration restriction is inherently abominable. Mattinson held a special focus group evenly divided between young, graduate Remain voters and older Leave voters with few educational qualifications. When she asked the members to anonymously vote for their main concerns, immigration was the second most voted for priority after the NHS. As Mattinson says, 'the numbers revealed that some Urban Remainers must have voted for it', and these were people who voted Remain in 2016, Labour in 2019, and lived in big cities. Everyone thought the immigration system should be 'open and transparent with clear rules – rules that are fairer and more generous to people who meet the criteria. Everyone could also agree that there should be a clampdown on ille-gal immigration and that there should be an "Australian-style" points-based system', based on skills. Urban Remainers 'were appeased by thinking that, once these grievances were addressed, immigrants would receive a warmer welcome'.[72] On this Ford and Sobolewska are clear: 'a selective migration system focused on the potential economic contribution of migrants as the main criterion for entry is consistent with the preferences of voters on both sides of the identity politics divide', as well as benefitting refugees by reducing hostility towards them.[73]

'Scousers Never Read the Sun'

Liverpool has a special place in the hearts of the Exonerators, and Scousers serve as a sort of 'Magic Proles': by any metric it is a largely working-class city, is still overwhelmingly white (unusual for large conurbations in the north of England), yet it is not only self-consciously left-wing, but exhibits a particular kind of politics that appears to reject the nationalism and cultural conservatism so prevalent among the English white working-class. Many Liverpool constituencies have demographics that elsewhere in England would suggest a drift towards the Right over the past twenty years: few graduates, low median incomes and few ethnic minorities. Yet they have not only resisted this right ward drift, but have actually moved towards the Left. At both the 2017 and 2019 general elections, the five safest Labour seats were all on Merseyside. (Of the remaining top ten in 2019, one was in Manchester, two in Birmingham, and two in London.)

The website Electoral Calculus breaks down the demographics and political culture of each of the UK's 650 constituencies. It ranks seats according to their political opinion on economics (Left vs Right), internationalism (Global vs National) and culture (Liberal vs Conservative), and designates them as one of various 'Tribes' such as Progressives, Traditionalists and so on. It also notes the class, age and nationality breakdown of different seats, and the percentage of people with A levels or undergraduate degrees.

The two London constituencies in the top-ten safest Labour seats are Walthamstow and Tottenham, both in north-east London and close to my own constituency of Hackney North. Both of these seats are Remain strongholds: only 36 per cent of people in Walthamstow and just 33 per cent of Tottenham voted for Brexit. They also have fairly low proportions of residents born in the UK, at 57 per cent in Walthamstow and just 48 per cent in Tottenham. Nonetheless, 41 per cent of people in Walthamstow and 39 per cent of Tottenham have qualifications at A level or above, and 53 per cent and 46 per cent respectively are in the ABC1 social categories. Electoral Calculus judges Walthamstow as 15 degrees Left on economics, 21 degrees Globalist and 3 degrees Liberal, while Tottenham is 21 degrees Left, 23 degrees Globalist and 7 degrees Liberal. So, the profile for Labour's most secure London seats are: quite Left economically, very internationalist and slightly culturally liberal. Only around one-third supported Brexit, they have an immigrant population of between 43 and 50 per cent, around 40 per cent have A levels or equivalent, and about half are middle class.

Similarly in Manchester Gorton, only 35 per cent voted for Brexit, two-thirds (67 per cent) are UK-born and 46 and 49 per cent respectively have at least A levels and are in the ABC1 socio-economic group. Electoral Calculus rates the seat as 14 degrees Left on Economics, 22 degrees Globalist, and 6 degrees Liberal. Therefore, the profile of Manchester Gorton (Labour's sixth most secure seat, and the safest outside of Merseyside) is pretty similar to Tottenham and Walthamstow: quite Left economically, very internationalist and slightly culturally liberal. Around a third supported Brexit, 33 per cent are immigrants, over 40 per cent have A levels and half are middle class.

From the two Birmingham constituencies, Ladywood is rated as 12 degrees Left, 21 degrees Global and 0 degrees in cultural position; 36 per cent voted to Leave and 60 per cent are UK-born; 39 per cent have A levels and 48 per cent are ABC1s. Politically, Ladywood is somewhat different from the two London constituencies and Manchester Gorton in terms of social and cultural beliefs, but is pretty much identical in terms of Brexit support, the percentage of immigrants and socio-economic class. Birmingham Hodge Hill is a little different from the four constituencies discussed so far. Only 9 degrees Left and 4 degrees Globalist, it is rated, perhaps surprisingly, as 17 degrees Conservative – unlike all of the previous four constituencies, it has been assigned the 'Centrist' tribe, whereas the others are all 'Progressives'. Here, 51 per cent voted Leave, 71 per cent are British born, merely 22 per cent have A levels, and only 30 per cent are ABC1. So, Hodge Hill is fairly unusual compared to other Labour strongholds, with a (tiny) majority supporting Brexit, fewer than a quarter possessing A levels, and just under one-third in middle-class occupations. Nonetheless, it does still have an immigrant population of 30 per cent.

Now let's look at the breakdown for the Merseyside constituencies. Liverpool Walton, the safest Labour seat in the country, is rated as 27 degrees Left, 3 degrees Globalist and 1 degree Conservative; 52 per cent voted Leave, a whopping 95 per cent are UK-born, only 25 per cent have A levels, and 36 per cent are ABC1. Knowsley is 26 degrees Left, 2 degrees Globalist, 2 degrees Conservative; 52 per cent voted Leave, fully 98 per cent are UK-born, 26 per cent have A levels, and 37 per cent are ABC1. Bootle is 25 degrees Left, 3 degrees Globalist, 0 degrees Social; exactly half of Bootle residents voted Leave, 97 per cent are UK-born, 29 per cent have A levels, and 43 per cent are ABC1s. West Derby is 26 degrees Left, 6 degrees Global, 1 degree Liberal; 48 per cent voted Leave, 94 per cent are UK-born, 29 per cent have A levels, and 41 per cent are ABC1. All four of these Merseyside seats are classed as 'Traditionalists', according to the Electoral Calculus formula.

So, politically, four of the five Merseyside seats differ markedly from other Labour strongholds in the top ten. They are slightly more economically Left than Tottenham, much more so than Walthamstow, Gorton, Ladywood and especially Hodge Hill; notably less internationalist than the others, and more socially and culturally conservative than anywhere apart from Hodge Hill. These four seats are also different demographically, with far fewer people having A levels or university degrees, and far fewer middle-class people than anywhere apart from Hodge Hill. The most notable difference, however, is in terms of immigration: on average, 60.6 per cent of the population of Walthamstow, Tottenham, Gorton, Ladywood and Hodge Hill are British born. For these four Merseyside constituencies the average is 96 per cent. Furthermore, large numbers of the British-born population of London, Birmingham and Manchester are from black, Asian or other minority ethnic backgrounds, whereas Liverpool is overwhelmingly white.

The constituency of Liverpool Riverside is a little different from the other four. The most demographically diverse of the Merseyside constituencies, it includes both traditional white working-class areas such as Vauxhall and Kirkdale, areas with a large number of black Liverpudlians such as Toxteth, and student halls of residence in the city centre and the Mossley Hill area. It is rated as 21 degrees Left, but 29 degrees Globalist and 18 degrees Liberal. Whereas the other four Merseyside seats are dubbed 'Traditionalists', the tribe assigned to Riverside is 'Strong Left'. Merely 27 per cent voted to Leave the EU, a relatively low 82 per cent are UK-born, an unusually high 53 per cent have A levels or university degrees, and fully 61 per cent are considered ABC1.

Yet even when Riverside is added to the calculation, the average percentage of British-born people in the Merseyside seats only drops to 93.2 – still over 30 points higher than the average for the other five constituencies that make up the top-ten safest Labour seats. Frankly, if you look at the demographics for Liverpool, with the low number of people with A levels, the even lower number of graduates, the overwhelmingly white British population, and the social and cultural conservatism (Riverside excepted), you would bet good money that they would be Tory-held seats, certainly after the collapse of the so-called 'Red Wall' in 2019. (According to the 2011 census, the 41

Red Wall seats that switched from Labour to the Conservatives were on average 97 per cent white, compared to the average across England and Wales of 86 per cent.[74]) So why is Liverpool different? If Labour can find out, and expand its success on Merseyside to areas with similar demographics, it could become the largest party in England for the first time since 2001, and once again have a chance of forming a parliamentary majority.

Yet Liverpool's status as the archetypical Labour city is relatively recently acquired. One hundred years ago, although overwhelmingly working-class and with some of the worst overcrowding, poverty and deprivation in Edwardian England, Liverpool was a resolutely Tory town. One reason for this was the casualised nature of dock work, a dominant occupation in the city, which did not lend itself to robust trade union organisation. Another was the sectarian divisions between the city's Anglican and Catholic communities, although this has been overplayed by some commentators.

As with Cardiff's Tiger Bay and other dockside districts, the history of Liverpool is often romanticised in the retelling of Exonerators. Because of their seafaring heritage, these areas were the most ethnically diverse places in the UK, and the main areas of settlement for people of colour before the post-1945 migrations. There were many mixed marriages and families, and people from all over the world lived and worked alongside each other in mostly pacific circumstances. Nonetheless, this does not mean that racial animus and violence were absent from these communities, and non-white settlers and citizens in towns such as Liverpool were vulnerable to discrimination and exclusion. In 1919, the same year as vicious attacks on black and Asian settlers in ports across the UK, mostly notably in Liverpool and Cardiff, over one hundred black factory workers lost their jobs when demobilised white soldiers returning from the First World War refused to work alongside them.[75] After the Second World War, there was a wave of anti-black riots in Liverpool in 1948, and later in other areas of black settlement such as Deptford in 1949 and Camden in 1954.

Liverpool tourism promotional materials will proudly tell you that the city has the oldest settled Chinese community in Europe, and the largest Chinese arch outside China, but are less likely to describe the historical hostility against the Chinese, who were regularly employed as strike breakers, and so 'anti-Chinese hostility from dockers and seamen was unremitting', according to literary historian Anne Witchard. In 1906 the dockers' trade union leader James Sexton initiated a public inquiry into supposed 'vice' in Chinatown, including prostitution, opium and the debasement of white women. Sexton had in the previous year won election to the council for the St Anne's ward on an explicitly anti-Chinese manifesto, and his pronounced Sinophobia led to complaints from, among others, the chief constable of the local police force, in a sadly-not-unique incident of the police being less racist than the trade unions.[76] After the Second World War, local pressures contributed to the deportation of more than two thousand Chinese seamen from Liverpool; many of them had wives and girlfriends in the city, but were deported so suddenly that many of their partners assumed they had abandoned them.[77]

By the 1980s, the once solidly Tory city of Liverpool had finally been captured for Labour. Yet as the journalist Dave Hill writes in his biography of John Barnes, even in the late 1980s it remained one of the most overtly racist cities in the UK. While most First Division football clubs had fielded black players, they were noticeably absent from the squads of Liverpool and Everton. After Liverpool signed Barnes, due to his brilliance on the pitch, racist hostility melted away from the terraces of Anfield, but not at Goodison; Hill makes the point, however, that the Evertonians would not have chanted 'N***erpool' and 'Everton is white' if they could not be sure that those taunts would hit their mark and wound the pride of the Liverpool fans.[78]

Describing a place called Guru in Darlington, Joe Kennedy writes of a 'herbally scented warren' that 'speaks of an aspect of provincial life rarely registered when London papers send correspondents to the north . . . namely the way the Sixties and the Seventies were experienced beyond the big cities'.[79] There was a similar place in Liverpool, a sort of alternative department store called Quiggins that operated on different sites from the late 1980s to the early 2000s. Its incense-scented halls housed a variety of shops selling bongs, ethnic jewellery and so on. It was closed in 2006 amid some outcry from its patrons, but with cool indifference from most Scousers; the displacement of a few sweaty goths was not something that aroused much outrage. Liverpool was and is a strange place, and one where more than many other places the legacy of the sixties and seventies lived on in working-class culture. On the one hand, it is a highly conformist monoculture, with tremendous pressure on youngsters to conform in manners of speech, dress, appearance, attitudes and habits. On the other, there has always been room for places such as Quiggins, and 'alternative' culture has found refuge in Liverpool even when shunned by the rest of the country.

Furthermore, despite its reputation as an archetypal working-class city, and less sympathetic portrayals as a hotbed of poverty and thievery, alongside many UK cities with universities, tourism and a large services sector it has grown and prospered over the past twenty years. None of this means that poverty and deprivation are absent from metropolitan areas; by various metrics, most of the deprived neighbourhoods in the UK are in big cities. But poverty and left-wing politics can easily coincide with rampant consumerism. The Direct Line insurance company estimates that relatively low housing costs mean that Liverpudlians have the highest level of disposable income in the UK, which in 2018 stood at an average of £1401 per month after tax and accommodation. This was followed by London (which has much higher average wages, but even more expensive housing costs) with

£1206, and Plymouth with £1183. This was just one survey, and I'm not sure of the methodical rigour behind it, but anecdotally there are huge numbers of people in Liverpool with money to spend on socialising, holidays, music festivals and – as is visually apparent on a night out in the city – cocaine. You'll be hard pressed to find anywhere in the UK with such long queues for the cubicles in the gents' toilets, and during the 2018/19 football season, there were thirty-four arrests for cocaine possession at Everton's ground and twenty at Liverpool's. In contrast, among all seven London clubs at that time in the Premier League, there were only seven arrests.

Since the late 1980s, these counter cultural attitudes have seeped into the city's politics, which are so atypical of places with similar demographics, and progressively brought the city closer to a middle-class Labour Party. The increasingly bourgeois membership and liberal policies have contributed to the party's estrangement from working-class voters elsewhere in England, but not in Liverpool. This also registers in the city's diverse and eclectic music taste; none more idiosyncratic than the enduring affection of young scallies for Pink Floyd.

Back in 1989 *The Face* magazine wrote of a hippy being chased down a darkened street by a group of teenagers: 'In most parts of Britain, what follows is likely to test his pacifist views sorely. In Liverpool, he's more likely to be nagged for tales of the Isle Of Wight Festival. Genesis are big in Merseyside. So is Zappa. But biggest of all are Pink Floyd.' This article went on to describe a Pink Floyd gig at Manchester's Maine Road stadium, where 'a crowd made up of students and social workers applaud[ed] the group's sleepy dexterity. Everything is as it should be. Except that the students and social workers can't relax. A massive contingent of young men from Liverpool slips through the crowd. The students keep their hands in their pockets.' The tension was broken 'by the thick Scouse accent which confronts one ageing hippy trying to keep track of the 25th guitar solo: "Hey, mate. Have you got any skins on yer?"'

The piece highlighted the unlikely composition of the audience at the Maine Road gig: Pink Floyd, and prog rock generally, were associated with a particular kind of person, and that person was not presumed to be a young, working-class man from Liverpool, 'the kind of young men who the world presumes must be into hip hop because they live on council estates':

> Outside the ground, the Manchester touts recognise that these people – most of them kitted out in a variety of expensive trainers – have little in common with any artist's impression of a typical Pink Floyd fan . . . Such events leave a trail of contradictions which will have most hip redbrick sociologists, with their clearly defined ideas about the haunts and habits of the post-casual generation, thoroughly confused.

A couple of weeks later, the writer attended a sort of 1960s tribute gig at Liverpool's Royal Court theatre, featuring performances from Robby Krieger of the Doors, Steve Howe from Yes, and 'two old men from Wishbone Ash' (me neither). Six scallies were skinning-up against a wall at the back, when a member of the road crew 'passes and stares for a few seconds, dazed and patently confused':

> He is passing through a city and a culture which is unique. A city where the early Genesis public school fantasies of old England seep from bedroom windows in Kirkby and Croxteth, a city where Waters is 'well sound' and Led Zeppelin are 'a belter buzz'; a city where 'real hippies' are treated with a mixture of awe and respect.[80]

However, the legacy of 1960s counterculture and the existence of places such as Quiggins in Liverpool, Guru in Darlington and doubtless many such establishments in places with an even more exclusionary working-class monoculture, qualifies but does not invalidate generalisations about working-class culture and politics. These places were clearly for a particular kind of person, people who were often mocked and abused by their peers. During the early 2000s, Liverpool's goths would hang out in front of the court buildings in Derby Square, and I'm sure there was a similar place for the few goths of Darlington – but their existence does not mean that they – and gay teens, nerds and so on – were not vociferously and often violently rejected by the majority of their peers. The mere fact of their existence does not make it impossible to make generalisations about working-class culture and politics. Kerry Hudson writes that during her time in Coatbridge, outside Glasgow: 'I had the wrong accent – half Northumbria, half Aberdeen, posh apparently, though it wasn't.'[81] Similarly, Jon Lawrence tells of the physical violence visited upon him in his Bristol schoolyard, as his classmates 'claimed to think [he] was American because my Bristolian accent was a little less broad than theirs'.[82]

None of this is to insult these communities – unless we think that cultural diversity and heterogeneity have moral worth in and of themselves. Nor is it to say that these things are fixed and unchanging. When I was a teenager, anything more than a short back and sides was beyond the pale; for the past few years, however, every self-respecting young scally is required to have a so-called *ketwig* of luxurious curls. Nonetheless, it does mean that cultural heterogeneity does not translate into the kind of progressive politics held by the Exonerators: in 2012 the founder of Quiggins, Peter Tierney, stood as a candidate in the Liverpool mayoral elections. He won 453 votes – for the National Front.[83]

Whatever we mean by the phrase 'working class', and whatever criteria used to define it, there is a developing realignment of class and voting behaviour. At the 2019 UK election there was a clear correlation between low incomes and voting Conservative: according to YouGov, 45 per cent of those with a household income under £20,000 voted Tory, compared to 34 per cent for Labour; for those with incomes between £20,000 and £40,000 it was 47 to 31 per cent. This was not uniform nationwide, and people of working age and on low incomes still tend to vote Labour, but if we include low-income pensioners as 'working class', then there is for now a clear working-class preference for the Conservatives. Meanwhile, in the United States, every $10,000 increase in median home value in a county results in the Republican vote falling by 0.3 per cent.

In these first two chapters I've been arguing that we should consider income, education and location in determining who is or who isn't 'working class', and that there are important if unpalatable cultural and political generalisations about what it means to be 'working class'. Of course, these generalisations have many exceptions. People are aware of attempts by academics, journalists, politicians and others to pigeonhole them, and they don't like it. In October 1968, one of the Wallsend shipyard workers, Ronnie Morris, told the researchers that he was on to them: 'You're out trying to put us all together and look at us as one group, aren't you? But we've all got different opinions. There's nothing in common with us at all.' Half a century later, one of Mattinson's focus group participants, Bob from Darlington, said something similar: 'being working class isn't a prison. It doesn't define me or how I think'.

Similarly, whatever we might try to define as 'working-class' culture or politics is impermanent, evolving, and often contains many contradictions and paradoxes. Lawrence writes of a Luton man who was fostering a mixed-race child, and whose wife got into a feud with a neighbour who had picked on the child, who was nonetheless relieved that Luton was 'like London' (i.e. white), as opposed to areas 'where there are black men & foreigners'.[84] As recently as 2005, Mattinson notes that most focus groups supported the statement that anti-immigrant sentiment in the Conservative manifesto was 'just trying to frighten people in this country and turn people against immigration. I agree with some of the things being said. I do worry about the amount of people coming into the country, but I don't want to pick on them.'[85]

Lawrence is sceptical of any attempts to generalise about different communities, past or present, and argues that within most working-class neighbourhoods of the past century there was a 'powerful ideology of independent selfhood', suggesting that 'rugged individualism can run in tandem with a strong commitment to personal autonomy and self-realization'.[86] Describing post-Second World War Bristol, he notes that opera and bingo clubs flourished side by side, 'and even managed to have some overlapping membership', albeit conceding that it was unusual for someone to be both an opera and bingo fan.[87] I agree with Lawrence's sentiment, but what happens when you lack the ability to 'realise self-hood', or when your rugged individualism is smothered early on by commitments to your family or dire need for steady cash? Within many working-class neighbourhoods there are many people who wouldn't be there, or who would be having very different lives, with different tastes and politics, if they could earn more money or secure investment or gain a qualification. Or if they didn't have to care for children or disabled or elderly relatives. As Mattinson notes, most of the people she interviewed talked of nearby cities such as Manchester, Liverpool and Newcastle as though they were another country, many had never visited London, and 'abroad was discussed as somewhere for an occasional holiday in the sun, rarely as somewhere that might offer career opportunities.'[88]

In Wallsend in 1968, a shipworker concluded 'money is the root, no matter what's said. We're all individuals outside that,' nicely encapsulating the way that the lack of money, the need for money, and how they had to acquire it was the defining characteristic of him and his mates, the one thing they all had in common and which kept them from expressing their individualism more fully. The researcher was impressed, scribbling in his notes that Morris was surprisingly intelligent, 'underneath an air of apparent stupidity which he puts on semi-deliberately to cover himself at work', revealing both the condescending attitude of these researchers and also the importance of popular philistinism endemic in such environments, and the need for bookish people to keep their heads down.[89] As Darren McGarvey writes of his childhood in Glasgow: 'The act of reading, and indeed all forms of academic achievement, were regarded by many of my male peers as either feminine or the preserve of posh people and freaks.'[90] Later on, he describes how he knew a family was not working class as the father used the word 'unfettered', and 'a working-class person wouldn't risk saying something so gay in public'.[91]

One of the implications of this, alongside the decline in trade unionism and local government as routes into politics, and the transference of the site of left-wing radicalisation from the shopfloor to the university campus, is that people from working-class backgrounds are under-represented in organised politics. Alison Baskerville is a former soldier and the world's first female combat photographer, who has documented the reality of war in places such as Afghanistan, Gaza, Mali and Somaliland. Now working as an artist, documentary maker and activist, she mixes with people very different to those she met in the military, but also to the working-class people she lived among while growing up. She says that she 'didn't know what class was until I left the military', pointing out that the focus on class and politics so prevalent in left-wing activism, academia and journalism is often absent among working-class people themselves. 'By the way I didn't know much about feminism either,' she adds. And of course there is plenty of class snobbery even among left-wing activists, often concealed in different ways; Baskerville recalls that when she got into social justice activism in Birmingham after the army, the activists she met were usually from a very different background to herself, and 'some of them wouldn't even talk to me' due to her military service.[92]

Aside from this kind of class antagonism, occasionally the apparent insecurity and lack of confidence of many middle-class left-wing activists can infuriate the very people they are trying not to offend. The journalist Afua Hirsch describes her husband, who is from a markedly less privileged background than herself, recalling his first interaction with her and her friends, a group of 'misfit Oxford graduates, sitting in a loose circle on the carpet . . . feasting on vegan food, painfully aware of the clichés' they embodied:

> In all his life . . . he had never seen a scene like this – people talking so earnestly, almost conspiratorially, in low, hushed voices, even eating the way we were eating, an array of strange plant foods being passed around on little plates.

He later told her of his disdain for them:

> sitting there with your herbal tea, all round in a circle . . . So tentative . . . so unsure of yourselves. Trust me, if a man like me had the opportunities you all had, there would be no stopping me. We'd be up in this country making some serious *money*.[93]

This nicely encapsulates the contempt that many working-class people have for the middle-class Left: if we had your money, we'd be eating fat steaks, not plant food; if we had your money, we'd be going to the Maldives and Dubai, not on carbon-neutral camping trips; if we had your family's resources, we'd be setting up our own businesses or paying for law school, not yet another postgraduate degree with no job at the end of it; even though we don't have your money, we're still wearing designer labels, or at least quality fakes, and not Oxfam hand-me-downs. While they might still have plenty of contempt for middle- and upper-class Conservatives, at least the latter spend their money and live their lives without apology, without performative hand-wringing that does nothing but assuage their own consciences.

'Aspiration' has understandably become a dirty word on the Left, implying as it does a desire to leave your class behind. Lawrence notes that of the various social investigations he sampled, no one used the word in the 1980s – out of 400,000 words of testimony it doesn't appear once. By the 1990s it was used 5 times in 220,000 words of testimony by workers in Luton. However, it was used 32 times in 230,000 words by workers in the north-east in the mid-2000s.[94] Yet many working-class people do not aspire to a different lifestyle, just to be able to better afford the one they already have. The historian Selina Todd has noted that when working-class parents were focused on giving their children a better life, they were not always talking about education and social advancement, but rather about simply having more fun.[95]

Understanding this is essential in order to understand the politics of the last decade. It is why so many working-class Americans – including blacks and Hispanics – appreciated Donald Trump: he may have been a billionaire, he may have inherited his money, but he was unapologetic about it, and spent it on the sort of things they might spend it on if they could afford it. It is why the Eton-educated David Cameron was implausibly able to pose as tougher and more-in-touch than the comprehensive-educated Ed Miliband, and why Eton-educated Boris Johnson was seen as infinitely more relatable than grammar school-educated Jeremy Corbyn. Even in areas where the Tories are still despised, in working-class areas of Scotland that vote heavily for the SNP, or in the increasingly few working-class areas that have Labour MPs – even in the magic prole city of Liverpool – the Left is able to win despite the existence of culture, not due to its absence. The Labour Party used to understand this: Harold Wilson – who sadly holds the distinction of being one of only three Labour leaders to win parliamentary majorities – was a grammar school boy from the lower middle class; an Oxford graduate and academic who substituted a pipe for his preferred cigars to cultivate a more rustic image; yet held no illusions about the sort of people who voted for his party. During the 1964 election he complained that the BBC was scheduling the popular comedy *Steptoe and Son* during the evening of the election, and when asked what he would prefer them to screen suggested they 'put on *Oedipus Rex*'.[96]

Can we distinguish certain beliefs and politics as associated with a particular class? To the extent that we can, for many working-class people, being involved in activism in the first place is seen as a bit posh: after listing various other factors about his extended family that indicate their deprived circumstances (such as no formal qualifica-tions, criminal records, etc.), McGarvey adds that 'zero are involved with an activist group'.[97] Thus the desperate attempts to rebrand working-class people as avocado-scoffing open-border advocates are politically suicidal; 'authentocracy' is not only compatible with Left politics – it is an essential element to its success.

The attempt to deny that newly minted Tory voters are working-class because they own their own homes is not only intellectually disingenuous, but is also highly patronising: McGarvey criticises those 'so certain of their own insight and virtue that they won't think twice before describing working-class people they purport to represent as engaging in self-harm if they vote for a right-wing political party' – I would say that denying that they do so in the first place is just as bad.[98]

There are, of course, many qualifiers to this argument. There are a great number of people from underprivileged backgrounds who dream of completing postgraduate degrees in esoteric subjects, couldn't care less about their personal appearance, and would love an eco-friendly camping trip. But invariably their identity is tied up with being exceptions to the rule, either as people who left where they grew up and never came back, or who carved out a small subculture within their otherwise monocultural and oppressive environment. A recent article in *Vice* about a hipster and music journalist returning to his home village of Driffield, East Yorkshire, is a case in point: it is not as though places such as Driffield don't produce people such as him, it's that they are considered unusual by the rest of the community.[99] It is impossible to talk about millions of people without generalising, but the existence of a large number of exceptions does not undermine the generalisation, and nor do these qualifications have powerful political implications.

As demonstrated by the popularity of Greggs's vegan sausage roll (which caused inexplicable consternation in some quarters), there is no reason why low incomes necessarily translate into narrow tastes. Many of the cultural distinctions around class might fade away if the material realities underpinning them changed. As McGarvey asserts, people from deprived communities are sceptical of 'culture, participation, the arts', but they are not really annoyed at conceptual art: they are annoyed at 'rising social inequality and how this expresses itself culturally'. When he inducted himself into the world of the Scottish middle class he realised that many 'irritating tropes of middle-class life, around veganism, cycling and healthy eating' actually were beneficial; 'trends and products [he] thought were for posh people and hipsters' were actually practical and good for you.[100] There is a strong argument that more resources and options would break down cultural barriers. But focusing on the unusual exceptions and denying cultural reality undermines any political attempts to change these material realities.

Conclusion: The Continued Relevance of Class

Class misunderstanding does not by itself lead to prejudice, and it is an open question whether or not people appreciate their own relative affluence or poverty. People tend to articulate their class position in relation to others, and contact with people from different walks of life can put your own status into sharp relief. In the introduction to her study of St Ann's, Lisa McKenzie tells of how she had been taught from childhood that working-class people were 'strong and proud, the backbone of the country', and that it had 'never occurred to me that "others" did not think the same way'.[101] It was only later on, as she came into contact with people born into more privileged positions, that she learned that these positive associations of 'working class' did not hold true for everyone.

Despite disingenuous attempts to claim otherwise, class snobbery and prejudice are simply not felt as painfully as other kinds of bigotry. Class snobbery is not a problem in the same way as class inequality, even though one can influence the other: according to Ford and Sobolewska, only 4 per cent of people say they believe somebody should lose their job for ridiculing a customer's poverty, suggesting that class-based bigotry is more acceptable than other prejudices.[102] A similar study found that of the characteristics a Remain voter would object to in a person living next door, unemployment was the most likely factor that would lead to the neighbour being shunned by them.[103] Nonetheless, as the journalist Cosmo Landesman writes, 'you don't find YouTube videos of passengers on public transport being subjected to vicious tirades about their cheap Primark clothes, vulgar jewellery or their dropped "h"s by a drunken snob'. Nor does snobbery 'create poor health, homelessness, family breakdown, mental illness, suicide or drug addiction', but is instead a product of disparities between the privileged and the disadvantaged.

What's more, there is no reason to suspect that this sort of class snobbery impacts its targets in a meaningful way; possibly because the attitude of many working-class people to 'the middle class' ranges from the mildly condescending to the bitterly hateful. In their book *Reacting to Reality Television*, Beverley Skeggs and Helen Wood analyse the reaction of working-class women to the often hostile and snobbish attitudes displayed on reality TV shows, and found that they responded with stoic indifference. Skeggs argues that the women who had been subjected to such abuse didn't 'care about a lot of these middle-class judgments being imposed on them', and 'just didn't notice it'.[104] Similarly, Lisa McKenzie found that the men of St Ann's think the opinions of outsiders are worthless, and couldn't care less how they are perceived. Having said this, most of the women to whom she spoke had an 'acute awareness of how they are known and represented in Nottingham and beyond', but this was because of the estate's association with violence and poverty, not because of cultural stereotypes or political opinions.[105]

This can be seen in the pride people have in their communities, no matter how troubled. McKenzie writes that, despite all the problems in St Ann's, she met very few people who imagined themselves being or living anywhere else: 'moving out was not an ambition in this neighbourhood as a method of acknowledging social mobility'. Instead, staying on the estate, belonging to it, 'and being respected and valued on the inside was always more important than leaving'.[106] One of her interviewees, Lorraine, claimed that if she won the lottery she would buy her house, make some home improvements, learn to drive and help out other people in the local community, but not move away.[107] This is an oft-found sentiment by no means exclusive to working-class or economically deprived people, and it is borne out by statistics: of lottery winners who move house, 65 per cent stay in the same city or town or only move up to five miles, and a further 13 per cent only move up to ten miles away.[108] There was one Irishman in Luton during the 1950s who moved there and took up work on the shopfloor at the Laporte chemical works after winning £20,000 – equivalent to almost one-and-a-half million in today's money – on the football pools.[109]

As McKenzie writes, government schemes and 'do-gooders' focused on improving people's self-esteem or how they can make a contribution to their local community miss the point; being respected in their community is not the problem. In fact, some women even tacitly encourage their children's criminality because they believe that the local value system is the best or only way that they can be valued.[110] It is wrong to understand their problems in terms of 'self-esteem'; many have plenty of esteem in terms of the value system of their neighbourhood. What struggling people need, in St Ann's and elsewhere, are money, resources and opportunities.

It is usually the people who have left one environment for another, or have to move between the two, who are most exposed to and most offended by prejudice and snobbery. Class hatred and bigotry matters far more to the working-class academic, barrister or surgeon than it does to someone who lives and works among the same people with whom they grew up. Speaking of the situation facing his fellow black Americans, the sociologist William Julius Wilson argued that racism was experienced in a very different way by the small black middle class, which encounters prejudice in its competition with whites for a few professional opportunities, than working-class blacks, for whom racism past or present is secondary to the institutionalised effects of multiple economic disadvantages. It is much the same for the working class in the UK. They do not care that middle-class people might sneer at their accents, or dress, or choice of leisure pursuits or holiday destinations; they often despise those people, and aspire to emulate them only in the sense that they want to have their wealth and security. Nonetheless, just because people refuse to act like or see themselves as victims does not mean that they are treated fairly. In an influential 1992 book, the French sociologists Pierre Bourdieu and Loïc Wacquant introduced the concept of 'symbolic violence', which they defined as 'violence which is exercised upon a social agent with his or her complicity'.[111] The sociologist Bev Skeggs applied this concept to working-class women who tried to adopt middle-class habits, often at psychological and financial cost, and still suffered from knowing that, no matter how hard they tried, they could still never quite do it right.[112]

Yet as Landesman argues: 'If anyone is to be pitied it's not the working-class person who is looked down upon, but the snob doing the looking. Believing in your own superiority – because of your birth or consumer choices – means that you are in the grips of a terrible and dangerous form of self-delusion.'[113] This is a very good point – any comfort provided by a sense of cultural or social superiority is small comfort indeed, a sort of 'wages of Waitrose' for those who are only marginally better off than the targets of their derision. But it is an attractive succour, and many people ostensibly on the Left, but in precarious positions, also console themselves for their precarity by hating the 'white working class'.

Even if you conclude that class is ultimately less significant than race, and that in white-majority countries even the most deprived white people are still 'privileged' compared to non-white people, it is essential for any project looking to address these inequalities to understand that they do not feel privileged. So, if parties of the liberal Left want to keep hold of or win back their votes, this needs to be acknowledged in their policies and language. It is no use to keep telling them that, if they only read X or considered Y, they'd realise that they were relatively well-off and should have more sympathy for immigrants/Muslims/trans people. It is particularly of no use to make this point via articles, television programmes, podcasts and social media accounts that only find an audience among people who already agree with you. At the same time, just because many people who suffer from the same disadvantages or worse *don't* fall into conspiracy theories, use racist language or vote for reactionary charlatans doesn't mean that we shouldn't try to understand and mitigate these disadvantages. It certainly doesn't justify implying that those doing so are motivated by racism or even fascism, or the sarcastic air-quoting of 'legitimate concerns'.

As Angela Nagle notes, portraying those who stress the role of economic anxieties and downward mobility in the rise of the Trumpian Right and similar movements around the world as excusing and thus enabling Nazis is not applied to historians of the actual Nazi period, all of whom consider the material and economic factors that led to the rise of fascism without being accused of blame-shifting.[114] At this point some readers might be shouting out: 'Aha! But what about all that research that indicates Trump supporters are actually better off than average!', and in this they have a point – although the same people would also be quick to stress that privilege and advantage are about much more than just wealth or income. And politically speaking, people's objective socio-economic position is less important than how they feel. As Nick Srnicek and Alex Williams write, a 'separation between everyday experience and the system we live within results in increased alienation: we feel adrift in a world we do not understand'.[115]

One recent incident provides an insight into this strange new world, in which globalisation and technological advances are rapidly eroding national, ethnic and economic power structures. In 2020, Indian police raided a call centre in New Delhi that was responsible for scamming thousands of victims in Britain, Australia and the USA. This shone a light on a small but booming industry of telephone scammers. A BBC reporter interviewed one, 'Piyush', to ask him about his techniques and strategies. Piyush told him that they used to target old people, as 'there are many old people in the US who don't have families, are alone and are disabled, so it's very easy to trick them'. They would use scams such as pretending to be the Internal Revenue Service, and insisting that they make payments on overdue taxes or they would face larger fines or arrest: 'We used to tell them that the police will go to their house and arrest them if they didn't pay.' Another scammer, 'Sam', told the BBC how he was surprised at the poverty of some of his targets, and 'is still in touch with some of the people he decided were too poor to be scammed, including a mother of three who worked in a fast food restaurant in the US, whom he now helps with computer issues. You could always work out someone's wealth, he says, from 'the way they talk [and] the sort of things they have on their computer'.

During some months, Piyush could make up to £40,000. Now, although he has left the world of telephone scams behind, he lives in one of the richest suburbs of New Delhi and sports a $400 watch – a gift from his old boss for meeting a target. However, he admits that the work could take a toll on his conscience, telling the BBC reporter of how he once forced a woman to hand over her last $100, a few days before Christmas, just so he could meet a target: 'I took that $100 and she cried a lot while making the payment. Yeah, this was the worst call I ever had.'[116] Piyush doesn't mention this woman's ethnicity. But she was elderly and, given the ethnic distribution among her age group in the US, there is almost a 90 per cent chance that she was white. If so, then in what sense is this elderly, isolated woman, handing over her last hundred dollars in the week before Christmas, 'privileged'? How, and according to what metric, is she more privileged than young Piyush, tech-savvy, perfectly equipped for the coming economy of the twenty-first century, living in a luxury apartment, with his whole life ahead of him? Only a racist, or, more charitably, a NeoOrientalist, who somehow thinks that being a poor white person in America is somehow better than being rich in India could think so.

Perhaps the woman drew some comfort from the 'wages of whiteness'. It could even have been that Orientalist associations of Indian voices with call centres reassured her and made her more susceptible to the scam. Either way, you would need a heart of stone or a head that can only accommodate theory to think that she was in any way 'privileged'.

Class – how much money you have, and what your prospects are for getting more – is the most essential factor that underpins and affects the meaning and significance of all other forms of identity. When the white woman Rachel Dolezal began living as a black woman she did not, as far as I'm aware, begin to suffer the same types of problems as genuine black people in the United States, which suggests to me that the most important discriminations and disadvantages to being black are not day-to-day racism but rather much deeper, life-long issues, which are inextricably linked to class. A key problem with our politics right now is that the Right pretends to care about class and many on the Left think talking about it is code for ignoring race.

Part II

Race

The man who adores the Negro is as sick as the man who abominates him.

Frantz Fanon, *Black Skin, White Masks*[1]

There's a generation of well-meaning 'liberals' out there who are seeking something real in this Web 2.0 world, and what can be more real than the plight of a marginalised minority?

Jeffrey Boakye, *Black, Listed*[2]

Around ten years ago I spent a year working at the University of York's disability service. This involved supporting disabled undergraduate students with a range of tasks, including notetaking in lectures and seminars, acting as a scribe in exams, and providing moral support and encouragement to students struggling with their mental health. It was a rewarding job, not only because sitting in on so many lecturers and seminars was almost like getting a second degree myself, but because of the many inspiring individuals I met. One student in particular stands out. Mohammed was a nineteen-year-old from Leicester who had lost his sight three years earlier. The sudden onset of blindness would be devastating enough for anyone, never mind a teenage boy – but Mohammed did not fall into despair, and instead achieved excellent exam results, gained acceptance to a leading university, and took up blind cricket, eventually playing for the England team.

I know that if I had gone blind at that age, my reaction would have been a lot less sanguine. Mohammed was a practising Muslim, and his faith was important to him – he even successfully lobbied his local mosque to pass a special *fatwa* to allow his guide dog, Vargo, to accompany him to prayers – the first time a guide dog (or any dog) was allowed into a UK mosque. All in all, he was a very impressive young man. During one of our lectures together, a professor – in the midst of explaining the arguments of John Rawls's *Theory of Justice* – called his name to ask for his input. Except, strangely, she pronounced it with a hard guttural sound on the 'h'. I thought this was odd, and not only because Mohammed's family was from Pakistan and Urdu speakers do not pronounce Mohammed in that way. More to the point, neither did Mohammed himself. He spoke his own name with the same East Midlands accent that he used for everything else – so why did she exoticise his name in this way?

This sort of thing is not uncommon. Jeremy Corbyn infamously did a similar thing with Jewish names, putting on a hammy Yiddish inflection so that Harvey Weinstein became Harvey Vine-shtein, and Jeffrey Epstein became Jeffrey Ep-shtein. Many people held this up as an indication of antisemitism, although personally I thought it was tin-eared rather than sinister: he was actually trying to endear himself to Jews by showing his learning and cultural sensitivity, too stupid to see it would have the exact opposite effect, and too stubborn to change when it did. Nor is this reserved for 'Oriental' names: many British football commentators make a special effort to accurately pronounce the names of Spanish-speaking players, with exaggerated rolling Rs and lisped Cs and Zs. (There also seems to be a kind of 'pizza effect' [see Chapter 4] going on here, as the British-based Spanish football journalist Guillem

Balagué sounds more like an English person doing a cod Spanish accent than any Spaniard I have ever met, although it could be that he actually has a lisp.)

Why do people do this? Specifically, why did the professor and Corbyn think that this kind of Orientalising was not merely appropriate, but actually endearing? The professor had almost certainly read Edward Said, and Corbyn almost certainly had not, but surely there were plenty of people around him who had. I think the answer is that both were aiming to impress on everyone listening the extent of their worldliness and the breadth of their cultural sympathies – as are the football commentators. But this is one of the key problems with today's NeoOrientalism: no matter how well-intentioned, it is often powered by a desire to augment the perception of one's erudition, and usually has the effect of exoticising and patronising the people it is ostensibly meant to benefit.

In 2019 I was on a tour of a Bedouin village in Israel's Negev desert. The Bedouin have had a great deal of difficulty proving their right to their land and property, with the result that they are easily dispossessed by the Israeli government or property developers. Our host was a chain-smoking sheik, who at length explained his family's history in the area and his long-standing legal struggles to protect his land. As he was offering us coffee, my friend Eyal – who works for an Israeli NGO supporting the rights of Bedouins – whispered that it was important to drink five cups of coffee, so as not to cause offence. The sheik overheard this and burst out laughing, exclaiming something along the lines of 'no one cares about that shit, drink as much or as little as you like'. So why do we do this? It is a way to show off how educated and cultured we are, and how sensitive we are to other cultures – but at the same time this essentialises other cultures, preserves them as unchanging relics, and is ultimately self-serving. Today, this 'NeoOrientalism' makes objects of 'non-Westerners' for the benefit of ourselves.

Edward Said wrote in *Orientalism*, first published in 1978, that 'an Englishman in India or Egypt in the later nineteenth century took an interest in those countries that was never far from their status in his mind as British colonies, [therefore] all academic knowledge about India and Egypt is somehow tinged and impressed with' this political fact.[3] For Said, even the most well-meaning academic Orientalist was hamstrung by the origins of the discipline in European colonial and imperial projects. Therefore, they could not appreciate 'Oriental' societies, cultures or peoples on their own terms, but instead always viewed them through the prism of European – and later American – interests. This inextricable connection with imperialism past and present meant that even benign and good-intentioned Orientalism was inherently and inescapably compromised.

Palestinian by birth, he approvingly cited French Orientalist Louis Massignon's criticism of Israeli 'bourgeois colonialism', yet argued that this critique was compromised through Massignon's binary way of understanding the world, which 'assigned the Islamic Orient to an essentially ancient time and the West to modernity'. For Massignon, 'the British seemed to represent "expansion" in the Orient, amoral economic policy, and an outdated philosophy of political influence', whereas what 'the Westerner' should really seek from the Orient was to recover 'what he had lost in spirituality, traditional values, and the like' due to the 'tradition of the Orient as therapeutic for the West'.[4]

Today, NeoOrientalist concern about and for people of colour is tinged by and impressed with the supposed weakness of the latter in relation to 'white people'. This is driven by various factors, including exploitation by the media and entertainment industry; the impera-tives of academic research funding; the solipsistic projects of the Western Left; and a desire to make oneself seem cooler and more authentic. It can be well-intentioned in some cases, but unfortunately the NeoOrientalist polarity between 'white people' and 'people of colour', or between a morally compromised 'West' and the idealised

'Other' of the Global South has the effect of reinforcing the distinctiveness and centrality of white people.

Said wrote of how 'the Orientalist provides his own society with representations of the Orient that bear his distinctive imprint, illustrate his conception of what the Orient can or ought to be, that consciously contest someone else's view of the Orient'. This places the Orient, and Orientals, 'out of reach of everyone except the Western expert'. Ultimately for Said, this served to provide Western discourse 'with what, at that moment, it seems most in need of, and that respond to certain cultural, professional, national, political, and economic requirements of the epoch'.[5]

Today, NeoOrientalists put their own distinctive imprint – well-educated, middle-class, mostly white – on to the Oriental object, who is imbued with the values of the former, whether they like it or not. This serves several purposes: cultural, in the sense that it allows the NeoOrientalist to appear as an interesting, multifaceted character; political, in that it allows them to advance their various projects; and economic and professional, in that it allows them to advance in academia, politics and the media, and raise profits for the food industry, tourism companies and the entertainment industry – all of which benefit from this NeoOrientalist gaze.

> Any deviation from what were considered the norms of Oriental behaviour was believed to be unnatural; [thus] Egyptian nationalism [was] an 'entirely novel idea' and 'a plant of exotic rather than of indigenous growth'.
>
> Edward Said, *Orientalism*[6]

In 1989 the historians Eric Hobsbawm and Terence Ranger published *The Invention of Tradition*, a collection of essays detailing the shallow roots of many traditions assumed to have ancient provenance, from the kilts and bagpipes of the Scottish Highlands to the elaborate ceremonies of the British monarchy. Hobsbawm and Ranger focused on how these traditions were used to justify and support conservative policies, but this exaggeration of the longevity of certain cultural traditions is not exclusive to the political Right and is a cornerstone of NeoOrientalism. Under this process, the 'West' is compared unfavourably to 'non-Western' societies and cultures, with the latter praised for having maintained communality, selflessness and a healthy relationship with their environment.

Perhaps the archetypal example of this are the Maasai people of Tanzania and Kenya. Instantly recognisable with their 'trademark' red cloaks and spears, these pastoralists are emblematic for a certain kind of Westerner of a people at peace with their environment, resisting the worst aspects of modernity. A letter to the *New York Times* describes how the author 'was horrified to learn that Tanzania is encouraging subjugation and ultimate obliteration of some of its oldest and noblest inhabitants, the once free and beautiful Masai'.[7] Meanwhile an article in the *Guardian* describes the Maasai as projecting 'a timelessness that speaks to notions of man's origins and the beginnings of time', and how 'centuries of survival in harsh lands gave them a strong sense of mutualism, but a culture of cronyism now pits the Masai against one another'. This culture of cronyism was not natural to the Maasai, but instead developed as a result of contact with 'the West', specifically with capitalism and mass tourism. In the same article, the writer describes how their solitude is interrupted by the arrival of tourists: 'We cut the engine and the silence is acute, [yet] one minibus has already pulled up on another sandy track a few hundred metres away and four heads are craning out of the roof. We sit and watch for the cheetah. All of a sudden white minibuses crest the horizon in droves.'[8]

This was what Said was talking about when he spoke of how Orientalism can 'reduce to a kind of flatness' and remove 'complicating humanity', so that 'the complex dynamics of human life ...

becomes either irrelevant or trivial in comparison with the circular vision by which the details of Oriental life serve merely to reassert the Orientalness of the subject and the Westerness of the observer'.[9] Even though this *Guardian* piece was written in the post-*Orientalist* world, and the writer seems to take care to avoid deploying obvious Orientalist tropes, they cannot help but construct a binary between the 'Westerness' of the tourists and the 'otherness' of the Maasai.

Yet Dorothy Hodgson's research into the Maasai has revealed that the archetypal 'Western' image of their lifestyle, which readers of the *New York Times* and the *Guardian* are eager to protect from the ravages and environmental despoilation of Western capitalism, is false, even down to the red cloaks: 'They wear an array of clothes depending on the context', says Hodgson. 'At home, some wear a long cloth knotted over one shoulder and fastened to the waist by a belt, while others wear blue jeans and T-shirts. All have pants, shirts, jackets, and shoes to wear to towns, political meetings, and other venues.'[10]

Furthermore, attempts to protect Maasai culture 'further reinforced and rigidified the distinctions between Maasai [culture] as traditional and others (whether British colonial administrators or Tanzanian elites) as modern'. As a result of this, writes Hodgson, 'Maasai women have not only lost economic rights of control over pastoralist resources and access to new economic and political opportunities, but they have been disenfranchised from a sense of Maasai identity as well'.[11] Although this NeoOrientalist essentialisation is most pronounced among Westerners, cynical Tanzanian politicians make their own contribution, and it has become '*de rigueur* for a visiting politician to have his photo taken with some traditional Maasai'.[12]

As with supposedly 'timeless' peoples or cultures, so too with religion. Many NeoOrientalists see the world's one billion plus Muslims as almost uniformly religious, with each article of their faith mattering deeply to each and every one of them, and insults to this faith considered intolerable. This is notably a mirror image of the view of the Islamophobic Right. Yet in reality a great deal of people who are nominally 'Muslim' pay little heed to the tenets of Islam, and do not subscribe to the political worldview assumed to be consistently held by all Muslims.

A clear example of this is the *rapprochement* over the past few years between Israel and various states in the Arabian Gulf, part of a larger and deliberate manoeuvre by the monarchies of these nations away from Islam as a means of ensuring national cohesion and their own continued rule. This also manifests itself in the recent papal trip to Saudi Arabia and the evolution of attitudes towards women's rights. One might argue that these are crooked dictators playing their people for chumps in exchange for greater wealth and power, but the average Qatari or Emirati has a worldview entirely different from that of their fellow religionists living in poverty in Egypt or Syria, and especially from displaced Palestinians in the refugee camps of Jordan and Syria. Even in Iran, as highlighted by Asef Bayat's influential article 'Revolution without Movement, Movement without Revolution', there was fairly little support for political Islam in the country before the 1979 revolution, which was able to succeed largely because the Shah (generously helped by the CIA) had hamstrung so much of the secular liberal and socialist opposition.[13] This NeoOrientalism is not confined to people outside the Global North, and is even applied to non-white people in white majority countries.

The Problem with 'People of Color'

In the outpouring of support for the Black Lives Matter movement in the wake of the death of George Floyd in May 2020, many white celebrities attempted to hitch their careers to its wagon, only to fall and be mangled under the wheels. One of the most prominent was the comedian and talk-show host Ellen DeGeneres, who damaged her reputation by tweeting that 'people of color in [the USA] have faced injustice for far too long'. An ostensibly unoffensive message, DeGeneres's mistake was her use of the term 'people of color', and it was soon made clear to her that – in this instance at least – the term was not appropriate: 'Seriously? Not people of color. George Floyd was black', was a typical response. DeGeneres quickly deleted her original tweet and sent a new message specifically referring to black people. She was not the first well-meaning white person to get in trouble with this term, although their grief usually arises from its similarity to the pejorative 'colored people' – a slip made in recent years by the likes of the actor Benedict Cumberbatch and the former Home Secretary Amber Rudd.

Yet this episode demonstrated the bigger problem with the term 'people of colour'. The phrase and its British equivalent, the even clunkier Black, Asian and Minority Ethnic, obscure the real and important differences between and within different ethnic minority groups. This not only makes addressing prejudice and structural disadvantages even more difficult, but it reinforces the idea of a colour binary, exacerbating the idea of 'white as default' and 'othering' black and brown people.

In the United States, the phrase 'people of colour' is used as a catch-all term to describe African Americans, Native Americans, Hispanic Americans, Asian Americans and all 'non-white' people. The broadness of this term undermines a focus on structural racism and systemic disadvantage by grouping together people with vastly different levels of wealth, income and education, who face completely different types and levels of pervasiveness of prejudice and discrimination. The US was founded on the enslavement of African Americans – the denial of their humanity was literally written into the constitution, with the infamous 'three-fifths compromise'. After eventually abolishing slavery, the US failed to reconstruct an economy, society, culture and political system all predicated on racist assumptions about black people. It is therefore inaccurate and offensive to elide the discrimination and prejudice faced by other ethnic groups with that suffered by African Americans.

Today, Asian Americans are the best educated, wealthiest and the highest-earning ethnic group in the US, but also have the greatest internal economic disparity among any ethnic group. In 2015, the share of adults aged twenty-five and older with at least a bachelor's degree ranged from 9 per cent among Bhutanese to 72 per cent among Indians; median household income varied from $36,000 among Burmese to $100,000 among Indians; and poverty rates were as high as 35 per cent among Burmese and 33 per cent among Bhutanese. There is also a persistent 'bamboo ceiling' whereby Asian graduates are disproportionately represented in lower-level positions across various sectors, including tech, law, media and finance, but under-represented at managerial levels or above. In the UK, while Chinese people attend university at a higher rate than whites, Chinese male graduates in 2005 could expect to earn 25 per cent less than white male graduates.[14]

Something similar can be said for Hispanic Americans or Latinos – a group which spans ultra-conservative Cuban émigrés who fled the Castro regime, to left-wing firebrands such as Alexandra Ocasio-Cortez. There is a huge disparity in wealth, income and educational level among Latino Americans, and this variety is also found in their politics and culture. Among Americans who identify as Hispanic, very few identify as non-white, and many Hispanics who move up economically stop identifying as Hispanic.[15] Any term which would consider US Senators Marco Rubio and Ted Cruz to have the same interests and concerns, and face the same problems, as recently arrived immigrants detained in camps on the Mexican border is clearly not fit for purpose.

To this day, African Americans remain notably less wealthy than other groups. While the large gaps between the incomes of blacks and whites have closed slightly in recent years, they remain considerable:

in 2016, blacks on average earned 65 per cent as much as whites, a small increase from 59 per cent in 1970.[16] As of December 2019 the unemployment rate for blacks was 5.9 per cent, compared to just 3.2 per cent for whites and only 2.5 per cent for Asians.[17] Even the children of black parents in the top 1 per cent are disproportionately likely to suffer downward social mobility or find it harder to maintain their position.[18]

This does not apply uniformly to all black people in America. For example, in 2018, the median income for households led by a Nigerian American was $68,658, compared with $61,937 for US households overall. Nigerian Americans are also more likely to be counted in the higher income brackets, with 35 per cent of their households earning at least $90,000 per year. They are also the best-educated demographic in the US, with a higher percentage holding postgraduate degrees than among any other group. In total, 37 per cent of Nigerian Americans have a bachelor's degree and 17 per cent a master's.

Although Nigerians account for less than 1 per cent of America's black population, they make up nearly a quarter of black students at Harvard Business School, and the first black woman to head the *Harvard Law Review*, Imelme Umana, was a Nigerian American (the first black man was Barack Obama). There is a similar trend in the UK where, according to the Runnymede Trust, there are three times as many Afro-Caribbean men in prison as at university, and this is particularly acute for men from Caribbean backgrounds: back in 2017, a picture of the fourteen black male students admitted to study that year at the University of Cambridge went viral, demonstrating the disproportionately few black Britons admitted to Oxbridge. Yet of the fourteen students, all but one – William Gore – had West African names.[19]

There are similar disparities when it comes to police violence. In 2019, 24 per cent of the Americans killed by police were black, despite their constituting only 13 per cent of the US population. In the same year, 2.5 per million white people were killed by the police, not far below the 3.8 per million Hispanics. For African Americans, however, it was 6.6 per million – almost three times the white rate and just shy of twice the Hispanic rate.[20] (Incidentally, the worst rate by far was for Native Americans, at 10.13 per million.[21]) This means that even the most privileged black Americans have genuine and well-founded fears that all their wealth and influence cannot protect their children from being gunned down by the police or an armed vigilante.[22]

Out of the high-profile cases of African Americans shot dead by the police, it is striking how many of them involve Hispanic, Italian-American or Asian officers. In 2014, Eric Garner died after being initially approached by police officer Justin D'Amico and placed in a chokehold by Daniel Pantaleo; his death was overseen by a female African-American NYPD sergeant, Kizzy Adonis, who did not intervene; in 2018, Chinedu Okobi died after being tasered multiple times by deputy Joshua Wang; Trayvon Martin, who in 2012 was not killed by police but by George Zimmerman, whose mother, Gladys Cristina Mesa, is from Peru, and who has a black grandfather; Philando Castile was shot dead in 2016 by officer Jeronimo Yanez; and Sandra Bland was found dead in her cell in 2015 after a violent arrest by state trooper Brian Encima.

Even in the 'original' example of police violence caught on video, the Rodney King beating of 1991, two of the officers involved – Theodore Briseno and Rolando Solano – were Hispanic. In fact, Briseno was publicly supported by Eric 'Easy E' Wright of hip-hop group NWA, who claimed that Briseno tried to help King and protect him from the other officers. Hispanic men are overrepresented in all law enforcement institutions in the US, including Border Patrol and Immigration and Customs Enforcement.[23]

In the George Floyd killing, two of the four officers involved were Asian Americans: Tou Thao, who stood guard as Floyd was kneeled on, had been sued for alleged excessive force back in 2017, with the

Minneapolis Police Department eventually settling out of court for $25,000. In total, six complaints had been filed against Thao; five were closed with no disciplinary action taken and one remained open at the time of Floyd's death.[24] Thao and the wife of Derek Chauvin – the officer who knelt on Floyd's neck – are members of the Hmong diaspora, refugees from Laos who settled in the US after 1975. Hmong Americans occupy a peculiar position: they fought alongside the US in Vietnam, but are 'people of colour'; they are disproportionately likely to be police officers, yet they are still immigrants. Furthermore, they do not fit cleanly into the country's broad-brush racial categories. Because so many came as impoverished refugees, they are more likely to be poor than many other Asian immigrants from places such as China and India who are often university-educated professionals.

Like many Americans of East Asian ancestry, the Hmong suffered from an increased level of hostility due to COVID-19: in May 2020, in the city of St Paul, an African-American teenager was recorded by his friend kicking a Hmong woman in the face while she sat waiting for a train. Yet as so many of them are small business owners or police officers, many Hmong found themselves on the wrong side of the protests that erupted after the Floyd killing. One member of Minneapolis's Hmong community, Gloria Wong, told the *New York Times*: 'We came to this country with nothing . . . I have been working my whole life for my building. Now it just takes one or two persons to trash it. I feel very down right now. My heart is just aching all over.' Ms Wong said that she was a supporter of the police, and her uncle had been one of the first Hmong Americans to join the force back in the 1980s.[25] The Hmong, like Nigerian Americans, demonstrate the complexity of race in the United States, and the meaninglessness of the term people of colour. As far as I'm aware, there is no evidence to suggest that Asian or Hispanic officers are more likely than average to kill black people – although black cops are as likely to shoot and more likely to arrest African Americans than their white colleagues – but the disproportionate number of Hispanic and African-American cops involved in high-profile brutality incidents also exposes the falsity of the people of colour–whites dichotomy.[26]

While there is a need for some sort of group noun for different ethnic minorities in majority-white countries, 'non-white' defines people by what they are not, and reinforces the idea of whiteness as default, so is clearly unsatisfactory (hence my use of 'people of colour' and 'BAME' throughout this book, even though those terms are problematic). Nonetheless, we need to move beyond easy catch-all terms that flatten and homogenise the multi-varied lives and experiences of millions of people, and create a binary between white and non-white.

Chapter 3

The Limits of the Rainbow

One of the key aspects of NeoOrientalism is the political essentialisation of people of colour. It is not just that black and brown people are assumed to have a homogenously radical politics, so that incidences of their support for conservative policies or candidates require explanation; but rather that political radicalism is assumed to be an essential element of not being white. In *Orientalism*, Said wrote that 'what mattered to the Western student was the supervening power of Islam to make intelligible the experiences of the Islamic people, not the other way around.'[1] That is to say, Islam provided the essential framework through which to understand Muslims; it was an all-pervasive feature of their lives, and Muslim people could not be understood except through its lens. For today's NeoOrientalists, political radicalism serves a similar function: non-white people are inherently radical, anti-imperialist and anti-racist, and can only be properly understood in this context.

Said argued that the noted Orientalist H. A. R. Gibb was interested in Islam as a 'transcendent, compelling Oriental fact', and didn't care about the complications of 'nationalism, class struggle, the individualising experiences of love, anger, or human work.'[2] If we substitute 'political radicalism' for 'Islam', we can say much the same about the political radicalism of people of colour today. For the NeoOrientalist, black and brown nationalisms, inter- (and intra-) ethnic hatred, class divisions and the myriad complications of human life are all of secondary importance to the 'transcendent, compelling fact' that people of colour are radicals and foot soldiers in the fight against the forces of reaction.

For some on the British Left, while white people are compromised by their racism and conservatism, ethnic minorities had the good sense to perceive and reject the false promises of Boris Johnson and remained solidly Labour. (Never mind the fact that many specific ethnic groups, such as British Indians and Jews, are more or less evenly split, and that even among the most pro-Labour groups a minimum of 10 per cent vote Tory.) Likewise, in the 2016 US presidential election, while the correlation along the lines of race was unmistakable, around one-third of Hispanic Americans and 10 per cent of African Americans backed Trump. Between 2016 and 2020, Trump even gained 4 percentage points with African Americans, 3 points with Hispanics and Latinos, and 5 points with Asian Americans. The problem here is not even the condemnation of white Americans as a group, but rather with anointing non-whites as the conscience of the nation and its only possible saviours. Needless to say, the reality is much more complicated than this, and in many areas different ethnic groups appear to be more conservative than white people.

There is evidence that suggests political identity trumps (no pun intended) ethnic identity: a University of Virginia study of three hundred Hispanic and Asian Trump voters found more than half agreed that the US 'needed to protect and preserve its white European heritage'.[3] In a 2017 Pew survey, fully 91 per cent of the mostly white group described as 'solidly liberal' agreed that 'discrimination is the most important reason why blacks can't get ahead', but only 40 per cent of the 'devout and diverse' group (people from a variety of ethnic backgrounds who identified as religious) did.[4] Political scientist Eric Kaufmann points out that even where whites 'are a majority and we might expect minorities to be on the defensive against them, a significant component of minority Americans express white ethno-traditional nationalism'. Part of this is a socio-economic response to perceived immigrant competition, but also reflects 'a minority conservatism which values the white narrative of American history and culture'. In a survey conducted in August 2017, immediately after the far-Right rally in Charlottesville, Virginia, around 30 per cent of Hispanics and slightly fewer 'Others' (mainly Asian) agreed with the view that 'America must protect and preserve its White European heritage'. This was only 3 points lower than the percentage of whites who said the same.[5]

The Politics of Ethnic Minorities in White-Majority Countries

It goes without saying that there is tremendous variety within and between different ethnic minority groups, and this is still compatible with the NeoOrientalist worldview, which accepts that minorities of minorities may vote for conservative parties, without compromising the fundamental essential radicalism of non-white people as a whole. At the same time, specific groups can and do change their allegiances; witness the shift in African-American support from the Republicans to the Democrats during the last century, or the more recent and much faster shift in Asian-American support in the same direction. At a micro-level, such changes can be even more rapid: in North Carolina's Robeson County, where Native Americans account for a majority of voters and which Barack Obama won by 20 points in 2012, Joe Biden lost by 40 points in 2020, while Texas's Zapata County – the second-most Hispanic county in America – was won by Obama by 43 points in 2012 and Clinton by 33 points in 2016: in 2020, Biden lost by 5 points. Nonetheless, there is plenty of evidence that the support of a majority of ethnic minorities in Britain and the US for parties of the Left reflects the anti-immigrant or racist reputations of the Conservative and Republican parties, rather than any political radicalism on the part of minorities.

The Latino population of the United States, far from fuelling the leftward shift of the Democrats in recent years, is a key reason why this shift may not be electorally wise in the long run, especially given the likely growth of this demographic in the coming decades. In California, for example, although only 23 per cent of Latinos voted for Donald Trump in 2020, and only around 15 per cent of California's Hispanic voters are registered Republicans, nearly one-third of Hispanics in the state say they are conservative, and another 30 per cent describe themselves as politically moderate. Furthermore, it is hard to make any easy generalisations about the reason for Latino conservatism, and it has much deeper roots than the reflexive anti-communism of Cuban migrants. According to historian Geraldo Cadava, the first Hispanic group formed to rally national support for a Republican, *Latinos con Eisenhower*, was founded in California by Mexican Americans, and Cuban Americans were not prominent within Republican politics until Ronald Reagan's presidency in the 1980s.[6]

Just before the 2020 election, Quinnipiac and Monmouth University polls found that while only 3 per cent of all voters were undecided, among Latino Americans that figure rose as high as 38 per cent in ten key battleground states. In the end, this wasn't enough for Donald Trump: while he held Florida, he lost the state of Arizona, and Joe Biden repeated Hillary Clinton's strong performance in Nevada and New Mexico. Nonetheless, given the solidification of party allegiance and decline in swing voting in the US, the apparent agnosticism of many Latinos will concern Democrats. As will the results of research by Ian Haney López and Tony Gavito, who asked eligible voters what they thought about conservative arguments with implicitly racist overtones, such as stopping 'illegal immigration from places overrun with drugs and criminal gangs' or calling for 'fully funding the police, so our communities are not threatened by people who refuse to follow our laws'. Almost three out of five white voters and African Americans, and an even higher percentage of Latinos, found these messages 'convincing'.

López and Gavito found that self-ascribed identity was the most important factor affecting these views: 'More than whether the individual was Mexican-American or from Cuba, young or old, male or female, from Texas, Florida or California, how the person perceived the racial identity of Latinos as a group shaped his or her receptivity to a message stoking racial division.' Significantly for the future politics of Latino America, only one in four Hispanics (at the time of writing) see themselves as 'people of color', and the majority reject this designation, preferring to see Hispanics 'as a group integrating into the American mainstream, one not overly bound by racial constraints but instead able to get ahead through hard work'. Furthermore, when asked to rate the attractiveness of various policies and slogans, the majority of Latinos rated left-wing economic positions – on issues such as government spending, welfare and the economy – as no more attractive than, or equal to, messages based on racial anxiety and resentment.[7]

This quantitative research is supported by anecdotal evidence. When the *New York Times* interviewed Trump-supporting Latinos just before the 2020 election, they found a variety of reasons behind their allegiance, all of which confound the worldview of the NeoOrientalists. Henry Cejudo, who won a gold medal in wrestling at the 2008 Beijing Olympics, is himself the son of illegal Mexican immigrants, and yet became an enthusiastic and high-profile supporter of Trump. Cejudo claims to have been a fan of Trump since watching him on the *Apprentice* TV show, and cites his apparent business nous as the reason for his support: 'We need a businessman, we need somebody like this to run our country.'[8] This should not be surprising: according to a 2019 survey by UnidosUS and Latino Decisions, Latinos are ultimately more concerned about jobs and the economy than immigration.[9]

For Paul Ollarsaba Jr, whose 2016 vote for Trump was the first time the forty-one-year-old former Marine had supported a Republican, he was persuaded by Trump's apparent commitment to the military. He proudly states that he is a Mexican, and that he believed for a long time his Mexican identity meant he should vote Democratic. His parents even criticised him when learning of his choice, asking, 'Why are you supporting a racist? You're Mexican, you have to vote this way.' But this response only solidified his support for Trump. He told his parents: 'No, it's my country. It's fear, people are afraid of saying they support the president.'[10] In this response there are similarities with a view expounded by immigrants and the descendants of recent immigrants in the UK, who appear to be converging with the white British population's attitudes to immigration, as we shall see. On a practical level, this suggests that the difficulties around immigration, nation and belonging that have plagued left-liberal parties in the Anglosphere in recent years will not be ameliorated by demographic change.

In fact, NeoOrientalist language and assumptions around the politics of Latinos appear to have encouraged many to support Trump and the Republican Party in the first place: Nathalie Nieves, from the New York chapter of the National Association of Hispanic Journalists, criticises the media's use of 'Latino' or 'Hispanic' as 'othering' them from their fellow Americans: 'If I'm totally honest, I only learned I was a Latina in the last few years. I still don't know what that means. Growing up, I thought of myself as Cuban, or maybe Caribbean. Eventually, I became a citizen and thus a Cuban-American. These days I think of myself as an American.'[11]

In contrast to Hispanic Americans, African-American support for the Democrats remains solid, with around 90 per cent voting for the Democratic candidate in presidential elections since at least the 1990s. Historically, of course, African Americans supported the Republican Party, the legacy of the latter's support for the abolition of slavery and extension of voting and civil rights after the Civil War. This results in some awkwardness with historical African-American figures such as Jesse Owens, who after taking three gold medals at the 1936 Olympics praised Hitler at a Republican Party rally, comparing him favourably to the 'perfidious' FDR.[12]

While African-American support for the Republicans today is much weaker than among Latinos, they are another group that, on the face of it, are much closer to conservatives than the NeoOrientalist worldview allows. As Chryl Laird and Ismail White argue in their book *Steadfast Democrats*, African Americans, like Hispanics, are mostly at the conservative end of the Democratic coalition. According to a Gallup poll from 2019, over two in five black Americans identify as moderate, and roughly a quarter of each identify as liberal or conservative. The political scientist Tasha Philpot even argues that the African-American electorate is politically conservative, just not Republican.[13]

During the 2008 Democratic primaries, polls suggested that most black voters initially backed Hillary Clinton over Barack Obama, as she seemed like a surer bet to take the presidency, before the strong performances of the freshman senator in Iowa and New Hampshire persuaded them that he was a risk worth taking. At one point in February 2020, polls showed that the billionaire Mike Bloomberg was the second most popular primary candidate among African Americans, a few percentage points behind Joe Biden. If this surprises you, it's possible that you are falling into the NeoOrientalist fallacy of assuming a connection between ethnicity and political radicalism based on the views of prominent academics, journalists and online activists: 23 per cent of all Democrats are black, but only 11 per cent of Democrats on social media. In an informal *New York Times* poll, only 2 per cent of its readers said they were black. Therefore, high-profile black columnists such as Charles Blow and Jamelle Bouie are not representative of black liberals; in fact, there is almost certainly a higher proportion of black people working at the *Times* than reading it.

Laird and White theorise that as part of an effort to increase their political potency as a minority within a majoritarian political system, black Americans prioritise group solidarity, 'whereby support for the Democratic Party has come to be defined as a norm of group behavior'. In other words, voting Democratic 'has come to be understood as just something you do as a black person, an expectation of behavior meant to empower the racial group'. This sounds pretty similar to the identification of many working-class Brits with the Labour Party; by the 2010s, they were continuing to vote Labour more out of habit and identity than any affiliation with Labour policies. What happened next should be of real concern for US Democrats.

Support for the Democrats among Asian Americans is a recent development: at the 1992 presidential election, it is estimated that less than a third of the Asian-American vote went to Bill Clinton. The percentage of Asian Americans voting Democrat has increased steadily since, to two-thirds in 2008 and 73 per cent in 2012. This fell back to two-thirds again in 2016, and fell again slightly to 61 per cent in 2020. It is believed that anger at affirmative action policies to aid black and Hispanic people, which they see as unfairly discriminatory against Asians, was one reason for the uptick in support for the Republican candidate at those last two presidential elections. In 2014, businessman Yukong Zhao filed a high-profile lawsuit challenging Harvard University's admissions policy, and in the same year Chinese-American groups lobbied successfully against a proposed California law that would have reinstated affirmative action at state universities.[14] These campaigns generated renewed support for Republican and conservative groups, some of which craftily portrayed their own opposition to affirmative action in terms of its effects on Asians.

Nonetheless, large majorities of Asian Americans still vote Democrat, and the high-profile (albeit unsuccessful) candidacy of

Andrew Yang for the Democratic nomination in 2020 has boosted the party's image in the eyes of many East Asian Americans. It also appears that anti-immigrant sentiment is more significant to the Asian-American vote than it is to Latinos. The political scientist Cecilia Hyunjung Mo recently conducted an experiment with Asian Americans, in which half were subjected to a 'seemingly benign racial microaggression' before the experiment began. A white researcher assisting Mo said to half of the participants: 'I'm sorry. I forgot that this study is only for US citizens. Are you a US citizen? I cannot tell.' The half who had this question directed at them were more likely to 'identify strongly as a Democrat' and were also more likely to view Republicans 'generally as close-minded and ignorant, less likely to represent people like them, and to have more negative feelings toward them.'[15]

In the UK, while the vast majority of black voters support Labour, there is plenty of evidence that this is based upon the Conservatives' reputation for anti-black racism. There are many reasons why black people, in terms of both economic and cultural values, might be won over to the Tories, and these are being elucidated by a new generation of BAME Conservative MPs, who are often on the Thatcherite or Johnsonite right wing of the party. In her maiden speech, Nigerian-born Conservative MP Kemi Badenoch described Brexit as the 'greatest ever vote of confidence in the project of the United Kingdom', and claimed that 'the vision of global Britain as a project is, as a young African girl, [something] I dreamed of becoming part of'.

While there are plenty of prominent people of colour who have consistently left-liberal views, all the evidence suggests that they are a minority, just like white radicals. And, just like white radicals, they usually come from atypical backgrounds. The rapper Akala, for example, attributes his politics to having politicised and 'militantly pro-education' parents, and attending pan-African Sunday school, but these are influences absent from the politics of most black Britons.[16]

Even on immigration, there are significant divergences from the NeoOrientalist viewpoint, which sees any desire for restriction of immigration as inherently suspicious, if not racist. Of people who emigrated to the UK before 1970, fully 48 per cent want immigration reduced a lot, and 22 per cent a little; for 1971–90 immigrants the numbers are only slightly lower, at 32 and 31 per cent.[17] A 2013 NatCen poll asked first- and second-generation immigrants in the UK whether they thought immigration was good for the economy, and only 26 per cent agreed, with 25 per cent saying it had been neither good nor bad, and 48 per cent claiming it had been detrimental to the British economy. The same survey asked whether they thought the numbers of immigrants should increase, stay the same or decrease. Only 8 per cent wanted immigration numbers to increase, 31 per cent wanted them to stay at the same level, and 60 per cent wanted the numbers to come down.

It is estimated that around one-third of BAME Britons voted Leave in the 2016 Brexit referendum: according to one online survey, 27 per cent of blacks, 30 per cent of Chinese Britons and 33 per cent of South Asian Brits backed Brexit. A thorough analysis of the opinions of BAME Britons by the Runnymede Trust found that black and Asian Britons cared less about the benefits of free movement than white people – although this varied with age, with younger BAME Brits more likely to travel to Europe on holiday or for work than older generations.[18]

A feature in the *Guardian* on BAME Britons who voted Leave included Mahmood, who came to the UK in 1989. He describes his nationality as Anglo-Pakistani and is 'aware of the irony' that, despite being from an immigrant background, he wants to make it harder for others to enter. Nonetheless, he insists that his views are valid: 'We have worked so hard to earn the right to live here and we contribute to the communities. What we don't want is more people coming in who won't bring anything positive and will just take.' Other people featured in the *Guardian* piece cite tales of violence and theft by Eastern Europeans against Asian people. Mahmood says that he, and people like him, are those 'on the ground' who will feel the result of increased European migration. He is fearful of the influx of poor immigrants into 'ghettoised' communities that he says 'are already struggling with a lack of housing and resources'. He complains that freedom of movement within the EU allows foreign criminals to enter the UK, and for scroungers to exploit the generous welfare state to send money back home.[19] It is sadly ironic that these comments echo the tropes used against Commonwealth immigrants in the 1960s and 1970s, and, as we can see in the Elizabethan complaint from Part I, used against immigrants since at least the sixteenth century.

The Runnymede study found that most black and Asian Britons held the same attitudes towards immigration as their white compatriots, although their personal experiences often meant that the reasons for holding those opinions differed. For example, many non-white Brits felt that when politicians, tabloids or drunks in the street talked about 'immigrants', they also essentially included them. That is to say, many British people from ethnic minority backgrounds felt that anti-immigrant sentiment was not merely restricted to actual immigrants, but often trickled down to, or was used as a substitute for, racist hostility to them and their children and grandchildren. This is why although they overwhelmingly wanted immigration to be reduced, they mainly focused on economic arguments against immigration, and were wary of language connected to 'culture'.

The Runnymede investigation found that many older migrants framed the issue in terms of fairness, particularly the unfairness of more recent immigrants from the European Union potentially receiving benefits that they themselves – older Caribbean, African or Asian migrants – didn't receive. Likewise, long-settled migrants often felt as though they had a hard time in Britain, at least at first, and resented the idea that more recent migrants had it easier. (This is sadly reminiscent of some women in middle age or older who are angry or resentful at the #MeToo movement since they had to deal with abuse and harassment in the workplace as a matter of course.)

Another reason that older migrants resent more recent arrivals is that they (rightly and understandably) see themselves as British, and not immigrants, which facilitates them holding the same anti-immigration sentiments typical of the white population, and in some instances even resenting immigrants for increasing hostility towards BAME Britons.[20] This should not be surprising. There are very few countries in the world where a majority of people favour increased immigration, and this does not appear to be a new trend. Even in specific situations when we might expect people to have welcomed more immigrants, we find the persistence of hostility. For example, during the early years of the existence of the state of Israel, when the country risked annihilation at the hands of its neighbours, many Israelis opposed the immigration of Jewish refugees from the Middle East and North Africa, citing the usual concerns around drains on resources and cultural incompatibility. On a global level, there are only a tiny number of people who support open borders and globalised free movement; the overwhelming majority are white; all but a negligible number are economically privileged and well-educated, and to assume that people might be pro-immigration because their ancestors came from another country is essentially a left-wing version of Norman Tebbit's infamous 'cricket test'.

One of Ben Judah's interviewees in *This Is London*, his acclaimed exposé of the lives of London immigrants, includes a Nigerian teacher living in Plaistow. After complaining about the number of immigrants in her neighbourhood, this teacher notes that when she came to the area twenty years previously it was still dominated by the white English: 'Now all the whites you see they are not English. They are EUs. The children they call them "freshies". They muck about and push them, laughing that they can't even speak English.' She also complains that while the black children 'become English', the Asian children who constitute most of her pupils 'try not to. The Muslims I don't think they will ever be English. They don't want to be at all.' Interestingly, this teacher also uses the same language of a too-rapidly changing neighbourhood when describing the changes affecting the black community in her area: 'I see the new generation of black people. Our kids we've had in this country they are beginning to think like English people and their skin colour it might not really be mattering. Maybe. The blackness is fading away. The blacks are trying to stay black . . . but there's no glue, no proper communication, no bond.'[21]

Many readers might be shocked by these remarks, but these opinions are common among many immigrant and immigrant-descended people in the UK, just as among the white British. It is more that we are less likely to hear them expressed from the former groups: we do not hear them from black and Asian anti-immigrant newspaper columnists, talk-radio hosts and politicians, because we have so few people of colour in these positions to begin with. It is also a matter of class. People of colour at the top of the media, politics, etc., are drawn from the same stratum of society as their white equivalents, and are therefore less likely to have those opinions, and certainly less likely to openly air them.

But just as earlier US immigrant groups, such as Irish, Polish and Italian Americans, and the descendants of Huguenot, Irish and Jewish immigrants to the UK, are not notably pro-immigration, it is only according to the NeoOrientalist worldview, which sees people of colour and immigrants as indelibly defined by their 'race' or immigration status, that we should expect to see black, Asian and recently arrived citizens of the US and European nations as inherently, inevitably and eternally pro-immigration. Already we can see different ethnic minority groups expressing scepticism towards immigration, not least the many non-white Brits who supported Brexit; correspondingly, there is no reason to suspect that the grandchildren of

Eastern European immigrants to the UK will be any more pro-immigration than the average Briton.

For many people like me, when we hear the word 'Christian', or 'Christianity', we might think of sour-faced bigots disappointed that they couldn't legally refuse a gay couple from staying in their B & B, or of a rootin', tootin', Stetson-wearing redneck off to bomb an abortion clinic in the Deep South. These crude and cruel stereotypes are not merely inaccurate, but also deeply Anglo-centric. The vast majority of today's practising Christians are people of colour, mostly living across Africa and Asia, but with many millions in the Global North.

A key aspect of NeoOrientalism is its failure to appreciate the significance of religion – particularly Christianity – to so many black and brown people in Britain and the USA. For example, in the middle of 2020, the release of Beyoncé's *Black is King* film generated a huge amount of excitement around the world, and perhaps especially among a certain type of extremely online young white women. In one scene, a woman proclaims: 'I can't say I believe in God and call myself a child of God, and then not see myself as a god', powerfully conveying the significance to Beyoncé, and many African-American women, of Christianity to their identity and sense of self. Given how much of the politico-cultural identity of young NeoOrientalist women – from their acrylic nails to their 'Slay Queen!' social media patter and their 'Educate Yourself' #BLM posts – is appropriated hook, line and sinker from African-American culture, it is curious they ignore arguably the most important aspect of that culture.

Yvonne Orji, one of the stars of *Insecure*, a comedy based on the lives of a group of black friends in Los Angeles, is a devout Christian and has pledged to refrain from pre-marital sex. This is in stark contrast to Molly, the character she plays on the show, but Orji is a successful, ambitious, politically liberal young black woman, who is nonetheless deeply religious. Such people are extremely common, and will become not only more numerically significant, but more prominent in arts, sports, literature and business in the coming decades. Given the NeoOrientalist association of 'blackness' with 'goodness', and the difficulty many NeoOrientalists have squaring religiosity in general and Christianity in particular with 'goodness', the increasing prominence of people like Orji will pose a challenge to this worldview.

In the UK, London is often assumed – with some justification – to be more liberal than the rest of the country, given that diversity is supposed to equate with liberalism. Yet it is also notably more theistic: 62 per cent of Londoners identify as religious, compared to 53 per cent of the rest of the country; 25 per cent attend a service at least once a month, compared with only one in ten outside London; and over half of the people identifying as Christians in London say they pray regularly, compared with under a third of such people elsewhere in the UK. This religiosity translates into more conservative values on some issues: a quarter of Londoners say that sex before marriage is wrong in some cases and 29 per cent say the same of same-sex relationships, compared to 13 and 23 per cent for the country outside London.[22]

It could be that racism faced by immigrants and ethnic minorities in white-majority countries leads to more conservative attitudes. Back in 1978 Amrit Wilson wrote that British society itself helped to keep the *izzat* honour code among Pakistani Muslims alive: 'The contempt for Asian culture, the constant shadow of racial hostility and the disregard for family and group identity provide[d] an atmosphere in which Izzat is constantly at risk and therefore is constantly charged and recharged. As a result, the women suffer; they are made the scapegoats of damaged Izzat.'[23]

Similarly, the increase in Muslim women wearing the burqa – relatively uncommon in the UK and almost unknown among South Asian Muslims until recently – might be seen as a depressing example of an increase in religious fundamentalism and a backward step for women's rights. Azadeh Moaveni writes that:

> Anyone who has spent time around young Muslim women while being charged to monitor veil-wearing as a possible sign of radicalisation – as academics like me are under the [UK] government's Prevent duty – realises that consumerism and peer pressure are the most important factors in the adoption of the headscarf . . . some Muslim girls start their first year unveiled, only to discover that hijabi fashionistas are the ruling clique on campus. They return for second year wearing a headscarf or turban. Hijabs are cool, just like beards are cool, just like Muslim piety is cool . . . It is the language of multiple rebellions: against keep your head down, 'coconut' parents; against the state that views your religion as a security problem; against a press that delights in your racist humiliation.[24]

In this sense, veils and other garments of religious significance are less about religion per se, still less about female subjugation, but are analogous to the posters on a student's wall, or tattoos or piercings, or their new favourite rapper.

There are some studies that support this idea. Professor Alison Shaw, an anthropologist at the University of Oxford, investigated the incidence of co-sanguineous marriage (marriage between cousins or other blood relations) among British Pakistanis. Somewhat dispiritingly, she found that this had increased from the 1970s to the 1990s, and was more common in Britain than it was in Pakistan. Yet Shaw argued that this apparently 'cultural' phenomenon had a rather more practical foundation: people in the UK were under tremendous pressure from their extended family back in Pakistan to marry their kids to one of their children, so that they could secure the immigration status to move to the UK. This burden usually fell upon the eldest child, and Shaw found that parents tended to fulfil their obligations with their first child and then let the younger ones choose their own partner, thus younger children were far less likely to marry blood relatives.[25]

As with attitudes towards immigration, when it comes to patriotism and national identity, the views of many people of colour disrupt NeoOrientalism. In Vron Ware's 2007 book *Who Cares About Britishness?*, she interviews several young Britons from BAME backgrounds, and finds that for all of them, some sense of British identity is important, from a British passport to cups of tea, and in some cases her interviewees lament a 'lost' Britishness in a style reminiscent of Peter Hitchens.[26] According to a 2009 study, Muslims in Britain are the most patriotic in Europe, with an average of 78 per cent of UK Muslims identifying as British, compared with 49 per cent in France and just 23 per cent in Germany. The report also found that the strength of religious belief made no difference to how patriotic British Muslims feel.[27]

In the wake of the beheading of the French teacher Samuel Paty, and further terrorist killings over subsequent weeks, French President Emmanuel Macron issued a crackdown on religious fanaticism. This was met with a predictable response by many NeoOrientalists, not least in the pages of the *New York Times*, who attacked Macron for stoking Islamophobia with his nationalist fervour. In response, a group of prominent French Muslims signed an open letter averring that no one 'could reasonably say that France mistreats its citizens of Muslim faith', except 'those who would like to instil the seeds of discord within the French national community'. The letter called for concord and union to prevail within the French national community, 'which is currently the victim of a series of unspeakable attacks which we all mourn'.[28]

Just as many ethnic minorities in white-majority countries demonstrate greater patriotic sentiment and support for immigration restrictions than many white people, they also tend to support law and order policies, even when they themselves are on the sharp end of police brutality and harassment. In response to Minneapolis City Council's 2020 announcement that it would disband the police department, Nekima Levy Armstrong – a civil rights lawyer and former president of the Minneapolis chapter of the National Association for the Advancement of Colored People (NAACP) – said they had shown 'a complete disregard for the voices and perspectives of many members of the African American community', who had not been 'consulted as the city makes its decisions, even though our community is the one most heavily impacted by both police violence and community violence'.

Other black Minneapolitans noted that it was particularly inappropriate to abolish the police force as it had a black police chief, Medaria Arradondo, for the first time in its history: 'Why now, when you have an African American chief who is highly regarded and trusted in the black community?' asked Steven Belton, the president and CEO of the Urban League Twin Cities. This was seconded by Pastor Brian Herron, of Zion Baptist Church, who said that while the police department was 'troubled', he felt it could really be 'transformed, and the culture of policing could change dramatically if [Arradondo] was given the proper support'.

Council Member Jeremiah Ellison, who represents a ward that is roughly half black, noted that 'the black community is not a monolith, and just because there's someone that might have a high profile doesn't mean that they necessarily speak on behalf of the black community of Minneapolis'. It shouldn't surprise us that many black people have such stark responses to the idea of abolishing the police. As Belton added, although the African-American community was overpoliced and subjected to excessive police use of force, 'at the same time we are also disproportionately victims of crime and witnesses of crime' and so 'you cannot talk of defunding the police if there is not a concomitant strategy of community safety in place as well'.[29] This is similar in the

UK, where only 2 per cent of black people, when asked to pick three options that would have the most positive impact on ethnic minority lives in Britain, included decreasing police funding.[30]

If these quotes surprise you, it's likely that you've been spending too much time in a milieu dominated by middle-class white post-graduates, or else assume that the black people featured on distinctively left-liberal newspapers and media are representative of black people as a whole, rather than being distinctively left-wing.

In recent years, politicians and commentators hostile to immigration and diverse societies have used concerns around cultural conservatism as a means to criticise ethnic minorities and immigrants. Many on the Left point out the irony of this, given how few of these individuals were previously known for their feminism or support for LGBT rights. At the same time, it is not as though cultural conservatism is ingrained in or essential to specific religious or ethnic groups. But the NeoOrientalist worldview is further undermined by suspicion of socialism and economically leftist policies among many communities of colour.

As Paul Gilroy observes in his seminal *There Ain't No Black in the Union Jack*: 'black Britons (who as a disproportionately underprivileged group, ought to be their stalwart supporters) remain suspicious and distant from the political institutions of the working-class movement.'[31] The sociologist Gargi Bhattacharyya concurs, arguing that the unhappy experiences of many black and Asian Britons when it comes to the state have led many 'dark-skinned folk of varying hues [to embrace] the promise of neoliberal subjecthood with enthusiasm' and that 'if anything, there is more vocal enthusiasm for some kinds of markets among black and minority populations' than among whites.[32]

Gilroy notes that 'many of the younger people in black cultural production haven't had any exposure to radical political movements at all. Their political essentialism often fits neatly with their entrepreneurial aspirations. They are sceptical of the left', and just like much of the broader population are open to the claims of free-market ideals, 'insights [which] look to them like good sense'. In an interview with bell hooks, the American author complained to Gilroy that black filmmakers of the 1980s and 1990s such as Spike Lee and John Singleton endorsed 'the myth that capitalism can work for you if you can work for it'. This is an attitude held by many black people on both sides of the Atlantic: they have worked hard for what they have, they have often had to try double hard because they are black, they deserve what they have, and they are not ashamed of saying it.[33]

Not that you need to read Paul Gilroy to work out that the appeal of consumerism and assumptions that capitalism is just 'common sense' are not exclusive to white people. Even Akala, who is decidedly of the Left, boasts that 'despite the household I was born into, here I stand, a self-employed entrepreneur', and there are many other people behind him with the same aspirations: 'As more young black people in London and elsewhere become materially successful, it will complicate class–race dynamics and continue to challenge people's expectations'.[34] Akala argues that 'black Britons' refusal to accept the class impositions of this society are in no small part what has made our presence here so challenging both for us and for Britain as a whole'.[35]

There is clearly some truth in this. Many people who would never consider themselves racist are nonetheless uncomfortable with a certain kind of blackness, or a particular type of black person. This can be seen in the vitriol directed at certain footballers, such as Raheem Sterling or Paul Pogba, who are lambasted in the press for what they spend their money on, how they dress or how they wear their hair – treatment that is not applied to white players or other black footballers who earn similar amounts of money but might be less ostentatious. Historically, many of the complaints made against second-generation black Britons focused on such provocations as 'walking jauntily' or even partaking in 'mass jollity'.[36] The American poet Maya Angelou had it right when she wrote in 'Still I Rise' (1978), her best-known work: 'Does my sassiness upset you?/Why are you beset with gloom?/'Cause I walk like I've got oil wells/Pumping in my living room.' Because for some people it is precisely this that offends them: they are more than happy with a certain type of black person, who acts, speaks and dresses in a certain way, who seems *grateful*; but are not prepared to extend the same approval to a black person who spends lavishly or vulgarly. They would never dream of thinking ill of a Barack Obama-figure but would not extend that same magnanimity to a young black man with his hood up on the back of a bus, or laughing loudly in the cinema.

Although criticism of the spending habits and lifestyles of some prominent black people, and the implication that excessive commercialism and consumption are somehow inherent to black 'culture', owe a great deal to racism, this doesn't take away from the fact that black and Asian people are no more likely than white people to be socialists. It also appears that lots of BAME Brits don't have the same hang-ups around private schools as many white people, as evidenced by the long list of BAME celebrities who attended elite private schools – including those with notably left-of-centre politics – such as the actor Riz Ahmed, the rapper Loyle Carner or the journalist Musa Okwonga. The YouTuber KSI, who attended Berkhamsted independent day school along with his brother, recalls that his parents 'worked so hard . . . and they put all their money into us', invoking the language of sacrifice and striving traditionally used by white conservatives to justify private education.[37]

Likewise, during the COVID-19 pandemic, the former England football player Eniola Aluko posted a series of tweets criticising the British government's furlough scheme – whereby workers were paid up to 80 per cent of their monthly wages by the state – as fostering a 'do-nothing' mentality and a 'culture of entitlement'. She later apologised and deleted the tweets, claiming they were 'a personal opinion on the future economy in this crisis'. Aluko's tweets contrast with the actions of Marcus Rashford, a black footballer who distinguished himself through his efforts to ensure that less privileged children remained well-fed during the pandemic – he himself had been a recipient of free school meals as a kid – and pressured the government into reversing its previous policies. The different positions of Aluko and Rashford demonstrate the diversity of opinions and attitudes among black Britons, and reminds us that just as bromides around self-reliance are commonplace across various cultures, societies and politico-economic systems, so too are beliefs around communalism and mutual support. But crucially, we cannot think that Rashford did this, or other black players do likewise, *because* they are black, any more than Aluko has her views because she's black.

Back in 1960s Wallsend, a labourer from Sierra Leone complained that there was nothing in the UK for his kids; in addition to the discrimination they would face due to their class and race, 'all they think about is [being] pop stars, guitarists or being shipyard workers! They don't want to be a professional man.' As Jon Lawrence points out, 'he was complaining that his children had integrated too fully into local working-class culture – adopting the low aspirations which he felt were endemic in English popular culture'.[38] Clear evidence if it were needed that these sentiments are not reserved to *Daily Mail*-reading Tory-voting suburbanites.

One of Kerry Hudson's interlocutors, a Turkish immigrant in Great Yarmouth, complained to her of the inhabitants of a nearby estate: 'I'm not saying all of them, but a lot of them, they're on benefits. And they don't have to do anything. They just get money. They get £300–400 a week.'[39] As mentioned, even the writer Aniefiok Ekpoudom, whose politics are very much of the Left, cannot resist noting that 'those who taunted [him] during school have moved from blue blazers to labouring jobs and building sites'.[40] This contrasts with the image of non-white politics painted by many on the Left, and contrasts in particular with the attitude of many white leftists.

This discrepancy leads to an awkwardness, whereby plenty of black people are much more comfortable talking about wealth and status than white NeoOrientalists. Spike Lee in particular is known for boasting to anyone who will listen that he is a 'third generation Morehouse man' – and his 2020 film *Da 5 Bloods* explicitly references the achievements of 'the House' – and many African Americans have an understandable pride in having attended elite institutions that sits uneasily with the culture of the UK Left. With one or two notable exceptions, it is difficult to imagine any white socialists boasting about having attended Oxford or Cambridge.

This attitude towards money, success and capitalism is not restricted to small-c conservative black people. Ru Paul, for example, could hardly be said to be conservative, yet is an outspoken fan of Hillary Clinton and the centrist tradition within the US Democratic Party: 'If you're a politician . . . there are a lot of things that you have to do that you're not proud of. There are a lot of compromises you have to make because it means that you can get this other thing over here. And if you think that you can go to fucking Washington and be rainbows and butterflies the whole time, you're living in a fucking fantasy world . . . what do I think of Hillary? I think she's fucking awesome. Is she in bed with Wall Street? Goddammit, I should hope so! You've got to dance with the devil.'[41]

Likewise, Killer Mike, who is one half of rap duo Run the Jewels, a pillar of the African-American community in Atlanta and a long-time advocate for racial and social justice, is also a small business owner and landlord, with several barbershops, a restaurant and about $2 million in property. He tells *GQ* magazine that he doesn't 'give a shit if Joe Biden the person has moved to the left . . . What I give a shit about is if your policies are going to benefit me and my community in a way that will help us get a leg up in America. That's it. Because we deserve a leg up, and I'm not ashamed to say it.' This didn't stop Donovan X. Ramsey, who interviewed Mike for *GQ*, from claiming his subject was deeply sceptical about 'how much a white supremacist, heteropatriarchal power structure built on the evils of capitalism will do to ensure his freedom', despite there being nothing in Mike's words, actions, lifestyle or indeed business plans suggesting he is critical of capitalism. Ramsey is at least black himself, although his Twitter biography boasts that he, like Spike Lee, is a 'Morehouse Man'. Killer Mike grew up in the Collier Heights neighbourhood of Atlanta, a prosperous black middle-class community, and his neighbours were mostly doctors, lawyers and entrepreneurs.[42] Incidentally, if a white person from such a background stood up as a tribune of the working class, the Authentocrats school would use their background to imply that they were inauthentic and disingenuous, irrespective of the accuracy of their comments. As far as I'm aware, no one has tried this with Killer Mike.

The Limits of the Rainbow

Many left-wing commentators assume that ethnic minorities – alongside women, LGBT and disabled people – are, or at least should be, on the same side in some grand coalition against the forces of conservatism. This is not only hugely patronising but displays a massive ignorance of the cultures and politics of different minority groups in Europe and North America. For example, California's Proposition 8 – which in 2008 banned same-sex marriages in the state (until it was overturned in court in 2013) – had the support of a majority of Latinos and roughly half of African Americans, but was opposed by a majority of white people; and there was a similar ethnic breakdown of support for related initiatives in Texas and Florida. Back in 1983, in a reactionary response to the growth of the Hispanic population, Proposition 63 proposed to make English the official language of the state of California. Despite the opposition of Los Angeles Mayor Tom Bradley – the most high-profile black politician in the state – fully 67 per cent of blacks supported the initiative, along with 58 per cent of Asians. This works the other way – in 2018, in Hialeah, Florida, a Spanish-speaking Taco Bell worker was fired after being recorded refusing service to an English-speaking African-American woman, Alexandria Montgomery, and threatening to call the police if Montgomery didn't leave.[43] Finally, at the 2020 election, California voters – a majority of whom are from minority ethnic groups – voted against an initiative to allow state agencies and universities to engage in affirmative action by more than 2.4 million votes.

As discussed in the next chapter, colourism, and particularly anti-blackness, is a problem throughout the world, giving little consideration to any Global North–South binary. And hostility to blackness among people from South Asia, the Middle East and North Africa does not immediately evaporate when they leave their home countries, and causes difficulties for second- or third-generation immigrants who form relationships with people darker than their own family. As the BBC's Ashni Lakhani reports of a British Bengali girl disowned by her family due to her black partner and mixed-race son, anti-blackness 'is as rife within this community as in many others', taking the form of 'casual comments throughout childhood such as "Don't go outside in the sun, you'll get dark," or "That fair-skinned girl will get so many marriage proposals". The mother of the girl in her story told her that black men 'only want to get you pregnant' and that she wouldn't 'amount to much dating one'.[44]

This anti-black racism among some South Asian people is not confined to personal relationships, but also seeps into politics: back in June 2020, during the height of the Black Lives Matter protests in Britain, one Asian Twitter user, who normally tweeted about Indian politics, posted pictures of a vandalised curry house, claiming it had been attacked by BLM protesters. A swift investigation revealed this was not the case – the restaurant had indeed been trashed, but there was no suggestion that BLM had anything to do with it. As the British Indian population grows in numbers and political significance, the anti-blackness of many British Indians may have unexpected and significant consequences.[45] It is also difficult to attribute this to the legacy of colonialism. Many Asian community newspapers in the UK from the 1980s had titles that positively appropriated 'blackness', such as *Kala Tara*, *Kala Mazdoor* and *Kala Shoor*, which suggests that there was more Asian–black solidarity during this period than today, and that factors other than British imperialism lay behind contemporary anti-Asian blackness.[46]

The attitude of many people of colour towards gender and sexuality is the most obvious gap in the rainbow. Despite the existence of a great many white homophobes, there is a bizarre assumption that non-white and LGBT people are natural comrades: 'LGBTQ people and Muslims should be allies: above all, because we share many of the same experiences and enemies', as one commentator has it.[47] In April 2019 the actor Shila Iqbal, who played a character on the popular British soap opera *Emmerdale*, was fired after old tweets surfaced in which she used homophobic and racist language. A month earlier a black actor, Seyi Omooba, who was due to play the bisexual character Celie in a stage adaption of Alice Walker's *The Color Purple*, was dismissed from the role after writing in a social media post that she did 'not believe you could be born gay [and] I do not believe homosexuality is right, though the law of this land has made it legal'.[48]

Just as religious devotion does not reflect any kind of cultural essentialism, so too with conservative views on sex and sexuality – although the contingent nature of these views does not mean that they do not exist. In February 2019, the Labour MP Shabana Mahmood spoke to education ministers to air her concerns that schools should follow government guidance for teaching relationships and sexual education, including engaging with parents and giving proper consideration to pupils' religious background. This was in response to a petition signed by 1763 of her Birmingham Ladywood constituents, who were concerned that their primary-school aged children were being taught about same-sex relationships. Hundreds of these parents went on to withdraw their children from school, and dozens picketed outside the two institutions – Parkfield Community School and Chilwell Croft – until the 'offending' lessons were cancelled.

Many of the parents were eager to stress that they were not homophobic, but merely felt the lessons were inappropriate for children of that age. LGBT campaigners countered that, on the contrary, it was important for these children to realise that same-sex attraction was normal at an early age, so that those who were gay would not be alienated from their own sexuality before they were even aware of it. The arguments made by the parents are redolent of the justification behind Section 28 of the Local Education Act 1988, which expressly forbade 'promoting homosexuality' within schools – although the latter was a top-down measure designed to win support for Margaret Thatcher's Conservatives from traditional Labour voters, rather than a response to a groundswell of Christian religiosity. My point here is not to say that Islam, or Muslims, are inherently homophobic – indeed many of the parents who withdrew their children from Chilwell Croft were Christians – but rather to suggest that these conflicts between religious rights and liberal universalism will remain contentious in the coming decades.

Unfortunately, NeoOrientalism undermines the liberal Left's ability to understand and come to terms with such conflicts. Nobody would suggest that acknowledging the atmosphere of virulent homophobia during the 1980s is an unacceptable slur against the people of that period, but the NeoOrientalist sensitivity with criticising brown people in general and Muslims in particular makes it difficult to say that, yes, in the same way that most Britons held homophobic views within recent history, a disproportionate number of British Asians hold such views today.

A 2018 BBC survey of 2000 British Asians found that while almost half (43 per cent) of respondents felt same-sex relationships were acceptable (down from 75 per cent of the British population as a whole), 36 per cent stated such relationships were 'unacceptable' (compared to 15 per cent of the UK as a whole). Somewhat dispiritingly, there was not much variation according to age: 42 per cent of those aged 55+ said they accepted same-sex relationships, compared with 43 per cent of the 35–54 age group, and just 44 per cent of those aged 18–34.[49] There is nothing inevitable about this, and as the revolution in attitudes to homosexuality among the British population as a whole over the past thirty years makes clear, these attitudes can and probably will change. But NeoOrientalist squeamishness does absolutely nothing to help bring this change about, and may even hinder it.

Nor are such attitudes limited to people of South Asian heritage. In 2020, the players of the US San Diego Loyal Soccer Club made the news through walking off the field en masse after a homophobic remark was made to one of their players, Collin Martin, during a game against Phoenix Rising. The perpetrator was the black Jamaican international Junior Flemmings, who was subsequently banned for six games. Martin reported that he 'never had a word said to me like that . . . I have heard homophobic language throughout my career and growing up but not to the point where it was directed at me like that. I felt personally attacked.'[50] Similarly, 'Hope', from Washington, DC, tells the BBC that she's 'starting to see black queer and trans people who are saying, "I don't want to march [for BLM]. I don't want to protest. I don't want to do anything because no matter what I do, black people don't want to march for black trans people" . . . We can't even talk to our black brothers and sisters because they feel the same way about us based on who we sleep with or how we identify – and that's a huge problem.' In the same article, 'Nic' from London says 'it's annoying because I feel like the conversations I'm having with white people about the right to life for black people are the same conversations I'm having with black people about the right to exist for trans people'.[51]

These anecdotes are supported by polling data. Support for laws to protect LGBT people from discrimination in jobs and housing ranges from 73 per cent of Asian Americans to only 65 per cent of African Americans – with whites and Hispanics in between at 69 and 70 per cent respectively. With regard to the different religious groups, support for these measures ranges from 72 per cent among Hispanic Catholics, 71 per cent among white Catholics and non-Evangelical Protestants, to 65 per cent among black Protestants, and just 60 per of Muslims and Hispanic Protestants. Although majorities of all ethnic groups support same-sex marriage (which in itself is very encouraging in terms of how much attitudes across the board have shifted in recent years), this ranges from three-quarters of Asian Americans, 65 per cent of Hispanic Americans, 62 per cent of white Americans, and just over half (56 per cent) of black Americans.

Among Democrats specifically, more than eight in ten (84 per cent) whites support anti-discrimination laws, slightly more than the 77 per cent of Hispanic Democrats, and significantly more than the two-thirds (68 per cent) of black Democrats. By way of comparison, for Republicans those figures are 56, 58 and 45 per cent respectively. Significantly, when broken down according to generation, there is much less variety across ethnic lines: 78 per cent of white Americans, 76 per cent of Asians, 74 per cent of Hispanics and 73 per cent of blacks under twenty-nine favour legislation to protect LGBT people; this compares with roughly six in ten whites, Asians and Hispanics, and just 54 per cent of blacks over sixty-five.

In the harrowing attack on a Bengali widow and her children described earlier, the *Guardian* article concluded by describing how an Asian man attempted to rescue them only for 'the white neigh-bours – assisted by two West Indian girls – hauled him into the court and beat him'.[52] This brief aside is an important reminder that the threat of violence can make vigorous perpetrators out of those who might otherwise be victims themselves, and an example of the many incidences of racist hostility by black people against Asian people.

X. Cambridge, writing in the *Black Liberator* in 1976, claimed West Indians had 'a far greater understanding of capitalist brutality than the Asians', and criticised passive and non-violent resistance. After claiming that their history was free of this, he added that West Indians were not 'pressed under by a caste system of duty and respect allied to, and substantiated by . . . passive and anachronistic religious forms one finds in India and Pakistan'. He added that 'we're mostly a trans-ported people, whereas the Indians have remained fundamentally indigenous'.[53]

Today, these frictions between black and Asian people remain, although in the US it is usually directed at people of East Asian ances-try. In an article criticising Westerners who might blame China for the 2020 COVID-19 outbreak, the American academic Andrew Liu highlighted 'a western exceptionalism that believed viruses and epidemics only happen "over there", in poor and non-white coun-tries.'[54] In this quote, and in the article itself, Liu created a dichotomy between 'Western' and 'non-white' countries. But this simplistic binary undermines the ethnic diversity of Western countries, typify-ing them as 'white', and assuming that 'non-white' people in these countries are immune to anti-Chinese sentiment or other kinds of xenophobia. A mere three days later, Oprah Winfrey – one of the most famous black American women in the world – confessed to *CBS News* that 'when this was happening in Wuhan, we thought it was "over there" . . . and then I talked to African Americans in Milwaukee, and folks were saying "we heard about it in Washington, but Washington is way over there, we didn't think it had anything to do with us"'. Thus giving the lie to any simplistic, NeoOrientalist dichotomy between white, Western countries and non-white countries, and the bizarre idea that black and brown people are somehow exempt from the parochial or even xenophobic tendencies of their fellow citizens.[55]

Among the huge increase in attacks on Asian Americans during the COVID-19 pandemic, one of the most serious occurred in Midland, Texas, where a family – including a two-year-old child – were stabbed and wounded. The suspect, nineteen-year-old Jose Gomez III, is a Hispanic American. As well as serious and violent attacks, there have been occasional surreal incidents, such as the picketing of a Washington, DC Chinese takeaway, Yum's, by the New Black Panthers in May 2020. There are all kinds of complicated animosities between Asian and black Americans, which may become more significant as the electoral significance of these communities increases.

As Robert Ford and Maria Sobolewska write of the UK, ethnic minorities are 'just as prone to ethnocentric thinking as the white majority' but less likely to manifest it politically – for now, at least. Ethnic minorities 'express some ethnocentric attitudes at similar rates to the white majority'; for example, 26 per cent of ethnic minorities and 40 per cent of white graduates think that 'those who do not share British customs and traditions can never be fully British.'[56] They are also far more religious, with socially conservative views on family, sexual orientation and gender roles. This means that while ethnic minorities 'align strongly with conviction liberals on identity conflicts, [they] do not share their broader socially liberal agenda'.[57] While for now, 'as long as the focus of conviction liberals' attention is on racial justice and extending anti-racist social norms, and ethnocentric conservatives are politically mobilised against migrants and minority groups, ethnic minorities have a strong incentive to align with conviction liberals, even though their views on many other social issues fundamentally differ'. But in the long run this makes for a 'volatile and potentially thin coalition' that could easily dissolve when arguments 'over gender equality or gay rights' take centre stage.[58]

At the 2015 general election the ethnic gap between the Conservative and Labour parties was 20 points, but in 2016 the gap between Brexit and Remain was 13 points. As Ford and Sobolewska point out, there were 'many more ethnic minority Leave voters in 2016 than ethnic minority Conservative voters in 2015'.[59] This suggests that the current support of ethnic minorities for parties of the Left 'is predicated almost entirely on white graduates' commitment to protect minorities and their rights, as on many other issues socially conservative ethnic minority voters and liberal individualist white graduates are poles apart'.[60] In Europe, right-wingers have been able to use LGBT and feminist sentiments to criticise immigration; the reverse could also work, whereby conservative culture warriors try to tap into ethnic minority conservatism. For now, the politics of different ethnic minorities in the West are complicated, varied and defy easy categorisation – just like the politics of white people. We should expect nothing less.

Chapter 4

The Tolstoy of the Zulus

'There's something casual and approachable and sociable and unthreatening about Black Guy that puts me on edge', writes Jeffrey Boakye in *Black, Listed*. I was pleased to read this comment by Boakye, because I had noticed the remarkable consistency with which liberal white people (like me) suffixed the word 'black' with the word 'guy', but feared it might be one of my petty and irrational grievances, as when British people use the hideous Americanism 'Can I get . . .' when ordering in a pub or restaurant.

Boakye points out that this formulation is 'intended to integrate and ingratiate' as ' "Black Guy" is a major softening of "Black", the "Guy" serving to throw a casual arm around the otherwise unapproachable other . . . It suggests an equality that speaks volumes to modern liberalism (because only easy-going, laid-back white people would see a black man as one of the guys).' I would add to this that its younger, hipper cousin 'trans folks' serves much the same purpose (see Part III). But Boakye's main concern with the term is that it supports 'the Cool Black Myth'.[1]

In May 2020, a post from the official Twitter account of British blue-eyed soul group Simply Red announced the 'Top 5 coolest cultures on planet Earth: 1. African Americans (they invented cool) 2. Working Class British Musicians 3. (A close 3rd) Jamaicans 4. Jewish Americans 5. Flamenco Gypsies'. This tweet was met with predictable mirth, not least because few of those cultures appear to have influenced the music of Simply Red. Other Twitter users pointed out the borderline racist nature of the post, reducing as it did millions of people to a crude stereotype around how 'cool' they were. This tendency is not restricted to middle-aged Mancunians; a central feature of NeoOrientalism is the belief that people of colour are not only morally better than white people, but inherently 'cooler'. Obama was ranked as the coolest US president by *Vice* due to his: 'supposed drug use; sexual proficiency; wearing sportswear; having notorious friendship circles; and, of course, being black'. Compared to this, Mick Hucknall's racial coolness hierarchy doesn't seem that bad.

One of the biggest problems with NeoOrientalism is that it promotes a resurgent cultural essentialism. Since the 1980s, academics and anti-racism activists have noted the shift in racism from a focus on supposed biological difference to apparent 'cultural' incompatibilities.[2] Therefore, well-meaning white people who obsess over 'black' or 'Asian' culture run the risk of exacerbating the very racism they think they are undermining.

There is a long history of this. As early as 1958, Jack Kerouac reported walking 'in the Denver coloured section wishing I were a Negro, feeling that the best the white world has offered me was not enough ecstasy for me, not enough life, joy, kicks, darkness, music'.[3] Since then, the globalisation of culture, and its increasingly American inflections; the increase in consumerism; the development of the internet and social media; and the sense that this kind of patronising attitude might actually be morally virtuous have spread this mindset way beyond hipsters such as Kerouac.

As Akala notes in *Natives*, 'an obsessive focus on essentialised cultural, ethnic and religious differences often serves many of the same functions as overt racism', which is why it's particularly important not to argue that black people are inherently good at specific things.[4] Few NeoOrientalists are so crude as to say that black people are inherently athletic or black men well-endowed, but they certainly give the impression that they are cooler and more talented. This is a prime example of what Gilroy called the 'postmodern translation of blackness from a badge of insult into an increasingly powerful but still very limited signifier of prestige'.[5] For many white people, especially young, left-wing whites, 'blackness' serves as tattoos or smoking once did for an earlier generation.

This cultural element of NeoOrientalism is perhaps its most insidious. The assumption that all 'people of colour' are political radicals may be patronising and result in strategic missteps by left-wing political parties, but the yearning for 'black' culture reinforces old racist stereotypes around black people. In the UK, there is a plethora of high-profile and respected black athletes, musicians, actors and comedians, but fewer authors and public intellectuals. While this is not the case in the US, people such as Toni Morrison or Ta-Nehisi Coates are still dwarfed by the profile of court jesters such as Kanye West.

Back in 1995, the sociologist Zygmunt Bauman described the changing relationship of individuals to their own body, whereby instead of merely being the thing within which we are contained, and that we can use to do useful things, the body was becoming yet another 'task' that we can and should master. At the same time, people could increasingly be *defined by* their body.[6] Building on this, Gilroy argued that the growth of identity politics meant that certain 'exemplary bodies' could become 'instantiations of community', so Michael Jordan, or Beyoncé, or Usain Bolt, become not just black people but 'blackness' itself.[7] Hence the profound discomfort of many African Americans with the changes inflicted by Michael Jackson on his own body, as memorably described by Ta-Nehisi Coates: 'you could see the dying all over his face, the decaying, the thinning, that he was disappearing into something white, desiccating into something white, erasing himself'.[8]

There is a long and tawdry history of the racist objectification of black and brown bodies, but recent decades have witnessed a development of this sinister fetishisation from a left-liberal perspective, among people who'd be horrified to be accused of racism. In Todd Shepard's *Sex, France and Arab Men*, the historian recounts how the 1970s French organisation *Front omosexuel d'action révolutionnaire* (FHAR) advocated for Arab rights through a sexual objectification of people of North African descent. For example, the 1973 publication *Three Billion Perverts: The Big Encyclopedia of Homosexualities* had a long entry under the heading 'Arabs and Us' exploring the sexual convergence of French 'homos' and 'Arabs'. This was criticised by heterosexual intellectuals such as Gilles Deleuze, who argued that 'Arabs and Us' was an unfortunate mixture of 'politically revolutionary' sentiments and 'perfectly fascist and racist' notions, which proposed the 'Arab' as an object of white male fantasies.

This sexualisation of North African men entailed not only desire but also the reproduction of racist stereotypes around the predatory nature and sexual virility of Arabs, combined with misogynistic attitudes to French women. When some of the women in the FHAR complained about harassment from North African men in the street, 'their male comrades replied that they would like nothing better'.[9] This intersection of racism and sexual desire has a long history, from the plantation to online pornography. Today, the British alt-Right internet personality Milo Yiannopoulos boasts about his 'very anti-white bedroom policy' and claims to oppose Planned Parenthood because 'they kill all those black babies', who 'in twenty years . . . could be my harem'. According to Yiannopoulos, in 2017 he married a black Muslim man.[10] For white heterosexual women, the adoption of the aesthetics of a particular kind of African-American woman can be seen as a similar kind of fetishisation and sexualisation, whereby people and their 'racial' identity are reduced to key stylistic signifiers. By adopting these, young white women can appropriate elements of

African-American culture without losing any of the advantages conferred by their whiteness. In her book *Brit(ish)*, Afua Hirsch memorably described a trip to a sex club frequented by white women with a sexual interest in black men (and by white men who pay to watch), but in the summer of 2020 this kind of fetishisation came out into the open, as white people on Black Lives Matter protests ritually kissed the feet of black people or self-flagellated their backs bloody.

Gilroy reckons that this 'aestheticization and spectacularization' of different ethnic groups has become an inadequate substitute for attempts to genuinely address racial injustice, and at the same time upholds 'unanimist fantasies', which have the power 'to destroy any possibility of human mutuality and cosmopolitan democracy'. So, the exalted reverence of Beyoncé's arse is not merely inappropriate fetishisation, but undermines any attempt at real anti-racist politics and progressing beyond 'race'. This was highlighted in the Jordan Peele film *Get Out*, when the protagonist Chris asks his captor why he preys on black people, and is told that they 'get the highest bids. For the last decade or so anyway. I wish it was less simple than that, but it's not. You're in fashion, baby!' As the poet Salena Godden writes, 'the festishisation of the sexuality of black people comes from centuries . . . it starts with sleazy old jokes that black men have huge cocks, or that black women are hyper-sexual and it festers to become something toxic and sinister. This continues now, mostly unquestioned, with the sexual objectification of women, rounded fat bottoms and full lips all across the media industry.'[11]

This is why the Kardashian-Jenners have particular relevance in the world of identity myths; it is not so much that they want to be black; but rather they want to have all the advantages of being black, while retaining all the advantages of being white. This is why Rachel Dolezal is one of the most important political figures of the twenty-first century. She represents the moment it started to become desirable for white people to 'pass' as black. Dolezal didn't pretend to be black because she was unaware of the particular difficulties faced by African Americans; she did so despite this, because in her world – and in my world – the kudos and cachet of being black, as far as white people like her are concerned, is so great that it makes even this kind of horrible deception worth it.

And the Dolezals of the world are Kardashians with postgraduate degrees, a sort of halfway house between the physical appropriation of the Kardashians and the more common politico-cultural kind. The Kardashian-Jenners essentialise and appropriate blackness through their aesthetics and choice of men; Dolezal did it through a combination of aesthetics – dyeing her skin and curling her hair – and politico-cultural affectations. Yet just because the thousands of white NeoOrientalists on university campuses and social media only practise it through their politics and cultural tastes does not mean that they are innocent.

The cultural fetishisation of NeoOrientalism can easily veer from the realms of poor taste into highly offensive behaviour. As the BLM protests moved through cities across the US (and in the world) during the summer of 2020, they were soon joined by 'influencers', less concerned with racial justice than with boosting their own image through association with a *cause du jour*, posing for photographs amidst a backdrop of angry protestors, police violence or burning buildings. Incredibly, some people went as far as creating 'I can't breathe' themed make-up and nail art, including artists in blackface or covered in fake blood, and nail designs featuring a black man with his mouth covered by the words: 'I can't breathe'.[12]

A key difference between this and the kinds of activities more usually labelled 'cultural appropriation' by angry student unions is that the ramen-eaters and yoga-practitioners of the latter kind are picking and choosing from the cultural smorgasbord of the modern, globalised world, and in most cases don't particularly care for Japanese cuisine or Vedic spirituality. In the former case, by contrast, white people using BLM for social media or real-life credibility are indeed claiming a higher knowledge of and concern for African-American politics and culture.

Back in 2016, the grime MC Skepta posted a video of himself singing along to 'Gold' by Spandau Ballet, in reaction to his album being certified 'Gold' in the UK. Jeffrey Boakye describes a white British radio DJ reacting to the video 'with a tone bordering on disbelief . . . that Skepta knows all the words'.[13] Boakye wondered exactly why a British person such as Skepta shouldn't be familiar with a bestselling song that has been a feature on classic pop radio and TV adverts for almost forty years. The implication of the DJ's reaction was that because Skepta was 'black', he shouldn't be aware of this kind of 'white' music.

In 2014 the (very white) journalist Josh Hall criticised the line-up for a music festival on the grounds that:

> the acts they've booked are those favoured by the children of people who commute from the Home Counties to a hedge fund job. The National and Midlake are two of the big draws – bands for people who are too discerning for Mumford, but who once applied for tickets to *Michael McIntyre's Comedy Roadshow*. Perhaps that's unfair, but questions of taste aside, the most remarkable thing about the inaugural 6 Music Festival is its whiteness.[14]

Doubtless Hall thought he was striking a blow for anti-racism, but in this linkage of 'people of colour' and musical credibility, he ends up doing the opposite.

He'd be in for a real shock if he ever found out what type of people formed the majority of the audience for black heavy metal bands like Ho99o9, or of classical musicians such as William Grant Still or Samuel Coleridge-Taylor. Wynton Marsalis, one of the most recent stars in the latter genre, made history in 1983 by becoming the first person to win a Grammy award in both the jazz and classical categories; a feat he repeated the following year. Marsalis is one of the most prominent talking heads in Ken Burns's magisterial twelve-part documentary, *Jazz*. In the antepenultimate episode the writer Gerald Early recalls that although white people had always listened to jazz, with the rise of bebop in the 1950s 'you have whites who have a certain kind of intellectual pretension listening to this music', people who 'suddenly are attracted to jazz because they think of it as a kind of analogy for what they're doing in literature, you have whites who are bohemian, who want to adopt a certain kind of lifestyle'.

This binary between 'black' music and 'white' music, and therefore between blackness and whiteness, has a sad effect on many black people themselves, from high-profile singers, such as Prince, Whitney Houston and most recently Lizzo, who are attacked for being 'too white', to millions of young black people, who are made to feel guilty or 'less black' for enjoying guitar-based or classical music.[15] As Akala notes, for young black men without the ability or inclination, 'the expectations to be tough, to run fast and to be a good rapper can be very damaging'.[16]

Many NeoOrientalists are sensitive to this and would never dream of doing anything as crude as implying that black people have better 'rhythm' or that black men are unusually athletic. Yet their glorification of 'black culture' is not merely homogenising, but also reasserts the 'coolness' of black people in more subtle ways. Gilroy alluded to this when he wrote of how 'the transgressive qualities in hip-hop' led to its being identified 'not as one black culture among many but currently as the very *blackest* culture – the one that provides the measure on which all others can be evaluated'.[17]

While it is great to have a broad taste in music, the concept of 'world music' often has essentialist tendencies that reinforce ideas of racial difference. In the words of Gilroy, it rekindles romantic ideas around 'primitives and noble savages'. Although there is nothing wrong with a 'hunger for cultural forms that stand outside the immorality and corruption of the over-developed world', 'imprisoning the primitive other in a fantasy of innocence can only be catastrophic for all parties involved . . . linguistic, traditional, and local particularities may all be in danger from the levelling effects of corporate multiculturalism', but 'we do not have to choose between fetishizing and therefore capitulating to unchanging difference and its simple evacuation or erasure'.[18]

There is a scene in *Born to Be Blue*, Robert Budreau's 2015 film about the life of the jazz trumpeter Chet Baker, where Miles Davis berates Baker for his 'sweet' playing style, and tells him he needs to 'live a little' to improve his sound. Baker interprets this as meaning that he needs to take more heroin, and soon spirals in addiction and debt, losing his teeth and having to relearn how to play the trumpet with his new, toothless mouth. Half a century later, the rapper Post Malone tells *GQ* magazine that the abundance of tattoos which disfigure his face come from 'a place of insecurity . . . Where I don't like how I look, I'm going to put something cool on there, I can look at myself and say, "You look cool, kid," and have a modicum of self-confidence when it comes to my appearance.'[19] These physical injuries more than fifty years apart are a manifestation of white people ultimately thinking that they are not 'black' enough to succeed in their genres where credibility is inextricably linked with 'blackness', and a particular kind of blackness at that. In the jazz scene of the 1950s, blackness meant childhood poverty, suffering from racism and police violence, and a serious heroin habit. For rappers in the 2010s, blackness meant childhood poverty, a career as a drug dealer, and a violent past.

All of this coincides with an industry where white people are still financially dominant, and black artists are often exploited and advised to appear less 'black' by toning down their lyrics, or their attitude, or their appearance. This is particularly a problem for women; very few black men try to straighten their hair today, but millions of black women around the world endure tremendous pain and discomfort trying to do so. The British singer Alexandra Burke was even advised to bleach her skin to boost her career.[20] This can go the other way: Amina Mama's research on black British women in the 1990s described the case of Mona, who faced repeated questioning about her straight hair. This led Mona to plait extensions into her hair 'in order to disguise it and make it look "natural", thus supposedly conforming to an Afrocentric ideal. The question of appearance is clearly central here, since Mona, in spite of having thought of herself as an "aware black woman" is now in the position of adding extensions to her own, unprocessed hair.'[21] Here we can see someone suffering to attain the look they feel they should have to be 'racially' authentic.

As Gilroy writes, 'the identification of black musical genius constitutes an important cultural narrative. It tells and retells not so much the story of the weak's victory over the strong but the relative powers enjoyed by different types of strength.'[22] This jeopardy, whereby a catholic taste in culture can actually serve to reinforce 'racial' difference, is compounded when 'the interests of the romantic consumers begin to converge with those of people inside the minority communities' who want to enforce a 'definition of invariant (and therefore authentic) ethnicity' to serve their own ends. That is to say, when there are people who stand to make money, or gain power, from cultivating cultural distinctiveness, hapless white NeoOrientalists can become useful idiots.

In one of the scenes in Richard Wright's *The Long Dream*, two African-American men are conducting an autopsy on the emasculated corpse of a lynching victim when one remarks to the other: 'You have to be terribly attracted to a person, almost in love with 'im to mangle 'im in this manner. They hate us, Tyree, but they love us too;

in a perverted sort of way, they love us.'[23] Today, the legacy of this paradox – fetishisation and fear; love and hatred – is found in the exaggerated reverence for 'black' culture, which makes it difficult to promote 'blackness' outside the well-worn avenues of entertainment, physical impressiveness, enigmatic 'allure' and 'coolness'.[24]

The historian Hazel Carby, writing of the 1970s, recounts how British schools would insist to children that 'we're all equal here', and if their black students claimed to be second-class citizens in 'housing, employment and education', the schools would complain about their 'negative self-image' and 'order some books with blacks in them'. Students would ask if they could talk about immigration laws or the National Front, and the schools would 'arrange some Asian and West Indian Cultural Evenings' instead.[25] Today, identity myths deploy black and brown cultures to a similar effect: they invite a focus on the importance of culture, rather than the specific disadvantages of individuals.

Despite my earlier comment about the rarity of biological racism, many people today still privately suspect there might be something genetically race related in terms of aptitude, mostly when they look at the men's 100m final at the Olympics or the roster of an NBA team. This is why the coolness myth is such a problem, because people who would rebuke themselves for thinking that some 'races' are more intelligent than others have no problem thinking that some are better at sport, or music, or simply 'cooler' than others. In the wake of the George Floyd killing, a poll by Monmouth University found that 76 per cent of Americans (including 71 per cent of white people) felt that racism and discrimination were 'a big problem', up from 50 per cent just five years earlier. This 26 point increase must owe something to the BLM movement drawing attention to such injustices, because there was not an increase in the police killing of African Americans during that period. But this change begs the question why only half of Americans felt it was a big problem in 2015, for there was plenty of media coverage of the killings of Michael Brown, Eric Garner, Freddie Gray and Tamir Rice, and of the protests that followed. I think part of the blame lies with the predominance of black people within so many aspects of popular culture in the United States – many whites might think, *Well, look how many of the top athletes and musicians and actors are black; can they really have it so bad?* This is one of the reasons why the reification of 'black' culture can be so damaging, and without many positives by way of compensation – as Lisa McKenzie wrote of the working-class inhabitants of St Ann's, they do not want for self-esteem; likewise, ethnic minorities in white-majority countries, just like the economically disadvantaged, need specific things (money, connections, resources) which no amount of identity amplification is going to provide.

Aside from this, culture is inherently flexible and resistant to categorisation. In 1970 a Hindu monk and professor at Syracuse University named Agehananda Bharati coined the term 'pizza effect'. This describes the process whereby an element of one nation or people's culture is embraced elsewhere and transformed in the process, before being readopted by the original culture. Bharati knew a thing or two about this; despite his adopted name and *swami* regalia, he was born Leopold Fischer in Vienna in 1923, and came to Indian mysticism through the auspices of the Nazi-sponsored Free India League, among other organisations.

Bharati noted that the original southern Italian dish of pizza was a simple flatbread with tomato sauce, but had been transformed in the United States into a variety of more complicated dishes, each with different toppings and flavours. This new concept of pizza was then transferred back to Italy in the inter-war period, where its popularity was boosted by its associations with American glamour and prosperity. Finally, during the latter years of the twentieth century, Italian pizzerias adapted to American tourists seeking 'authentic' pizza, and began to concentrate on simple, thin pizzas with few ingredients. These American tourists, delighted at having discovered 'authentic' Italian pizza, brought it back to the hipster bars and restaurants of the States.

In sociology and religious studies, this process is also known as the 'hermeneutical feedback loop', 're-enculturation' and, notably, 'self-Orientalisation'. Far from being restricted to pizza, this process has shaped understandings of religious faith, food, film, music and more, and fatally undermines the NeoOrientalist belief in the special value of certain cultures, and the existence of 'authentic' culture in the first place.

According to Bharati, the legendary Indian director Satyajit Ray's 'Apu Trilogy' – broadly considered to be among the greatest Indian films of all time – were originally unacclaimed within India itself, and were only re-evaluated as masterpieces of Indian cinema after the acclamation of Western film critics. Similarly, elements of 'Indian' cultures or religions, from transcendental meditation to the significance of the *Bhagavad Gita* to Hindus, only latterly achieved their current prominence on the subcontinent as a response to their significance in the West. Mohandas Gandhi himself first read the *Bhagavad Gita* in an English translation, and much of his understanding of Hinduism was informed by his time spent in London.[26]

In many cases hybrid forms such as chicken tikka masala, formed from a combination of South Asian and British culinary influences, or salsa music, created by Puerto Rican musicians in New York, have been successfully exported back to their supposed countries of origin. Likewise, St Patrick's Day, styled into its modern form by the Irish diaspora in the United States, was eventually exported back to Ireland, with Dublin holding its first St Patrick's Day parade in 1931, fully 169 years after the first recorded St Patrick's Day parade in New York.

Every October in the UK and Ireland you'll find plenty of people moaning about how Hallowe'en is an American festival, but much of the current iconography of Hallowe'en was brought to America in the nineteenth century by Irish immigrants, who adapted their traditional carved turnips to use pumpkins instead.[27] More recently, the 'Day of the Dead' parades in Mexico City were given new popularity by the James Bond film *Spectre*.[28] Connectedly, culture and brands associated with whiteness in the UK are often viewed very differently elsewhere. For example, the shoe company Clarks, associated in the UK with school shoes in which no fashion-conscious NeoOrientalist would be seen dead, is massively popular in Jamaica. Even more counterintuitively, the 1960s British sitcom *Dad's Army*, described as 'deeply corrosive' by the *Guardian* newspaper because of 'the crippling and still pervasive nostalgia for the war', is hugely popular in Jamaica among people who presumably don't have the sort of post-imperial melancholy the *Guardian* believes infects the UK.[29]

American hip-hop pioneer Luther 'Luke' Campbell was a huge fan of the British comedian Benny Hill, who influenced his lyrics and vocal style; as Gilroy writes, the fact that Benny Hill influenced something so profoundly black as hip hop 'should have provided a last nail in the coffin of any ethnocentric account of its origins and development'.[30] Use of the word 'shade' to disrespect, as in 'throwing shade', was popularised by African-American culture, but the first record of 'shade' being used in this manner, hilariously, comes from Jane Austen's *Mansfield Park* (1814), when one character remarks that 'with such warm feelings and lively spirits it must be difficult to do justice to her affection for Mrs Crawford, without throwing a shade on the Admiral'.

This kind of cultural exchange is usually beneficial for all involved; Salman Rushdie believes that this type of transference is how 'newness enters the world'.[31] Nonetheless, the 'pizza effect' can appear in more sinister forms. For example, Iranian nationalists have adopted the term 'Aryan' – itself of Indian origins before its use by Nazi racial theorists – to stress their 'racial' distinctiveness and superiority.[32]

Today, billions of people around the world view the UK not as an obnoxious post-imperial kingdom of nostalgia, but instead as a vibrant place with an enviable culture, precisely because of centuries of this kind of transference. When art historian Neil MacGregor asked Berliners what they thought of the UK, he was struck by the centrality of music to Germans' impression of Britain – music which owes an immeasurable debt to colonialism, globalisation and immigration. This impression is not restricted to Germans. Wole Soyinka, the first Nobel Literature laureate from an African nation, tells MacGregor that Handel's 'Hallelujah' chorus is inextricably linked with his memories and associations of Britain. Perhaps surprisingly, the 'Hallelujah' chorus was at one time the most requested piece of music on Nigerian radio – and Handel himself was a German immigrant to the UK.[33]

When the US soul singer James Brown visited Nigeria in the 1960s and spent an evening at the Lagos nightclub of the legendary Afrobeat singer Fela Kuti, Brown remarked that 'some of the ideas my band [got from Kuti's band] had come from me in the first place, but that was okay with me. It made the music that much stronger.' A century before Brown's visit, slaves who returned to Nigeria from Brazil brought with them music which later would be thought of as 'authentic' African music.[34] Later on in the nineteenth century, African-American nationalists, such as Martin Delany, exported back to Africa the 'civilising mission' of white Europeans; Delany argued that elevating the black American was inseparable from elevating and enlightening 'the uncultured Africans by offering them the benefits of civilised life: cesspools, furniture, cutlery, missionaries', and so on. As Gilroy points out, the name of the eponymous hero from Delany's novel *Blake* has clear resonances of 'an earlier, explicitly Atlanticist radicalism'.[35]

In April 2020 the British chef MiMi Aye posted a link to a *New York Times* recipe for hot cross buns, a traditional British treat eaten around Easter time. Suffice to say, the recipe was not a recipe for 'hot cross buns' as commonly understood in the UK, and the monstrosities featured in the accompanying photo were unrecognisable to any British person. To add insult to injury, the subtitle for the article (which was subsequently changed after Aye's tweet) insisted that they were 'essentially' the same as Chelsea buns – an entirely different type of baked good. This was an unusual moment, as while there have been plenty of cases of British chefs criticised for 'culturally appropriating' recipes from other cuisines, it is extremely rare for the boot to be on the other foot: possibly because there are so few dishes that are 'authentically' British; possibly because there are so few non-Brits who would want to cook them.

Either way, Aye's tweet initiated howls of anger from her British followers, and garnered over 1500 'likes'. She sardonically followed this up by noting how 'everyone is getting mighty upset about someone from another culture f*cking up one of their national dishes – weird, right?' Because this is a key offence with 'cultural appropriation': the claiming of a different dish or item of clothing or whatever by its original name. If the *New York Times*'s food writer had simply called them an 'Easter bun', no one would have cared. Likewise, if the British chef Jamie Oliver had called his version of paella 'rice, chicken and chorizo stew' or similar, he wouldn't have received so much abuse from thousands of angry Spaniards.

The key offence in these cases is not in the imitation, but rather in bastardising the original and claiming it is the same. It suggests that you don't care about the original cuisine, or culture. And people are incentivised to do this by the NeoOrientalist belief that other cultures are more inherently interesting or valuable than their own. It's not that wanting to eat, say, original Parma ham, or valuing it, is the problem. It's thinking that it says something positive about you in terms of your cultural refinement, and especially in terms of your politics. Correspondingly, the 'gammon' who doesn't care for these things is not a reactionary and not worse than you. We wouldn't say (hopefully) that the person with narrower tastes is culturally backwards, so why do we infer that they are conservative? Why is this so important to people? They are fetishising and using a people or culture for their own psychological ends. Instead of the NeoOrientalist desire for the authentic, and the valuing of particular types of cuisines (or cultures) above others, we should appreciate how privileged we are to be able to know of and enjoy all this different food; especially when a huge number of people around the world, including in the UK, have never set foot in any kind of restaurant.

The food writer Jonathan Nunn complains that, in London's Soho, 'world cuisines [are] being sanitised, homogenised and then sold back as something new and exciting', but it was ever thus.[36] As fellow journalist Joanna Fuertes points out in her response to Nunn's blog, the more novel development is the rapid increase in rich Western travellers seeking an 'authentic' food experience: in 2018, Tripadvisor reported that demand for cooking classes and culinary tours had grown by 57 per cent from the previous year, while Airbnb launched a local cooking experiences service after a 160 per cent increase in bookings of its food and drink experiences. Fuertes recalls one instance at a taqueria in Costa Rica, where her (American) dining companion rejected the 'Westernised' items on the menu and 'started yelling, in English, and clicking his fingers at the staff, asking for the *real*, off-menu delicacies we should be trying'.[37] As George Reynolds wrote in his critique of the late Anthony Bourdain, 'it's pretty rich for a white American to come to an underdeveloped country and strip-mine it for delicacies . . . on the condition that the country swears not to get too developed in the meantime'.[38] This kind of practice, of the search for 'authentic' cuisine or music or whatever, restates racial difference through being suggestive of pristine, authentic, 'local' culture, as opposed to the polluted and devalued 'white' culture of 'the West'.

143

In his bestselling *Between the World and Me*, Ta-Nehisi Coates recalls Saul Bellow's sneer: 'who was the Tolstoy of the Zulus?' and over several pages recounts his own realisation that Tolstoy was the Tolstoy of the Zulu. Likewise, Robert Hayden and Richard Wright and Toni Morrison and even Coates himself are not just the property of African Americans, or even black people in general, but of everyone. As Gilroy argues, the 'politics of cultural conservation' is inherently conservative. 'It is to subscribe to a doggedly positive and always over-integrated sense of culture and/or biology as the essential reified substances of racial, national, and ethnic difference.'[39] We have difficulty describing, never mind theorising, intermixture, fusion and syncretism without suggesting the existence of original 'uncontaminated' purities, the 'stable, sanctified conditions' to which one day it might 'be possible to return'. Ultimately, 'we must be prepared to give up the illusion that cultural and ethnic purity has ever existed' and get over 'the modernist obsession with origins'.[40]

The genius of white writers and composers and athletes stems not from their whiteness, but rather from their human-ness. So too with black writers and composers and athletes; their genius is not a tribute to nor reflection of the qualities of their 'race', but rather of the whole of humanity. As Toni Morrison writes of 'black' music, 'we don't have exclusive rights to it', and as Thomas Chatterton Williams says of his mixed-race, French-American daughter and black American artists such as Syl Johnson, John Coltrane and Nina Simone: 'these are also her sounds if she wants them'.[41]

Chapter 5

The Myth of 'Western' Exceptionalism

In an acclaimed essay on the COVID-19 pandemic published in the middle of 2020, the public intellectual Pankaj Mishra criticised 'the skeletal welfare states of Britain and the US' which 'can't even secure supplies of gowns and masks for its hospital workers', and argued that 'neither Britain nor America seems capable of dealing with the critical challenges to collective security and welfare thrown up by the coronavirus'. Yet by the end of 2020 Britain had spent over £12 billion on personal protective equipment, while in March 2021 President Joe Biden signed a $1.9 trillion stimulus bill, in the greatest expansion of federal government spending since the New Deal era. Mishra was far from alone in making hasty inferences from the pandemic that supported his political views: commentators from across the spectrum found vindication for the ideology in the crisis. We know now that we cannot draw easy lessons from how different nations handled the pandemic: some democracies did well, as did some authoritarian regimes; some countries headed by women did well; others less so, and so on.

The main problem with Mishra's article is that it asserts a bizarre 'Anglo-American' exceptionalism that does not exist in reality, and which reasserts artificial and unhelpful dichotomies. It is particularly strange to see this from Mishra, as his book *Age of Anger* masterfully demonstrates the historical and geographical spread of chauvinism, anti-intellectualism and authoritarianism. Nonetheless, in this article he writes of German Chancellor Otto von Bismarck's social insurance system, which 'wasn't only retained and expanded in Germany as it moved through two world wars, several economic catastrophes and Nazi rule; it also became a model for much of the world', noting that 'Japan was Germany's most assiduous pupil'. Yet he will have known that Bismarck's social insurance system and the corporatist German economy was inextricably linked with militarism and national chauvinism. Likewise, he writes that the German sociologist Max Weber had 'a tough-minded understanding of the unforgiving world that forced a latecomer like Germany to catch up expeditiously with Britain and the US. "We cannot pass peace and human happiness on to our descendants," he wrote, "but the maintenance and up-breeding of our national kind."'

In this respect Japan was Germany's 'most assiduous pupil' in more ways than one; Mishra later writes that 'the Japanese, in turn, inspired China's first generation of modern leaders, many of whom spent years in Tokyo and Osaka. Despite the defeat and devastation of the Second World War and the US occupation, Japan has continued to influence East Asia's other late-developing nation-states: South Korea, Taiwan, Singapore and Vietnam.' For some reason, he neglects to mention the devastation Japan wreaked on East and South-East Asia, killing a comparable number in that section of the world to those killed by the various combatants in Europe, and far more than the number of Japanese killed by the Americans. Mishra concludes by arguing that 'slavery, imperialism and racial capitalism . . . made some people in Britain and America uniquely wealthy and powerful, and plunged the great majority of the world's population into a brutal struggle against scarcity and indignity'.[1] While the first part of this sentence is undoubtedly correct, the second part is obviously false: the great majority of the world's population were already in a brutal struggle against scarcity and indignity, and would likely have remained so without the rise of European empires and the transatlantic slave trade.

Back in 2008, the economist Michael Cembalest produced a graph charting the rise and fall of global gross domestic product over the past two thousand years. Given the timespan involved and the contested nature of GDP figures even today, this graph was based on estimates, yet nonetheless had significant lessons. The most striking revelation is the economic predominance of China and India for most of the first fifteen hundred years, a dominance to which China – and to a lesser extent India – has almost returned. In contrast, the share of the world's GDP contributed by the United States escalated sharply in the twenti- eth century, but is now very much on the decline, while the economic ascendancy of Britain and France appears as a mere blip. The unmis- takable impression created by this graph is the long-term economic dominance of China and India, and despite this being challenged for a couple of hundred years towards the end of the last millennium, it now appears that normal service is very much resumed.

The dominance of 'the West' over 'the rest' was for a very short time in the great span of human history. Yet so much of the NeoOrientalist worldview is predicated on an assumption that this dominance is entrenched and permanent. Much of the Anglophone Left's writing about 'Sinophobia', for example, would have been appro- priate during the period of the Opium Wars or the Boxer Rebellion, but certainly isn't today. The racio-economic power structures estab- lished in the eighteenth and nineteenth centuries won't last for ever, and the effects of this history on the modern world diminishes year by year. Anyone who thinks, for example, that Chinese people see themselves as 'victims' and Westerners as somehow 'superior' has clearly not met many Chinese. The Chinese even have a word – *baizuo* (or literally, the 'white left') – which is used to mock Westerners who continue to apologise for their supposed privilege or act as though China is somehow subservient to their nations. *Baizuo* is specifically deployed to refer to people who 'only care about topics such as immigration, minorities, LGBT and the environment'; 'have no sense of real problems in the real world'; and are hypocritical humanitarians who advocate for peace and equality only to 'satisfy their own feeling of moral superiority'.[2]

In terms of its political, military and economic clout, China is returning to the pre-eminence enjoyed until it was rudely interrupted in 1839. Its investment in overseas infrastructure, through the famous Belt and Road Initiative, spans from East Asia to Eastern Europe; it is building a highspeed rail link from the Greek port of Piraeus (which it owns) to Budapest, where the authoritarian Viktor Orbán has fewer qualms about dealing with China than prevaricating liberal leaders. When Gideon Rachman writes in the *Financial Times* that 'China had challenged American power in the Pacific, by building a chain of military bases across the South China Sea', this represents a thoroughly Western-centric view that discounts the priorities and fears of Japan, South Korea, Vietnam, the Philippines and other nations whose security is challenged by Chinese expansion in the area.[3]

Equivalence between the US, bloodstained as it is, and China is morally and geopolitically inaccurate. China alone sustains the North Korean regime – one of the most reprehensible the world has seen – and for no apparent strategic reason. Likewise, the treatment of the Uighurs, Tibet, the fostering of an us-against-them xenophobia; the list of Chinese Communist Party (CCP) sins is great. The corollary of this is US actions in Afghanistan and Iraq, Guantanamo Bay and extraordinary rendition; yet the key difference between the likes of the US, Britain and France and the Chinese state is that the actions of the former arouse domestic disgust and repudiation by students, politicians, journalists and academics. In China, the latter are non-existent, or forcibly silenced.

The political scientist Zhang Weiwei claims that

China is now the only country in the world which has amalga-mated the world's longest continuous civilization with a huge modern state . . . Being the world's longest continuous civilization has allowed China's traditions to evolve, develop and adapt in virtually all branches of human knowledge and practices, such as political governance, economics, education, art, music, literature, architecture, military, sports, food and medicine. The original, continuous and endogenous nature of these traditions is indeed rare and unique in the world.[4]

China means business. It sees the period 1839–1947 as an aberra-tion which interrupted the Middle Kingdom's rightful pre-eminence among the nations. In particular, it sees 'the West' as the perpetrators of this national humiliation, and this plays a central role in the Communist Party's control over the population.[5] Many people in Western nations may be ready to put the power politics of the past behind them and embrace a new, post-national order; the CCP is not. As a result of this, many Muslim-majority countries have been conspicuous in their silence over China's treatment of the Uighur Muslims. Fifty countries, including Iran, Pakistan, Saudi Arabia, Iraq, Syria, the Palestinian Authority, Algeria, Egypt and Somalia, signed an August 2019 letter to the UN Human Rights Commission *praising* the policy of the Chinese government in Xinjiang.

As mentioned in the previous chapter, some voices denounce link-age of the COVID-19 pandemic with the actions of the Chinese state as irresponsible at best and quite possibly racist. Certainly there were incidents of citizens of China and other East Asian countries, or people of Chinese or East Asian descent, being insulted or even attacked during the period of the pandemic, yet these despicable actions should not prevent fair criticism of the Chinese government, and specifically of the CCP, in handling the outbreak. Portraying crit-icism of the Chinese government's handling of the outbreak as 'racist' is not just misleading, but also lets the Communist Party off the hook for the suppression of its own citizens and medical staff who attempted to warn about the dangers of the virus. Most infamously they include the Wuhan doctor Li Wenliang, who was denounced before he ultimately died of the virus himself.

Other whistleblowers were similarly silenced or arrested, and seven weeks elapsed between the discovery of the virus and the Chinese authorities implementing a lockdown in Wuhan, during which time the mayor estimated over five million people travelled out of the city.[6] The CCP also engaged in a misinformation campaign, trying to blame the US military for creating and spreading the virus, using inflammatory language that would rightly be denounced as racist and irresponsible had it come from the mouth or Twitter account of Donald Trump.[7]

A World Health Organization team arrived in Beijing in mid-February 2020 but were forbidden from investigating the source of the virus, and pressure from the Chinese state forced the WHO to countermand their researchers on the ground. According to the *New York Times*, China 'extracted concessions' that 'helped the country delay important research and spared its government a potentially embarrassing review of its early response to the outbreak'. Wang Linfa, who had helped identify bats as incubators of the first SARS coronavirus, announced that it had become 'a political investigation', with priorities and implications beyond public health. Perhaps as a result, the head of the WHO, Dr Tedros Adhanom Ghebreyesus, was effusive in his praise for Chinese disease prevention and President Xi Jinping personally.

When six WHO officials – three Chinese and three from overseas – were eventually allowed to enter Wuhan, they were expressly forbidden from entering and collecting samples from the Huanan Seafood Wholesale Market where the virus is believed to have originated.[8] We would expect this kind of obstruction and evasion from shameless characters such as Donald Trump, but we would hope that officials within the US government, or agencies such as the Centers for Disease Control and Prevention, would have the professional pride and moral integrity to speak out, and it is for this reason why moral relativism between the US and China is inappropriate: the US, for all its manifest faults, has mechanisms to restrain executive power and protect whistleblowers – in China these do not exist.

There were serious consequences to misplaced squeamishness around 'racism' accusations: the Italian government withdrew plans to quarantine a large group of schoolchildren returning from a trip to China after criticisms that the move amounted to 'populist fearmongering'. Hence the fear that worrying about the virus or taking prudent precautions could be seen as 'racist' almost certainly cost lives. Naturally the Chinese government had no such qualms, and enforced vigorous lockdowns with its usual efficiency and disregard for human rights.[9]

As in China, most people in India see the idea of Britons as powerful and Indians as victims as an absurd anachronism. The BBC reporter Justin Rowlatt wrote on the seventieth anniversary of Indian independence of how:

It is sobering to learn what young Indians think of Britain today. When I ask a group of 16- and 17-year-olds at Amity International School in Delhi which of the two countries is most powerful, all but one says India . . . 'It is our economy that is growing at a much faster rate,' says Sarthak Sehgal. Doha Khan draws on history to justify her view, saying: 'Before Britain came to India it gave 22 per cent of GDP to the world and when the British left we were no more than 4 per cent. So, I would say that India was much more important to Britain than Britain to India, even then.' Another girl says it is a question of demographics. 'India is the second largest population, so even by numbers India is much greater. We are young and we have great ideas', she says to giggles from her classmates.

Similarly, in Vron Ware's *Who Cares About Britishness?*, she observed a group of Indian students in a roleplaying exercise, in which one young woman gave a satirical impression of a well-educated, young Englishwoman, putting on a deliberate 'warm and jolly manner', and claiming, 'I would like to talk to you about ways in which we can help you. We feel so terribly sorry for what happened in the days of the British Empire. We want to be your partners in this new era instead of dominating you.'[10] This patronising, self-abasing attitude does no good to anyone. It does not make any attempt to reverse the material consequences of imperialism, and the best that can be said for it is that it is therapeutic for a certain type of white person. The philosopher Slavoj Žižek describes it as a 'process of self-blame which is the inverted form of clinging to one's superiority' through the idea that the complex problems of the world today are 'merely reactions to our crimes'.[11]

In 2020, an Indian child poverty charity named Akshaya Patra opened the first of three planned soup kitchens in the UK, with the goal of tackling child poverty and hunger. The chief executive of the charity, Bhawani Singh Shekhawat, admitted that while 'It might seem strange to some that this model is imported from India . . . we are bringing a tested model from a country that has dealt with this problem with speed and at scale.'[12] In many ways political developments within India have depressing parallels with the United States and Europe, in terms of rising nationalism and the debasement of political debate through an increasingly polarised media. The economist Vasuki Shastry laments the similarities between India and the US, including the intersection of class and ethnicity. In India, says Shastry, police brutality is widespread and so-called 'encounter killings', where people die in police custody, are commonplace. At the same time, Prime Minister Narendra Modi's Bharatiya Janata Party (BJP) has attempted to undermine the criminal justice system on several occasions. 'In India, the proximate reason for the harassment is caste and economic class; in America, it is race and economic class. Despite being separated by geography, a police officer in urban America today has a lot in common with his counterpart in Delhi or Mumbai.' Fox News and right-wing talk radio have their counterparts in India's pro-Modi 'commando channels', so-called because anchors wear military fatigues. As Shastry writes, 'the political spectacles in Houston in September 2019 and Ahmedabad, India in February 2020, where Trump and Modi showed up at campaign-style rallies before an adoring audience, further cements America's Indianization'.[13]

Neil MacGregor, former director of the British Museum, interviewed people across five countries – India, Canada, Nigeria, Egypt and Germany – all of which had close links with Britain and had even been occupied by British troops in their history. He was surprised to find that their knowledge of the UK was for the most part 'accompanied by a deep fund of goodwill and genuine affection for modern Britain', and the most widely admired achievement of the modern UK was itself supposed openness to the world. The Afrobeat singer Yeni Kuti reminisced about three men – English, Arab and African – helping her carry her granddaughter's pram down the stairs on the London Underground. 'It could happen, she insisted, only in London', for it is 'the city that, because of our colonial past, now belongs to the world'.[14] As the rapper and actor Riz Ahmed notes, 'the reality of Britain is vibrant multi-culturalism, but the myth we export is an all-white world of Lords and Ladies. Conversely, American society is pretty segregated, but the myth they export is of a racial melting-pot solving crimes and fighting aliens side by side'.[15]

Akala argues that 'Euro-America's ability to dominate black people' is understood by some conservatives not as merely 'one more chapter in a long history of human exploitation and domination, but rather as permanent racial superiority and inferiority'. Yet this idea is also central to NeoOrientalism, which treats the period of European colonialism and the Atlantic slave trade as not one era of history among many, but as the defining historical era, eclipsing all others, and key to understanding all aspects of the modern world.[16] This relates to a paradox within NeoOrientalism, which rightly highlights the value and contribution of a whole host of cultures, and correctly asserts that there is more than one version of modernity, and at the same time asserts that 'Euro-America' has shaped and continues to dominate the modern world. Clearly there are different versions of modernity, and therefore different peoples, nations and cultures that have 'built' the modern world. If there is a culturally or ethnically specific origin and architect of modernity, then how can we explain the different and competing visions?

When James Baldwin writes in *Notes of a Native Son* of the Alpine yokels, staring slack-jawed at the first black man they have seen, 'these people cannot be, from the point of view of power, strangers anywhere in the world; they have made the modern world, in effect, even if they do not know it', this neglects the vast contributions of the Ancient Egyptians, Chinese, Mongols and numerous other peoples to constructing the world that we know today.[17] It excludes the learning of Timbuktu and Alexandria, Mayan astronomy and Arabic mathematics; it ignores the non-white heritage of philosophy, literature, arts, architecture, music, medicine, linguistics, astronomy and other disciplines. Paper, gunpowder, ceramics and mass-produced textiles are all central to the modern world and all with decidedly non-European origins. Columbus's pilot, Pedro Niño, was African – therefore the very opening up of the 'New World', with all of the genocide and slavery and imperialism that was to follow, was conducted with the active involvement of 'people of colour'.[18] The very word 'Caucasian' apparently derives from odalisque paintings of fair-skinned slave women from the Caucasus in Turkish harems, and so the term most commonly used as a substitute for 'white' comes from a context of white subservience.[19]

Fortunately, the power relations and racial hierarchies of the eighteenth and nineteenth centuries are not frozen in time forever. Although they cast a long and grim shadow, continuing to affect the lives of millions – or even billions – of people around the world today, the days of the transatlantic slave trade and European imperialism are in chronological terms a mere blip in the history of humanity. The resultant power structures are not set in stone. Indeed, they have already begun to shift. As Akala points out, 'less than a century ago, the Chinese in British-ruled Hong Kong lived in squalid, segregated ghettoes . . . today [they] are on average some of the richest people on the planet'.[20] Now the Chinese living across the Shenzhen Bay have their eyes set firmly on ushering in a new era of Chinese global dominance – or at least their government does.

And it is not only China and India, but also a whole host of other countries, large and small, that takes issue with the idea of continued Euro-American or Anglo-American predominance. In a speech marking the centenary of the Treaty of Trianon (which dissolved the Austro-Hungarian Empire and created modern-day Hungary), the Hungarian prime minister Viktor Orbán asserted that 'the United States is no longer alone on the throne of the world, Eurasia is rebuilding with full throttle', and declared that 'a new order is being born. In our world, in our lives as well, great changes are banging on our gates.'[21] Around eight hundred miles to the south-east of Hungary, a resurgent Turkey – viewing itself as the key power in the Middle East and the rightful leader of Islamic nations – has been busy expanding into Syria, Libya, Azerbaijan and various other areas. In 2020 Turkey's interior minister Süleyman Soylu boasted of how the growth in refugees aiming to enter the European Union from the south-east would result in the destruction of the EU: 'Europe cannot endure this, cannot handle this . . . The governments in Europe will change, their economies will deteriorate, their stock markets will collapse.' In a separate speech, Soylu outlined Turkey's vision of the new global order, in which it would 'embrac[e] the entire world with our civilisation, holding the West and East with one hand, the North and South in the other, the Middle East and the Balkans in one hand, the Caucasus and Europe in the other.'[22]

In this context, the NeoOrientalist focus on Anglo-American national chauvinism and the legacy of the British Empire seems not merely misguided, but even a type of anti-national onanism, focusing on how terrible your own country is even as it fades into irrelevance and ignoring the rise of new powers due to their ethnicity or their brief (in the cases of China and Turkey, exceptionally brief) subservience.

One academic at the University of Oxford wrote in April 2020, 'If my university is the first to develop the [COVID-19] vaccine, I'm worried that it will be used as it has been in the past, to fulfil its political, patriotic function as proof of British excellence.'[23] While British NeoOrientalists were publicly willing their own country's vaccine programmes to fail, despite the potential loss of life, the Chinese and Russian governments genuinely were intending to use their vaccines to further their own geopolitical ambitions. In October 2020 and with the US presidential election on the horizon, Speaker of the House of Representatives Nancy Pelosi looked to dampen anticipation of a COVID-19 vaccine emerging, given that Donald Trump, however implausibly, would have taken the credit. She did so by criticising British regulatory standards, suggesting that any vaccine approved for use in the UK would not meet US regulatory standards. 'My concern', said Pelosi, 'is that the UK's system for that kind of judgment is not on par with ours. So if Boris Johnson decided he's going to approve a drug and this president embraces that, that's the concern I have.' As the journalist Oliver Wiseman pointed out, there was a certain irony that people who in another context 'would scoff at the suggestion that there was a meaningful difference in pharmaceutical standards between the US and a developed European country like the UK, or that only American scientists could be trusted to rule on the safety of a vaccine' found themselves making exactly that argument, and bolstering 'US chauvinism because it fits the anti-Trump narrative'.[24]

The idea that the white men of the West are railing against their nations' perceived decline is also pretty spurious; in the US, for example, Americans with the lowest level of education are those most likely to reject the idea that 'Western Civilisation' is under threat or in decline. Even when it comes to school history syllabuses, claims of 'Western' exceptionalism have little empirical basis. While it is true that the visceral horrors of, say, the Atlantic slave trade and the European empires are toned down in school textbooks, film and television portrayals, all of history is whitewashed in such a way. When children or adults learn about ancient Egypt or Greece or Rome, or medieval Europe, the violence and cruelty of the time – of virtually all of human history – are not accurately conveyed. Even in post-colonial states, the change in political control does not always filter down to the level of the schoolroom: in Kenya, almost seventy years after independence, school textbooks report that a German missionary 'discovered' Mount Kenya, and their texts have not been 'decolonised', despite the nationalistic, anti-British sentiment of post-independence Kenya – as many British Asians of a certain generation can attest.[25]

Finally, the legacies of empire can potentially be a source for combatting racism and injustice. In Kennetta Hammond Perry's book *London Is the Place for Me*, she argues that the post-emancipation colonial experience 'made it possible for someone like [the Trinidadian singer] Aldwyn Roberts to refashion himself as Lord Kitchener and imagine that London, the urban epicentre of the British imperial enterprise that made him a colonial subject, could indeed represent a place of belonging to which he could lay claim'.[26] Likewise, the historian Marc Matera notes that, before the 1950s, black intellectuals and activists in the UK sought a devolution of sovereignty within the British Empire, rather than independent nation-states.[27]

Obviously, I am not somehow implying that empire was a good thing, any more than are Perry or Matera. But I am saying that this history and its legacy can be used to undermine the structures of racial exclusion and hierarchy it was based upon. In *This Is London* a young Nigerian immigrant confesses to Ben Judah that, after meeting an old Jamaican who had been appointed to the Order of the British Empire, 'what got me, was that in this country . . . this old black guy can meet the Queen . . . I thought, OK, this guy did it . . . I can make it too.'[28] And similarly Sabir, an Afghan newsagent in Neasden, suffixes a racist tirade by conceding that nonetheless 'you must not say about the black person the truth [for] the Queen she wants there to be peace in London and this is the only way. I think this is a very good idea', demonstrating the syncretism of two different ideas of British identity, one from the not too distant past and based on racial hierarchy, and the other contemporary and based upon the imperative of tolerance and multiculturalism.[29]

NeoOrientalism doesn't just concern majority black or brown nations, but can also be applied to the majority-white nations of Western Europe. A favourite motif of many British and European opponents of Brexit is that the vote to leave the European Union represented a post-imperial midlife crisis, or a desire to return to an imagined glorious past. When advanced by British citizens, this often appears as a kind of nationalist masochism, deriding British economic, political and diplomatic prospects, even though these issues were irrelevant for many Brexit voters.

It is more understandable from non-British critics, such as the Irish journalist Fintan O'Toole – after all, there are *some* blowhards who see Brexit in such a light, and they are particularly obnoxious, perhaps especially for an Irishman like O'Toole – yet it still lacks factual justification. For example, defence spending is consistently a low priority for most Brits, even during periods when opposition to the EU or immigration is high. This (along with lack of support for spending money on overseas aid) suggests that arguments around immigration, political sovereignty and a 'little Englander' impulse to concentrate on domestic problems were more important to the Brexit vote than any 'global Britain' neo-imperial fantasies.

As Stephen Bush, political editor of the *New Statesman*, points out, it's hard to claim that the Netherlands has fully come to terms with the Dutch Empire: 'blacking up' is still widely tolerated in the Netherlands, and while UK Prime Minister Tony Blair apologised for Britain's role in the slave trade in 2007, the Dutch Prime Minister Mark Rutte is still resisting calls to do so.[30] Nonetheless, there is very little appetite for 'Nexit'. So too in France, Belgium and Spain, all post-imperial nations that have significant problems with racism and yet show little appetite for leaving the EU.

People who advance such a view usually have a blind spot for the failings and shortcomings of European countries, which are just as numerous as those of Anglo-America, and in some cases more severe. For example, while there are clearly many admirable things about the modern German nation, there are nonetheless several aspects of German politics and political culture that would cause a great deal of concern, to put it mildly, if replicated in Britain or the US.

First among these is the attitude to immigration. Angela Merkel attracted plaudits for her decision to allow the entry of millions of refugees in the mid-2010s, and the warm welcome extended by many ordinary German citizens was admirable. Nonetheless, this *Willkommenskultur* occludes deeper neuroses around immigration. At the end of 2020, it was two German scientists of Turkish descent, Dr Uğur Şahin and Dr Özlem Türeci, the co-founders of the chemical engineering company BioNTech, who announced the discovery of the first COVID-19 vaccine. They were lauded around the world, including in Germany, but in their home country much of the coverage was laced with anti-migrant sentiment, implying that Şahin and Türeci were unusual examples of the benefits of immigration due to their professional success and apparent adaptation to 'German' culture. Writing of the conflicted coverage of Şahin and Türeci, German journalist Anna Sauerbrey argues that 'when it comes to immigration, Germany is uneasy even with its most spectacular successes' and 'resentment against immigrants over the past decade has become pervasive in German public life'. In 2010, the book *Germany Abolishes Itself* by Thilo Sarrazin – formerly a senior politician in the Social Democratic Party – claimed that the educational gap between immigrants from Muslim-majority countries and Germans was rooted in genetic differences, and that immigration would threaten Germany's economy by decreasing overall education standards. The book was a bestseller and can still be found on the bookshelves of middle-class, liberal Germans.[31]

Personal anecdotes support the idea that Germany, for all its successful post-Holocaust soul-searching and welcoming of refugees in the 2010s, retains attitudes to race that are now thankfully rare in Britain or America. Back in 2013, the British journalist Bim Adewunmi wrote of how, despite her happy times in Berlin, 'Berliners seemed oddly at home with staring. They stared at me at the airport, at the train station, on the tube and on the bus, and as I selected bread rolls at the supermarket. One small child in a school group almost walked into a wall as he stared at me.' In two separate incidents, German men actually touched and pulled her hair while she was travelling on public transport. For Adewunmi, while the image of Berlin as 'really hipsterish, really international and multicultural' was accurate, 'its internationalism is starkly monochrome'.[32]

Across the Rhine, the brutality of the French police would be inconceivable in the UK, especially in mainland Britain, where the police are not permitted to use crowd control weapons such as water cannon, rubber bullets or tear gas. During *gilets jaunes* (yellow vests) protests that began in France in 2018, a teenager in Strasbourg lost an eye, and an elderly woman in Marseilles died after being hit by a rubber bullet. As recently as 1961, police in Paris killed up to three hundred unarmed protesters marching for Algerian independence. Without wanting to downplay the extensive racist violence practised by American police officers, it is hard to imagine a US police department killing three hundred black civil rights marchers in the 1960s, and if that did happen, it would be seared into the global consciousness, whereas the 1961 Paris Massacre is relatively unknown outside France.

The 2013 legalisation of same-sex marriage in France brought thousands of protesters to the streets marching in opposition and, alongside many other majority-Catholic nations, it retains a twelve-week limit on abortion. There is no chance of a Conservative government in the UK trying to restrict abortion in this way, and attempts by Republican lawmakers to do the same are seen as indicative of the exceptional evil of the American Right. Back in Germany, Angela Merkel opposed same-sex marriage, and despite presiding over Europe's largest economy, spends less on international aid than the UK government (although this may change if the UK goes ahead with its mooted decrease in the overseas aid budget from 0.7 to 0.5 per cent of GDP).

Many people in Anglo-America, and not just NeoOrientalists, assume that much of continental Europe, particularly the northern-most countries, are havens of liberal social democracy. There are sound reasons for this, but as usual the reality is more nuanced. As the journalist Ed West points out, in Denmark ambulances are privatised, and there are three times as many private health operations per capita as the UK. Denmark has far tougher immigration restrictions than the UK, and they were passed by the left-wing Social Democracy party.

These restrictions do not mean that Denmark has suddenly become a hotbed of racism; Danes remain among the most tolerant people in the world, but it highlights how the inextricable association of immigration control with racism is really restricted to the Anglophone Left, and in fact might be called the real post-imperial hangover.

Generally, there appears to be far more hostility to racial minorities in most of continental Europe than in the UK: a 2016 poll for the EU Agency for Fundamental Rights found that 63 per cent of black people in Finland, 51 per cent of those in Ireland, 48 per cent in Germany and 41 per cent in Sweden had experienced racial harassment in the past five years. Of the twelve countries surveyed, the UK was second to last, with 'only' 21 per cent of its black citizens reporting racial harassment, behind Malta with 20 per cent. Furthermore, Britain is unique among European countries in having a tiny education gap between the children of natives and immigrants, whereas in every continental country it is still considerable.[33]

This Europhilia is not unique to Brits, but also extends to some Americans. Many black American writers, from James Baldwin to Ta-Nehisi Coates, have found some sort of refuge from racial oppression in France but, as Thomas Chatterton Williams points out, African and Caribbean blacks do not mistake France as some sort of haven for blacks; this is because in France African Americans are understood first as American – with all the economic, cultural and political signifiers that entails – rather than black.[34]

The Universal Appeal of National Populism

As mentioned in Part I, the fact that different politicians, from Trump to Johnson to Netanyahu to Putin to Erdoğan to Bolsonaro to Modi, have been able to use a similar combination of nationalism, anti-intellectualism, and appeals to 'common sense' to secure popularity in such a wide variety of polities, economies and societies, indicates the widespread appeal and potency of this kind of politics. Yet in addition to an understanding of geopolitics that sees some countries as obnoxiously nationalistic and others as perpetual victims, NeoOrientalism attributes special morality to citizens of the Global South, assuming them to be socialists, anti-racists, feminists, LGBT allies and so on. When faced with the overwhelming evidence that this is not the case, it argues this must be due to the legacies of European colonialism.

The geographical spread of laws against same-sex relationships is an obvious refutation of the NeoOrientalist depiction of the inherent goodness of the Global South, but legislation alone tells a partial tale. After all, in many places in the Global North it might not be illegal to be gay, but it is still pretty dangerous, and attitudes to homosexuality in countries such as Britain and the US were highly retrograde merely a generation ago. At the same time, as argued by Jasbir Puar, 'gay rights' have been used by Western right-wingers as a cover for racist or Islamophobic rhetoric, including by people who cared little for gay rights or feminism before 11 September 2001. Nonetheless, the charge of 'homonationalism' should not deflect from the observation that many people in the Global South are notably homophobic. As the example of Britain and the US shows, this is not inherent or fixed in time forever, but it is the case today, and appears to affect young people as much as their elders.

A casual glance at social media can confirm this: in March 2020, a Twitter post by a practising Muslim announcing her engagement to her partner saw her inundated with abuse from young Muslims, from Nigeria to Pakistan to Malaysia. Goodluck Jonathan – the behatted former president of Nigeria, who won international plaudits for his peaceful transition of power to Muhammadu Buhari in 2015 – oversaw a 2014 law banning gay marriage and making 'amorous relationships' between same-sex couples an offence punishable by imprisonment for up to fourteen years. For many in Nigeria, irrespective of ethnic or religious heritage or political persuasion, homosexuality is seen as a 'Western import'.

Aside from homophobia, the anti-intellectualism and national populism that have made headway in the US and parts of Europe in recent years are not confined to those living in white-majority countries. In India, Narendra Modi's BJP has a great deal of support among young Indians and students, and combines nationalistic, anti-Pakistani rhetoric with attacks on so-called 'Naxals', a derogatory catch-all term for Marxist intellectuals and liberal elites. As the Indian journalist Annie Zaidi points out, the Indian press writes about Muslims, lower-caste Hindus and members of the 'scheduled' tribes with a scandalised and voyeuristic tone that would be recognisable to anyone familiar with the British tabloids.[35] Somewhat counterintuitively, the BJP has even been making inroads among the country's Muslim voters, particularly Muslim women, possibly as a result of the government's criminalisation of 'triple talaq' instant divorce in 2019 (in which a male can legally divorce by simply uttering or writing the word *talaq*, Arabic for divorce, three times): ahead of the 2019 parliamentary elections, the party set up over one hundred legal aid centres to help Muslim women who had suffered destitution as a result of triple talaq.[36] Donald Trump's politics – brash, aspirational, nationalistic and anti-Islam – won him millions of fans in India, and some even worshipped him as a god. Literally: one such man, Bussa Krishna, created a shrine to Trump in his home in the state of Telangana, complete with a six-foot-tall statue, and in 2020 had a fatal heart attack after hearing that Trump had contracted COVID-19.[37]

In addition to the Indian Muslims voting for the BJP, and the estimated one-third of US Muslims who voted for Donald Trump in 2020, it is believed that around 5 per cent of French Muslims voted for the explicitly Islamophobic Marine Le Pen in the 2017 French presidential election. While this figure is within the realms of a polling error, it is notable that a non-negligible number of French Muslims were sufficiently attracted to other aspects of her conservative and authoritarian programme to overlook her blatantly anti-Muslim attitude.[38] Intra-Muslim discrimination and violence are also a real and growing problem: in Pakistan, for example, Ahmadi Muslims are excluded from much of public life and often denied the protection of the state, leaving them materially marginalised and vulnerable to attacks.

One of Ben Judah's interlocutors, Mukhtar, is a Somalian man living in Harlesden, north-west London. He tells him how he feels very isolated: 'I feel like I don't belong in Harlesden any more ... London's changing ... and it's not all of London, it's only certain areas. It's become weird. People were friendly once. People were welcoming. They are not like that any more. Because they don't know anyone. Everyone moved.'[39] Another interviewee, a Pakistani who sells fruit at Rye Lane market, laments that 'there is no order in Britain', and that in his six months of living in the UK, 'blacks beat me three times ... [the] police they do nothing to control these blacks'.[40] Nor is this racial antipathy unique to Asian immigrants: Grace, a Nigerian cleaner, complains that black hospital cleaners are being replaced with Poles and Romanians, who 'are bringing in their own. The nurses will come in and notice whole teams of Sierra Leoneans have vanished from the building. They have been replaced by white people, from Poland, Lithuania or other places they have never heard of.'[41]

Anyone even vaguely familiar with the language deployed by those hostile to immigration into the UK over the past seven decades will be struck by the consistency of the language. Complaints about change, violence, loss of community and people favouring their own groups; all are today found among immigrants themselves as much as among the settled population. The political implications of this may be profound. Certainly, there are plenty of reasons to suspect that immigrants, and particularly their children and grandchildren, will move closer to the politics and values of British liberals, but in the meantime the anti-immigrant hostility and racial stereotypes of migrants may prove fertile ground for the politics of reaction.

That so many recent immigrants to the UK have these attitudes should not surprise us, given the hostility to immigration around the world. A comprehensive survey by Pew Research asked people in twenty-seven different countries whether they would like to see immigration increase, stay the same or decrease. In Europe, Greece and Italy were the least receptive to increased immigration, with 82 and 71 per cent respectively saying they would like numbers to decrease or stay the same. The percentage of people wanting fewer or no more immigrants coming to their country was higher in South Africa (65 per cent), Argentina (61 per cent), Kenya (60 per cent), Nigeria (50 per cent), India (45 percent) and Mexico (44 per cent) than it was in Australia (38 per cent), the UK (37 per cent) or the US (29 per cent).

A 2017 survey by Ipsos MORI asked people around the world whether they thought their country would be 'strong' if it 'stopped immigration' entirely. Just under one-third (31 per cent) of Britons agreed, slightly up from 30 per cent of Australians and less than the 37 per cent of Germans who answered in the affirmative. In contrast almost two-thirds (61 per cent) of Turks and nearly half (45 per cent) of Indians said the same. There was a similar disparity when asked if they felt as though they were 'strangers in their own country', to which 57 per cent of Turks, 54 per cent of South Africans and 39 per cent of Indians agreed. This contrasts with 38 per cent of Germans and 37 per cent of both Britons and Australians. The greatest discrepancy came when people were asked if employers should 'prioritise locals' over immigrants when hiring, to which 74 per cent of Turks and 62 per cent of Indians assented, compared to 58 per cent of Americans and only 48 per cent of Brits.

There is plenty of anecdotal evidence that chimes with these statistics. Akala draws attention to hostility towards Jamaicans of South Asian heritage by the black majority, for whom the relative economic prosperity of the former is made harder to bear due to their more recent presence on the island.[42] The black population of South Africa is among the most hostile to immigration in the whole world, with regular violent attacks against migrants from elsewhere in southern Africa. The language used by some black political leaders is reminiscent of the discourse of the European far-Right, as when a Zulu king described migrants as 'vermin'.

In the Middle East, the 'Kafala', which controls migrant labour, mostly from East African nations, is effectively modern slavery in another form. In one particularly egregious example from April 2020, an Ethiopian domestic worker was sold alongside furniture on a Lebanese 'buy and sell' Facebook page. As the Argentinian-Lebanese journalist Joey Ayoub wrote on Twitter: 'I spent the first 24 years of my life in Lebanon' and had 'personally seen this dozens of times. Migrant domestic workers are traded like objects.'

On a global level, as migration increases over the coming years, the spread and intensity of this hostility may increase, and those of us living in the West who believe in and want to promote the free movement of people need to change our understanding and vocabulary of race and disadvantage in order to deal with it. Citizens of the 'Global South', like 'people of colour' in the West, are rhetorically used as or assumed to be potential future foot soldiers in campaigns for the priorities of well-educated Western liberals: against racism, against misogyny, against homophobia, against ableism, etc., and also for social justice and democracy and equality and so on. But billions of people have other ideas and will refuse attempts to press gang them into progressive politics.

Another central tenet of NeoOrientalism when applied to the global stage is the significance given to racism – nationally and culturally specific, a product of European colonialism and the Atlantic slave trade, only a few centuries old – at the expense of colourism – universal, transcendent across cultures, societies, economies and political systems, and pre-dating European empires and transatlantic slavery by several hundred years.

Clearly, within white-majority countries, the more particularistic racism is a bigger problem – for now. Yet in many non-white countries, from South Korea to Sri Lanka, colourism is a much more important issue than 'racism', as understood in the West. As the global power shifts underway today accelerate over the next century, the global significance of colourism may well increase. Even within white-majority countries, colour, shade and 'darkness' are integral to racial hierarchies and injustices. As kihana miraya ross wrote in the *New York Times* immediately after the George Floyd killing, 'racism' alone is not appropriate to understand why so many African-American men die in such a manner. Racism, while far from a meaningless term, is 'a catch-all that can encapsulate anything from black people being denied fair access to mortgage loans, to Asian students being burdened with a "model minority" label'. Instead, ross insists that we need to see such violence as specifically reflecting 'anti-blackness'.[43]

Colourism intersects with class, but also with gender: as the UK grime artist Lioness argues, there are plenty of successful dark-skinned men in the music and film industries, but few dark-skinned women.[44] In the song 'Black Hypocrisy', the Jamaican dancehall singer Spice notes that 'the same black people dem seh I'm too black/And if yuh bleach out yuh skin dem same one come a chat'. This is the fate that befell Khadija Ben Hamou from Algeria's southern Adrar region, who won the 'Miss Algeria' competition in 2019 and was subsequently inundated with abuse because of her 'dark' skin colour.[45]

Notably, colourism exists in countries that have never known colonisation by white Europeans. In South Korea, for example, pale skin has long been an idealised beauty standard; you can see clips on the internet of members of Korean pop bands such as BTS and EXO teasing each other about their supposedly 'dark' skin, and applying high-factor sun cream. One of my friends, a white British man who lives in Osaka, Japan, with his Japanese wife, was recently stopped in the street by someone who complimented them on their child's 'white, foreign' skin, and he tells me that this reverence for white skin is 'not to the same degree as in Korea and certainly not to the same degree as in China'. The pervasive anti-blackness in that latter country sometimes cuts through to Western audiences via incidents such as the infamous laundry detergent commercial in which a black person is 'washed clean' or when a sign barring black people from entering was put up in a McDonald's in the Chinese city of Guangzhou during the COVID-19 pandemic.[46]

In 2019, the Bollywood star Esha Gupta was watching a football match involving her favourite team, Arsenal, and posted on Instagram a screenshot of an exchange with a friend. Her friend had said that Arsenal player Alex Iwobi – a black man from Nigeria – looked like a 'gorilla', and a 'Neanderthal', for whom 'evolution had stopped'. Gupta uploaded this to her 3.4-million followers with a simple caption: 'hahaha'. Ironically, Gupta had herself complained of similar experiences, telling the *Times of India* in 2017 of how 'in Europe, brown skin is celebrated', and that she was 'proud' of her looks, but 'in India, I have to face discrimination for my complexion. It's sheer hypocrisy. I am made to feel bad about the way I look when 90 per cent girls in India look like me'.

The NeoOrientalist would simply say that colourism in India is a legacy of colonialism, but this does not explain why this kind of overt racism is today so unacceptable in nations such as France and Britain, unless we think that nations such as India are a few decades 'behind' the former. It is patronising and unsatisfactory to say that the former countries are more 'advanced', and that the likes of India are in the process of 'catching up'. At the same time, India by no means has a specific or unique problem with anti-black racism or colourism, and it is obviously not the case that these phenomena are somehow inherent to the subcontinent and will never change. Nonetheless, it remains a pressing problem for now.

Around the same time as Gupta's Instagram post, the Pakistan cricket team captain, Sarfraz Ahmed, was banned for four matches after being caught using a racist slur against the South African player Andile Phehlukwayo.

The secretary-general of the Association of African Students in India, Ezeugo Nnamdi, said he was 'not surprised' to hear about Gupta's post: 'Racism is not something which is very hidden here', he told the BBC. 'It is something very open. They call you "habshi" [a derogatory term for black people], and a lot of other words and racial slurs. Here, you are regarded as a cannibal.' This is borne out in popular culture. In the award-winning 2008 Bollywood film *Fashion*, the aspiring-model heroine played by Priyanka Chopra descends into drink and drug addiction, but only reaches rock bottom when she sleeps with a black man.[47]

Sabir, the Afghan newsagent in Neasden interviewed by Ben Judah, insists that black teenagers are happier in prison as they get 'free burgers'. He feels guilty about saying this, in fact he 'knows he is not supposed' to say it. This is because he has recently become a British citizen, and tells Judah that on the 'unforgettable day' when he first received a British passport, the lines 'Her Britannic Majesty's Secretary of State Requests and Requires' had a profound effect on him: 'The Queen, he explains, has given him rights. But in exchange, he elaborates, the Queen requests her subjects to speak kindly of all her children', including black people.[48]

This vignette not only reflects the profound sense of anti-blackness held by billions of people across the globe, but also serves as a useful corrective to the NeoOrientalist view of people such as Sabir, which understands him and other Afghan migrants as fundamentally and irrevocably victims of British imperialism who – whether they like it or not – are part of a struggle against racism and nationalism (and also, even more bizarrely, ableism, misogyny, homo- and transphobia, etc.). This is almost a mirror image of the right-wing view of Sabir, which sees him as a member of an international *umma*, defined by his religious identity, and likely to betray his new country at any moment.

South Africa is one place where the history of white supremacist racism clearly continues to shape non-white views around race. Anti-black racism existed in South Asia and the Middle East long before the European colonial period; hence their enslavement of black Africans centuries before Vasco da Gama rounded the Cape. But in South Africa this type of racism is clearly a European import. The apartheid era only formally ended in 1994, and continues to cast a long and malevolent shadow, most obviously in terms of wealth and opportunities, but also in terms of perceived racial hierarchies.

In 2020 the BBC ran a story about a young South African couple – Tumelo and Ithra – from a black and Asian background respectively, whose parents were due to meet for the first time. In South Africa – and in much of the Global South – black and Asian relationships meet with a disapproval that might not be applied to black–white or Asian–white couplings. Both Tumelo and Ithra report that they 'received fewer stares' when they dated white people, and are the only such couple out of more than three hundred students in their class at university.

When Ithra announced to her family that she was dating a black man, there was a 'mass exodus' from the family WhatsApp group, and it appears that her family is not unrepresentative; according to a survey by the Institute for Justice and Recognition, only 47 per cent of South Africans approve of mixed-race relationships; a percentage unchanged since 2003. Ithra's mother thinks 'Blasian' relationships are more difficult due to the religious differences: with white and black South Africans, both couples are likely to come from a Christian background, whereas Ithra's family is Muslim. Nonetheless their inaugural meeting went off without a hitch, with the shared significance of family, food and faith building bridges between the two families.[49] For most of the world's non-white majority, this is surely how future relationships and understandings between people of different ethnic or religious backgrounds will be built: not with reference to books or theory, but upon shared commonalities.

Thus far we have seen how the NeoOrientalist tendency flattens and homogenises billions of people. However, it also polices the boundaries of exactly who should or should not be considered 'white', often without regard to the complex history, culture and politics of such people. This policing is the focus of the final chapter of Part II.

Chapter 6

Policing Whiteness

The greatest race of the East End, after the Cockney, and in numbers, is the Jewish.

'East End with Tom Harrisson', *BBC*, 1939[1]

In August 2011, a group of protestors gathered in Charles Clore Park near the waterfront of southern Tel Aviv. The demonstrators had been marching against the mistreatment of the several thousand East African refugees who have settled in south Tel Aviv, who are denied even the most rudimentary protections by the state, and subjected to racist hostility from the police and their neighbours. Apart from the refugees themselves (the vast majority of whom are Sudanese or Eritrean), the protest was made up mostly of young Ashkenazi Israelis, descendants of the European Jews who emigrated to Israel in the years either side of the state's founding in 1948.

In the days before the protest, missiles fired from Gaza at southern Israeli towns had left one dead and thirty injured, and at the conclusion of the march a moment of silence was held to commemorate these casualties. Afterwards, a succession of short speeches was made, during which muted heckling began from the edge of the crowd:

A group of about five men with distinctively Mizrahi accents demand that the speakers denounce the missile barrage. Their heckling increases when an Arab speaker approaches the podium. The audience loudly applauds his words about the shared fate of Jews and Arabs in times of economic stress. In contrast, the hecklers' leader shouts: 'It's become a leftist protest.' A demonstrating activist replies: 'If you don't like it, leave.' In response, the heckler yells: 'Shut up, you queer!' which is answered by: 'That's right, I like screwing ass.'

After this exchange, the atmosphere becomes increasingly vitriolic. At one point, a protestor tells the Mizrahis to 'Go back to the zoo', to which the leader of the counter-protestors shouts: 'You son of a bitch. Hitler didn't kill enough of you.'[2]

In some ways, this incident could have taken place in many different countries: A crowd of mostly young, middle-class, 'white', university-educated people protests in solidarity with a group of people different from themselves. They are criticised by working-class men, who accuse them of being insufficiently patriotic and who imply that their concern is a result of their 'privilege'. Yet because this is Israel, there is one important difference: the group of working-class men are themselves from a group historically and currently mistreated and disadvantaged within their own country due to their ethno-national background and the colour of their skin. Ever since the migration of Mizrahi Jews to Israel from across North Africa and the Middle East, they have been mistreated. From being placed into squalid camps upon their arrival and then disbursed to peripheral towns, there was also a scandal whereby the children of Yemeni Jews were taken away from them and given to childless Ashkenazi parents, in an episode redolent of the mistreatment of Aboriginal Australians and First Nation Canadians.

In Israel, the association of 'whiteness' with support for nativism, Islamophobia, militarism and so on, and the assumption that 'brown' people are for some reason against this, is turned on its head. Class, race and education are correlated in such a way that the descendants of the original Ashkenazi immigrants occupy the most socially and economically privileged positions, and make up the vast majority of the support for the Israeli 'Left', such as it is. In contrast, poor and working-class Israelis are almost uniformly later arrivals from the Middle East, Ethiopia and the former Soviet Union. This is most starkly and visually brought home by the sheer number of black and brown faces wearing military fatigues and lugging M16s around downtown Tel Aviv – the majority of Ashkenazi Israelis are able to avoid frontline infantry positions and occupy elite positions in the air force, military intelligence, special forces and so on, all of which have lower casualty rates than the checkpoint fodder units.

Virtually all of the people killed by the Israeli police are Muslim Arabs, Ethiopian Jews or Mizrahim – and yet while Muslims are, understandably, implacably opposed to the Likud party that has governed Israel for most of the past four decades, Ethiopians and Mizrahim are among its biggest supporters. In fact, Yigal Amir – who in 1995 assassinated Prime Minister Yitzhak Rabin in response to what he saw as the 'betrayal' of the Oslo Accords – was radicalised at least in part by the experience of being a Mizrahi student at an Ashkenazi Yeshiva, where he was badly bullied.

This characterisation shouldn't be taken too far: firstly, it ignores the ultra-Orthodox, many of whom are Ashkenazi and most of whom are poor (although this owes something to their belief in the religious imperative to have as many kids as possible and for men to study the Torah in lieu of working). Furthermore, just because the vast majority of the Left is Ashkenazi and middle class does not in any way mean that most Ashkenazi middle-class people are on the Left. You do not need to go far in south Tel Aviv to find a hipster with all the right opinions on climate change, trans rights and police violence against black people who will nonetheless casually inform you that 'all Arabs are terrorists'. Finally, it doesn't consider the millions of Arab Muslims with Israeli citizenship, who overwhelmingly support the Left in terms of opposing the Occupation, although they tend to be less keen on other left-wing priorities such as gay rights.

Nonetheless, an incident of one Jew saying to another 'Hitler didn't kill enough of you' is a stark reminder of the complexity of identity and politics *within* specific religious or ethnic groups. It is also a warning for the Western Left: the current support of the majority of people of colour for left-wing politics is contingent and by no means permanent. It is easy to see the current alliance between 'white identity liberals' and ethnic minorities breaking down over the next few decades, with the result that the Left in the UK and the United States could become just as isolated and impotent as it is in Israel.

In September 2011, on the tenth anniversary of the 9/11 attacks, Nathan Eccleston – a footballer currently plying his trade at Nuneaton Borough, but at the time a youth player for Liverpool – was placed under investigation by the club after tweeting: 'don't let the media make u believe that was terrorist that did it. #OTIS'. 'OTIS' is an acronym for 'Only The Illuminati Succeed', and Eccleston's tweet was my introduction to the growing popularity of this antisemitic conspiracy theory among working-class youth.

A few years later this kind of 'left-wing' antisemitism, which positions Jews as having a leading role in perpetuating socio-economic and racial hierarchies, received fresh attention due to the increase in incidences of such antisemitism within the Labour Party during the leadership of Jeremy Corbyn. One of the most high-profile incidents was Corbyn's own defence of an antisemitic mural, which depicted prominent Jews playing cards on a table supported on the backs of black and brown people. Sadly, black people are just as susceptible to this kind of hatred as white people, despite the disproportionate support among Jews for the US civil rights movement, the South African anti-apartheid struggle, many other anti-racist and social justice crusades – including anti-Zionist campaigns – and the relatively high rate of inter-marriage between Jews and black people. There is a proud tradition of black socialist solidarity with Jewish people, such as with James Baldwin, who despite his steadfast opposition to Israel emphasised that Jews had been historically instrumentalised and disposable according to the development and prerogatives of Western capitalism. The common subordinate position of blacks and Jews has led both to be pilloried: the Trinidadian activist Michael X was himself at one point an enforcer for Jewish slum landlord Peter Rachman.

Black antisemitism reached new heights in the summer of 2020 in the wake of the killing of George Floyd, when some black celebrities – understandably outraged by the fate of Floyd and numerous other African Americans killed in similar circumstances – inexplicably used the moment to link Jews to the injustices faced by black people. The American football player DeSean Jackson even went so far as to post a screenshot of a quote, falsely attributed to Hitler, declaring that Jews 'will blackmail America . . . will extort America, [and] their plan for world domination won't work if the Negroes know who they were'.[3] The first thing to say about this is that you know you are really antisemitic when you are making up things that even Hitler didn't say, but what kind of black person hates Jews so much that they would invoke *Hitler*, as though he didn't also harbour evil beliefs about black people? While Jackson's outburst is an extreme example of the conflation of Jewishness with anti-blackness, even Alexandria Ocasio-Cortez pulled out of an event honouring Yitzhak Rabin, lest she somehow be seen to endorse Israel, and thereby endorse racism.

Aside from acting as though the treatment of black and brown people in the Middle East is somehow an offshoot of the racial histories and hierarchies of the United States, rather than the latter being one small component of a long and varied history of anti-blackness across the globe, the understanding of Jews as 'white' and the Holocaust as 'white-on-white' crime demonstrates an extremely American-centric, chrono-centric understanding of race. In the context of the millennia of persecution faced by Jews, it is very recent indeed that they have been considered 'white'. At the dawn of the last century, antisemitic diatribes by European politicians or journalists usually claimed that the very 'Orientalness' of Jews made them incompatible with European civilisation. The German nationalist politician Heinrich von Treitschke said of the German Jewish composer Heinrich Heine that he 'never wrote a drinking song' as 'the oriental [Jew] was incapable' of 'carousing in the German way'.[4]

At the same time, the antisemitism of leading imperialists such as Herbert Spencer was also taken up with gusto by many anti-colonial activists. For example, in his 1909 text *Hind Swaraj*, Gandhi favourably quoted the leading antisemite G. K. Chesterton. This attitude was also taken up by many Jews: Max Nordau, who co-founded the World Zionist Organization with Theodor Herzl, criticised the emasculation of European men in the years before the First World War, blaming the nefarious influence of Émile Zola and Oscar Wilde, among many others. As Mishra explains, he became obsessed, like other Jews reading Spencer, with the idea of creating '*Muskeljudetum*, literally muscular, virile, warrior-like Jews'.[5]

Conversely, as Mishra points out, many anti-colonial struggles in the Global South took inspiration from the Zionist movement. Martin Delany used Jewish experiences of dispersal as a model to understand the history of black Americans and to argue for his proposal of a black American colonisation of Nicaragua or elsewhere.[6] The Iranian intellectual Jalal Al-e-Ahmad felt that the Spartan community and values of the young Israeli state offered a template for how Iran should develop in a decolonising yet Western-dominated world: 'Israel, despite all its defects and despite all contradictions it harbours, is the basis of a power: The first step in the promise of a future which is not that late . . . Israel is a model, [better] than any other model, of how to deal with West.'[7]

Today, as Gilroy writes, blacks 'appear to identify far more readily with the glamorous pharaohs than with the abject plight of those they held in bondage.'[8] The podcaster Ash Sarkar has argued that antisemitism is not really the same as other racisms, effectively because Jews are privileged. Or, as she phrased it, do not face 'systemic disadvantage in either the jobs market or the criminal justice system'. Firstly, and obviously, not all Jews are privileged. Around the world, a great many are very poor, and you don't have to travel too far to find poor Jews. A short walk from my flat in Finsbury Park is the largest community of ultra-Orthodox Jews in Europe, most of whom live in poverty. Aside from housing, wealth and income, Jews are also susceptible to some of the inequities faced by other minorities: for example, during the coronavirus pandemic, Public Health England found that Jewish men over sixty-five died at twice the rate of Christians, even after adjusting for socio-demographic factors.

Secondly, just because many Jews now support right-wing politics, this does not mean that they somehow lose their 'ethnic minority' status, any more than do the large and growing numbers of other minorities who express conservative views and vote for parties of the political Right. If many ethnic minorities do move over to the British Conservative Party in coming decades, we can expect to see this attitude to be extended to them. It is a continuation of the postmodern inversion of base and superstructure we saw in Part I, whereby objectively middle-class people consider themselves working-class because of how they feel. So it is too for NeoOrientalists: non-white people are politically radical activists in a global struggle against racism (and misogyny, homophobia, transphobia, ableism, classism, etc.) and so those who are not must really be white.

How the Irish Became White

Ta-Nehisi Coates writes that 'the history of civilization is littered with dead "races"' sometimes created by themselves, other times imposed from without and 'later abandoned because they no longer serve their purpose'.[9] Of these, the Irish have served the interests of racial separatists for almost a thousand years, which perhaps accounts for the plentiful historical examples of association between Irish and black people. Crispus Attucks, widely believed to be the first American killed in the War of Independence, was black, of African and Native American descent, and was said to associate with a 'motley rabble of saucy boys, negroes, mulattoes, Irish teagues and outlandish jack tars'.[10] This association was not always voluntary: in post-1945 Britain, signs outside pubs or hotels declared that 'No blacks, no dogs, and no Irish' would be permitted to enter.

To this day, remnants of anti-Irish prejudice remain, and sometimes in surprising places. Even in ostensibly internationalist groups such as the Campaign for Nuclear Disarmament, anti-Irish prejudice could still find open expression as late as the 1960s. As revealed by the historian Jodi Burkett, a delegate to one CND conference announced that 'the Irish folk, especially the Catholics, are a bitter, hating, illogical, murderous, unforgiving obstinate lot'. While this was a minority opinion, Burkett notes, it was not unheard of 'both within and outside the CND or across the British left'.[11] At the 1976 Grunwick strike in north-west London – which has a special prominence in the history of the labour movement as a landmark case of South Asian industrial militancy and cross-ethnic cooperation on the picket line – one of the Indian protestors nonetheless remarked on the presence of the Special Patrol Group with 'What are they doing here? Do we look like terrorists? We're not Irish!'[12]

Memories of this history of anti-Irish hate and discrimination have now largely faded, so that the kind of Irish-baiting that would rightly provoke outrage if aimed at other groups passes largely unnoticed. For example, the former Labour MP Stephen Pound waged a career-long effort to have the statue of Oliver Cromwell outside the Houses of Parliament removed from its prominent position on account of his massacres and atrocities in Ireland. Not only was he unsuccessful, but parliamentary authorities placed a smaller bust of Cromwell outside Pound's office, and trained a CCTV camera on it to check that no one moved it. You cannot imagine the placing of a bust of, say, Reginald Dyer, known as the 'Butcher of Amritsar', outside the office of an MP of Indian heritage, much less a bust of Robert E. Lee outside the office of an African-American Congressman, being covered in the same mischievous tone.

Today, many Irish people subscribe to anti-racist politics, as a legacy of their own struggle against imperialism, and Sinn Féin is consistently left-wing across a whole host of issues, from abortion to gay rights to climate change. This was not always the case, and much of this liberalism is fairly recent: Ireland only legalised divorce in 1995, and the referendum was won with just 50.28 per cent of the vote.[13] Back in the 1840s, the Irish revolutionary John Mitchel combined his opposition to British imperialism in Ireland with a full-throated endorsement of slavery, denying that it was 'a crime, or a wrong, or even a peccadillo, to hold slaves, to buy slaves, to sell slaves, to keep slaves to their work, by flogging or other needful coercion.'

This was good politics for Mitchel: Irish nationalist movements have long depended on support from donors and politicians in the United States, and taking up against slavery risked jeopardising this goodwill. At the same time, something peculiar seemed to come over Irish people when they emigrated to the United States. While the famous Irish nationalist Daniel O'Connell attacked slavery and said he would never visit America while slavery existed, the Irish who emigrated to America soon made their peace with the institution.[14] As the historian Noel Ignatiev argues, the racial hierarchies in the US were not 'a pattern they were familiar with and they bore no responsibility for it; nevertheless, they adapted to it in short order'.[15]

It was exacerbated by the fact that much of the American abolition movement was motivated by a kind of Protestantism that was also implacably opposed to Catholics, and there were intersections of support for abolitionism and African-American rights with temperance.[16] In Philadelphia in August 1842, the Irish led a horrific attack on a black temperance parade celebrating the anniversary of the abolition of slavery in the Caribbean – the combination of temperance and implicitly pro-British sentiment being perfectly calibrated to infuriate the Irish.[17]

Nonetheless, in some mid-nineteenth century working-class neighbourhoods – such as Moyamensing, Pennsylvania, where up to one in thirty people were estimated to be mixed race – there appears to have been a lot of social mixing of Irish and blacks. The Twelfth Presbyterian Church in Philadelphia had an African-American minister in 1837, and baptismal records suggest that about one-third of the congregation was Irish. 'So many of the pioneers of blackface minstrelsy were of Irish descent,' wrote Ignatiev, 'for the Irish came disproportionately into contact with the people whose speech, music, and dance furnished the basis, however distorted, for the minstrel's art.'[18] In Philadelphia's Walnut Street prison, roughly half of the prisoners in the 1820s appear to have been Irish or black, and they were entirely integrated; 'race' was not a social definition within the prison.[19]

The deprived position of Irish immigrants to America among free labourers probably contributed towards their developing hostility towards blacks, and this was adroitly encouraged by savvy slave-holding politicians. James H. Hammond of South Carolina, a lieutenant of the senator and slavery defender John C. Calhoun, made a famous speech against 'wage slavery' and received letters of thanks from Northern workers, with Irish prominent among them.[20] These tactics won the Irish vote for the *ante bellum* Democrats. According to

Ignatiev, the Irish did not vote Democratic 'out of sentimental attach-
ment to those who gave them the vote', but rather because the
Democrats 'eased their assimilation as whites, and more than any
other institution, taught them the meaning of whiteness'. Conversely,
the Republican cry of 'free soil, free labor, and free men' had little
attraction to the Irish: 'Unable or unwilling to avail themselves of the
white-skin privilege of setting themselves up as independent farmers',
they stuck by the Democrats, which protected them from nativists
and guaranteed them 'a favored position over those whom they
regarded as the principal threat to their position, the free black people
of the North (the only group as 'free' of either property or marketable
skills as the Irish)'.[21]

Today, there is a clear division between Irish Americans and actual
Irish when it comes to the politics of Donald Trump, with the former
mostly in favour and the latter firmly against. The transition of Irish
people from immigrants received with hostility and racism to people
who receive immigrants with hostility and racism is an important
qualifier to NeoOrientalist ideas of immigrant descendants as somehow inherently welcoming of migrants. Interestingly, people currently
living in Ireland are more in favour of gay marriage and reproductive
rights than the Irish diaspora, indicating that 'Irishness' as a diaspora
identity is quite conservative in important ways. Nonetheless, as
Angela Nagel points out, there is a long list of prominent Irish voices
that expressed bigoted and hate-filled views, from Constance
Markievicz to George Bernard Shaw and W. B. Yeats and Patrick
Pearse. The Irish 'right of return' is a specifically ethno-nationalist
policy that discriminates in favour of those of Irish ancestry, like its
Israeli equivalent. In fact, for some time in the twentieth century,
there was mutual admiration between Irish republicans and Zionists;
not something that Sinn Féin likes to brag about today. Yitzhak
Yezernitsky (who later became Prime Minister 'Yitzhak Shamir'), a
leader of the *Lehi* which fought against the British occupation of

Palestine, adopted the codename 'Michael' in homage to Michael Collins. As Geoffrey Wheatcroft argues, 'despite some myth-making, almost no self-styled anti-colonial movement took Irish republicanism as a model, with the exception of Revisionist Zionism'.[22]

The essentialising nature of NeoOrientalism is twofold: on the one hand, it positions entire groups of people as victims, not merely in a specific structural sense, but existentially. This leads to outbursts such as the American actor Rosanna Arquette tweeting 'I'm sorry I was born white and privileged. It disgusts me. And I feel so much shame.' Or the journalist Laurie Penny confessing, in the aftermath of Trump's victory, that while she'd 'had white liberal guilt before', it was 'the first time I've actually been truly horrified and ashamed to be white'.[23]

This allows NeoOrientalists to don the garb of sainthood through their attempts to redeem the unfortunates. At the same time, it puts entire groups on a pedestal, implying that they are not just morally better, but ultimately just better people. While this could be a positive thing, this sort of patronising essentialism contributes to racism just like the 'positive' values applied to black and brown people by the original Orientalists.

It is common to see white NeoOrientalists assert that black people cannot be racist as the victims of racism are themselves immune to suffering from racism. Gilroy has no truck with this kind of argument. 'This kind of reasoning was reduced to nonsense in the vulgar formula that suggested racism could be defined as the simple sum of prejudice and power. The proposition that only white people could be racist became confused with the different notion that black people could not be racist.' This does not stop the *Guardian* columnist Owen Jones from asserting, simply, that 'racism is prejudice plus power'.[24]

For Gilroy, to say racism can only be a consequence of power and so, as blacks have no power, as a 'race' they cannot be racist is a 'tautology' that glosses over the 'jump between individual action and societal patterning'. It is possible to interpret this and similar statements as 'a means to solicit racial identification and endorse the principle of racialized difference as a valid means to classify and divide human beings', thus creating the danger of a situation 'when a favoured group seeks or is endowed with a special or unique status because of past experiences of victimage', for they can claim that 'normal standards of judgement can be suspended as restitution or reparation for past suffering'.[25]

Similarly, the British journalist Afua Hirsch, who is of mixed Ghanaian and Jewish descent and grew up in an affluent suburb of London, draws a contrast with her husband, whose parents were both Ghanaian and who was brought up in a poor area. Writing in her book *Brit(ish)*, she notes that although she was 'profoundly shocked by the material deprivation' of her husband's childhood, she thinks that 'when it comes to identity . . . he was born with the equivalent of a silver spoon', and notes how her 'parents . . . often joked that I would rather have grown up on a council estate. [This] contained a grain of truth'.[26]

It could be that NeoOrientalism is particularly pronounced among diaspora peoples. In April 2020, in response to an article by the Dutch historian Rutger Bregman about a group of Tongan schoolboys, a young Australian writer hit out at Bregman for hijacking their story, but in the process committed classic Orientalism, albeit against her own ethnic group:

Tongans are taught to share from the beginning. You're also taught to treat everyone like family. You're taught to survive together not 'Everyman to himself'. It's hard to exist without community. So when one person is ill or hurt, it's an automatic reaction to help. To heal and to use knowledge passed down to you. This is seen in every aspect of how the boys survived. They created a community, a small family and worked together.

With a few changes, this could have come from the pen of R. M. Ballantyne or Rudyard Kipling.

This paradox is similar to the paradox of antisemitism – Jews were held to be both vermin and all-powerful – except that it is ostensibly well-meaning. Nonetheless it is both patronising and exploitative: people of colour are not plaster saints, to be loudly appreciated to add kudos to an otherwise boring whitey; nor are they pawns to be moved around on the chessboard of Western politics: they are players themselves. In the words of Gilroy, 'blacks are not after all a permanently innocent people' but rather 'modern folk who can think and act for ourselves'.[27] To fight the anti-racist battles of the twenty-first century, it is vital that we avoid conflating disadvantage with sainthood – or of privilege with villainy.

None of the essentialism described above is ill-intentioned. In fact, many of the worst culprits of NeoOrientalism are among the staunchest advocates of anti-racist movements in the West. It might seem obtuse or cynical to focus on well-meaning, inadvertent stereotyping when there are so many more serious problems to tackle: so what if the language of anti-racism promotes 'essentialism' – why is this necessarily a bad thing? I believe there are three reasons why this sort of positive stereotyping is not only crude, but actually counter-productive.

In her bestselling 2017 book, *Why I'm no Longer Talking to White People about Race*, Reni Eddo-Lodge took aim at white liberals and leftists whose idea of combatting racism was 'wallowing in guilt'. In contrast, Eddo-Lodge argued, 'white support looks like financial or administrative assistance to the groups doing vital work. Or intervening when you are needed in bystander situations . . . Don't be anti-racist for the sake of an audience. Being white and anti-racist in your private or professional life, where there's very little praise to be found, is much more difficult.'[28]

A few years ago, I was at an academic conference when, in two separate incidents, white academics – one Canadian and one

Australian – prefaced their talks when presenting a paper with a 'land declaration', acknowledging that the land that their universities were built upon was stolen from the indigenous people through a process of genocide. I thought this was interesting as, if they were to perform this ritual in a lumberjacks' bar in rural Saskatchewan or at a truck stop in Western Australia, I would have nothing but respect and admiration – certainly I would be too cowardly to do such a thing. But at an academic conference in the UK, where virtually everyone in the room fully agreed with and endorsed the message, invited something analogous to contempt.

This performative anti-racism is both a key element and an unfortunate by-product of NeoOrientalism. It is perfectly possible to be an anti-racist without being a NeoOrientalist. You can do this through recognising the specific structural disadvantages of particular ethnic minorities in specific contexts, the complex intersection of race and class (and other factors such as gender, age, sexuality, etc.), and doing whatever you can to combat this.

You do not do this through lumping all 'non-white' people together, assuming perpetual victimhood, and making narcissistic social media posts. For all these reasons, the racial essentialism of NeoOrientalism is not merely crude or mildly patronising, but counter-productive and self-serving. It actually reinforces the racial differences it seeks to undermine, at the same time as allowing white people to burnish their 'anti-racist' credentials and cultivate their social media image.

Ultimately, NeoOrientalism idealises and exoticises non-white people, with the result that it further reinforces ideas of 'racial' difference. It allows white people and privileged ethnic minorities to appropriate the suffering and disadvantage of poor black and brown people around the world. Paradoxically, it both codifies the victimhood of specific groups, and puts them on a pedestal; it is both patronising and instrumentalist. Although ostensibly well-intentioned, it is just as false and self-serving as the Orientalism Said described over forty years ago.

Back in 2013 the American comedian Chelsea Handler, reflecting on her brief relationship with the rapper 50 Cent, claimed she had 'always had a little thing for black guys. [They] are very, very masculine, and I really like that.' She told the radio DJ Howard Stern that when she broke up with 50 Cent, she 'called him the worst thing you could say to a black person short of calling him the N-word. I said something like you're like a street person basically. Something along the lines of being a gangster, and it was really, really offensive.' Asked whether she said he was 'ghetto', Handler responded: 'I said something like that. I said, "You have no business even talking to someone like me."' Here is someone who fetishises black men, and then deploys racist tropes against them when the relationship goes sour. Seven years later, after 50 Cent tweeted he would support Donald Trump in the 2020 presidential election, Handler announced that she 'had to remind him that he's black', thus demonstrating a linkage of classic Orientalism and NeoOrientalism.

The cause of anti-racism is undermined by NeoOrientalism as it undermines universalism, solidarity and comradeship, and also makes assumptions about the homogeneity and radicalism of different ethnic minorities. As Gilroy wrote in 2000, an exclusive focus on ethnic difference and 'non-white' victimhood means that the tactics produced in the struggles against slavery and racism 'have become utterly exhausted' and led to the situation whereby 'the spurious certainties that were once the exclusive stock in trade of European raciological thinking' can now be found on the supposedly anti-racist Left.[29]

NeoOrientalism does this because it focuses on the particular at the expense of the universal, undermining bonds of cohesion and reasserting 'racial' or ethnic differences and hierarchies. As Said wrote, 'such divisions are generalities whose use historically and actually has been to press the importance of the distinction between some men and some other men, usually towards not especially admirable ends'. Therefore, when 'one uses categories like Oriental and Western as both the starting and the end points of analysis, research, public policy . . . the result is usually to polarize the distinction – the Oriental becomes more Oriental, the Westerner more Western – and limit the human encounter between different cultures, traditions, and societies'.

For today's NeoOrientalists, their use of demographic and pheno-typic categories to make crude, generalised politico-cultural groups such as 'white people' and 'people of colour' serves the same ends, increasing the binary between 'white' and 'non-white', emphasising the whiteness of the former, the non-whiteness of the latter, and increasing the distance between both. Said criticised 'any view that divides the world into large general divisions, entities that coexist in a state of tension produced by what is believed to be radical differ-ence'. He argued that it was impossible to 'divide human reality . . . into clearly different cultures, histories, traditions, societies, even races, and survive the consequences humanly'.[30]

A focus on identity undermines the fight against racial inequity by reasserting difference, encouraging defensive responses by blurring the line between the structural and the personal, and papering over the significant differences within various ethnic and religious groups.

Part III

Sex

Chapter 7

Men

With sex, as with class, some forms of identity have greater potency than others. As we'll see over the next three chapters, the designations of 'woman' and 'LGBT' are highly contested, both in the sense of who is allowed to be called one and in terms of what they should stand for. Men and masculinity, as identities, occupy a much smaller space in public and media debates, and the contestation of male identity is infinitely less fraught than the contest over womanhood and femininity.

Concerns about mental health (suicide is the number one killer of men under forty), economic deprivation and political radicalism have encouraged treatises on the state of masculinity, such as Grayson Perry's *The Descent of Man*, Martin Robinson's *You Are Not the Man You Are Supposed to Be* or the comedian Robert Webb's *How Not to Be a Boy*. Therefore, there is clearly no shortage of literature on the condition of modern manhood, and what 'masculinity' does to men – but politically and culturally the identity has limited significance. Even in circles where people are quick to point out the intersection of race and class with masculinity, there is less debate around exactly who or what is a man. There is a growing literature on the interaction of 'masculinity' with race and class to produce all kind of things, from support for national populism to UK grime music. But when academics or commentators talk about, say, 'white working-class men', although they might be accused of trying to racialise class, no one says: 'Er, don't you mean white working class *cis*-men??'[1]

The two most common types of identity myths around manhood and masculinity are those who blame feminism and the retreat from 'traditional' ideals of manliness for an apparent 'crisis in masculinity', and those who proselytise the idea of a 'toxic masculinity' which is harming men, women, the planet and everything else. (One article in the *Guardian* from May 2020 was headlined: 'Men are less likely to wear masks – another sign that toxic masculinity kills'. Six months later, another column by the same author was headlined 'If women are hesitant about the vaccine, it's because the health industry hasn't earned their trust'.[2])

There is no shortage of critiques of the Jordan Petersons of the world, and there is little point in my adding to them, but it is worth appreciating that the concepts of masculinity that have been challenged in the past decade or so are themselves national-, ethnic- and class-specific, and in many cases have a very shallow provenance.

For example, there is plenty of work by historians interrogating the longevity of contemporary notions of masculinity. In the UK, research by Helen Smith on same-sex relationships among working-class men in industrial Britain has found that varying local mores affected the nature and acceptability of gay sex and culture. In metropolitan areas such as Birmingham and London, men on the gay scene would usually travel into the city from the surrounding areas, and came from a variety of different places and locations, which made it easier to transcend the cultural norms of the Brummagem working class. Consequently, argues Smith, 'they felt able to engage in camp behaviour, and display this more overtly' than men in smaller communities, such as the steel and coal towns of South Yorkshire.[3]

In these latter 'traditional, working-class communities', says Smith, understandings of what a man should do 'placed illegitimacy and affairs at the top of the list of unacceptable behaviour' and therefore getting women pregnant was more problematic 'than anything that could be hidden'. So if through having sexual relationships with other men you could avoid having (straight) sex before marriage and risking an illegitimate pregnancy, then as long as you were subtle about it, you could 'satisfy sexual urges and remain within the boundaries of the local community'. Aside from their sex lives, these men had nothing to do with 'the camp aesthetics' of men on the gay scene in metropolitan areas, and the masculinity of these men, and even 'in most cases, sexual identity' was not in question. At the same time, in areas where illegitimate children 'were accepted as part of the community, same-sex relationships may have been more of an issue of concern'.[4]

If the masculine identities and sexual mores of the recent past are much more complicated than we might assume, the same can be said about modern relationships and gender relations. In many cases, something which could be viewed as an example of 'toxic masculinity' could easily be seen as a heartwarming example of modern love, depending on the perspective.

In 2017, Sindy Chikadaya and Vanel Abramsamadu found fame on the internet after Vanel used social media to track down Sindy, after briefly meeting her in a bar and taking a selfie with her. 'Yo Twitter,' he wrote, 'This year i was out in Shoreditch one night. Took a random selfie with this female, we got a vibe for like 5 mins but she took off and got on the bus before i could even get her name. I beg you Guys RT so i can find her plz'. The internet duly responded, and within a couple of days he had tracked her down. By the time the BBC covered this story in 2020, they were a couple raising two young children, and it was reported as a heart-warming, inspirational story. But this could just as easily be interpreted as an entitled man obsessing over and stalking a woman who once showed a brief interest in him; it could even be construed as indicative of the type of attitude that leads men to commit violence against women.

A few years ago, a New Zealand gannet – apparently named Nigel – was found dead next to a concrete sculpture of a female gannet.

According to the local press, Nigel had been trying to mate with the sculpture for several years, having been disowned by the broader gannet community. As with the Abramsamadus' case, the story quickly went viral. However, not everyone on the internet sympathised with Nigel. One US journalist said the whole story was 'an example of rape culture', as 'the concrete bird did not owe Nigel her affection . . . Maybe Nigel was ostracized from the other gannets for REASONS. You don't know. Maybe he was the pedophile in the last bird community he was in.' She concluded that while 'this might be harsh since Nigel is now dead', nonetheless 'even concrete birds do not owe you affection, Nigel. Stop wooing a bird who is not interested.' There are two prisms through which to read these interactions: one is through the lens of patriarchy and male domination over females; the other is through human interactions and sexuality.

So too when it comes to so-called 'pick-up artists'. Sympathy is in short supply for men who at best can be described as oleaginous leches, and at worst as violent misogynists. But what about the men who are neither? What about those who have real difficulty meeting and talking to women?

For many of the so-called 'incel' (involuntary celibate) community, their problem is not so much that women won't sleep with them; it's that the type of women they feel entitled to won't sleep with them. For some men, it is probably the case that, as Jia Tolentino argues, 'they suddenly found themselves unable to obtain sex by default' as 'the sexual marketplace began to equalize'.[5] But this is clearly not the case for all men, not least because many men have always found it difficult to obtain sex 'by default', even in highly patriarchal cultures where arranged marriages are common. Fans of the Israeli comedy *Shtisel* will appreciate that even among ultra-Orthodox Jews – by no means a feminist culture, and where couples are put together by a match-maker – men considered to be low-status according to the values of the community find it hard to marry, and may even have to settle for a woman who converted from secular Judaism. As argued by the blogger Scott Alexander, himself unfairly traduced as an incel sympathiser, many 'nerdy people *really are* bad at talking to the opposite sex. They're not making it up. They really are disadvantaged.' And nor are these issues ultimately immaterial: writing of the criticisms levelled at Alexander, Tom Chivers notes that 'love, sex, intimacy and affection' are all important things in human lives, and their absence can have devastating consequences.[6]

There are, of course, many women who find themselves similarly dispossessed (and this intersects with race; in the US, marriage rates for black women are notably lower than for women of other races – and for those of black men), and yet they do not resort to the kind of hatred and brutality characteristic of the incel community. My point here is not to defend men who use their lack of success in sexual and romantic relationships as an excuse for misogyny or violence, but rather to emphasise that such men are a small minority of the sexually disenfranchised. The majority of loveless men are no more responsible for 'toxic masculinity' than homeless people are for the ills of capitalism. At the same time, it is very difficult to argue that strength, physical prowess, and pursuit of wealth and status are examples of this kind of toxic masculinity. None of these things is limited to men, nor to a particular kind of masculinity, nor are these things necessarily toxic. Instead, they reflect a complex interaction of power, prestige and class.

It may be that the strictures of masculinity may make this situation one of the rare areas where men have it worse than women: to be sure, dating for women is mostly terrible, with women at risk of sexual assault or violence at worst, and at best of being deemed as too desperate, needy, crazy, fat, ugly, smart or dumb. Yet single women with difficulties finding partners or having sex at least often have the comradeship of other women, and feel able to express it on social media, where they will usually be met with sympathy; this comradeship and sympathy are less forthcoming for men. And while even unfortunate-looking, socially inept men have advantages that women don't have, or more pertinently don't suffer from disadvantages that these women might, a key theme of this book is that the absence of disadvantage is not experienced as privilege; it is difficult for a forty-year-old male virgin to derive comfort from thinking, *Oh well, at least I'm not being raped or paid less.*

For many men, it is not their sense of entitlement holding them back, but rather their appearance, social skills, economic position or some combination of the above. These men are not driven by hate, but rather by fear, sadness and loneliness. Back in 2005, long before anyone had heard of incels, the journalist Hugo Rifkind went along to a 'pick-up artist' training session, and described his fellow participants as 'not even Ed Miliband-style geeks [but] the real ones . . . who saw futures stretching ahead of them full of takeaways, computer games and not having a girlfriend. Men already into their late twenties, perhaps, who had almost given up on losing their virginities before they lost their hair.' 'We don't hear much about young male loneliness, despair and self-disgust', except as the butt of jokes, added Rifkind, 'yet it's real, and devastating'.[7] In fact, the evolutionary psychologist Diana Fleischman hypothesises that as robots become ever more human-like over the next few years and decades, many men will give up on trying to form relationships with real women, and turn to sex robots, for which they will presumably be further shamed and castigated.[8]

Away from the area of sexual relationships, it seems that masculinity, toxic or otherwise, does not manifest itself in the political choices of men. For example, in the 2020 Democratic primary, female candidates such as Kamala Harris and Elizabeth Warren drew more support from men than they did women. In fact, in her home state of Massachusetts Warren came third among registered female Democrats, behind both Joe Biden and Bernie Sanders. On the day that I am writing this in 2021, a poll has just been released on the opinions of New York state voters on the current governor Andrew Cuomo, who has been accused of sexual harassment by several women. According to the Siena College poll, women voters were 5 points more likely than men to say that Cuomo shouldn't resign from his post (52 per cent compared to 47 per cent), and were also 5 points more likely to call his apology satisfactory (59 per cent versus 54 per cent). Even though this may owe something to partisanship – men are more likely to vote Republican, and therefore more likely to oppose Cuomo, a Democrat – it shows the complexities of how gender interacts with politics and even views on sexual harassment.

Today, the areas of the UK where men are most likely to kill themselves correspond almost exactly with the former industrial areas, suggesting that male depression and 'crises of masculinity' correspond with economic deprivation and hopelessness in important ways. In Jon Lawrence's book *Me, Me, Me*, he includes photographs of the former shipbuilding town of Wallsend in Tyne & Wear in the 1970s, and at the sight of the huge hulls of the container ships alongside the terraced houses, it struck me as profoundly incongruous that such vast emblems of technological modernity were made in the now firmly post-industrial areas of the UK. To adapt Zhang Enlai on the consequences of the French Revolution, it is far too soon to tell what effect this move from world-leading industry to the provision of fake-tanned, veneer-toothed meatheads for reality television and social media will have on the men of these areas, but it would be foolish to assume that this huge transformation within two generations has not had an important impact already. A gym owner in Sunderland told Grayson Perry how the appearances of his young lads were maintained with a great deal of effort, expense and attention to detail, 'like a miner's wife obsessively scrubbing the front step', and for the same reason.

Similarly, as Wesley Yang reminds us, hardcore pornography was ostensibly illegal across much of the US as recently as the early 1990s, difficult to access for most boys, and decidedly one-dimensional. It is far too early to tell what effect this has had and is having on masculinity, and yet talk about porn is often framed as moralising prudery.[9]

Having some kind of 'identity' is pretty crucial to the modern world. Denied the identity that used to be provided by a steady job, it is no surprise that some men fall back on masculinity when it is all that they have – especially if they do not have another kind of identity, such as black or gay or even 'working class', given the decline in the political and cultural clout of that identity in recent decades. At the same time, many men have been raised from a young age to think and act as though this identity is somehow powerful and important, and that they have an obligation to think and act in a certain way. In *The Descent of Man*, Perry writes that 'the current state of masculinity is biased in favour of white middle-class men with nice jobs and nice families', but of course many of those suffer too from desperate aspiration to unrealistic ideals.[10] Identity myths around masculinity are not only harmful to women, or 'non-masculine' men, but to all men. As Perry also notes, although men 'might plead that their muscles, big cars and sharp suits are for attracting women, really they are for impressing male rivals. The only validation a man craves for his masculinity is from those who really understand his achievement: other men.'[11] So even those who are most successfully realising various elements of idealised masculinity – professionally, physically, sexually, etc. – are themselves wracked with insecurity.

My point here is not to argue that 'men can't do right for doing wrong' – while many men are having a tough time right now, so are many women, young people in general, older people without savings or property, people who haven't had steady work in decades, parents with disabled children, etc., etc. My point is that many of the problems of men today stem from economic insecurity and the desperate scramble to earn and acquire, rather than from any form of identity.

Chapter 8

Women

If the contestation of male identity has relatively little political or cultural significance, the same cannot be said of femininity and feminism. There are fierce debates around exactly who is or what constitutes a 'woman', what women believe, and exactly what a feminist looks like.

Of all the groups implicitly considered part of the rainbow coalition of left-liberal demographics, the presence of 'women' is the most bizarre. In terms of socio-economic views, since women bear most of the care responsibilities (paid and unpaid) worldwide, have less well-paid jobs and less secure and more part-time employment, they are often more supportive of robust welfare provision and other left-wing economic imperatives. But there is no reason to think that half of the human species should have an affinity with particular disadvantaged minority groups, much less to assume that they are more sympathetic to 'identity politics' than the other half.

There is often widespread surprise in the UK when prominent women – Mary Berry, Adele, Kate Bush, even Melania Trump – make statements that are considered inconsistent with left-liberal values. Perhaps the most extreme example of this came in a speech in the House of Commons by former actor and then-Labour MP Glenda Jackson in response to the death of Margaret Thatcher. Jackson finished her speech by stating that Thatcher was 'the first Prime Minister denoted by female gender ... but a woman? Not on my terms', thereby implying that Thatcher's politics precluded her from being considered a 'real' woman.

It is true that in many democracies there is now a 'gender gap', with men tending to favour conservative parties and women parties of the Left, but this is often contingent and, in many cases, a recent development. In fact, it has been estimated that if women were barred from voting in UK elections, the Labour Party would have won every contest from 1945 to 1979, such was the preference of women for the Conservatives. In her history of female conservatives, Beatrix Campbell argued that dominance of Thatcher, Ronald Reagan and the 'New Conservatism' of the 1980s were only made possible by the discomfort of millions of women with the social and cultural liberalisations of the 1960s and 1970s.[1] Today, it has been argued by academics at the London School of Economics that the most significant factor for women supporting Trump was not a belief that they would benefit materially, but rather that they shared his prejudices.

The historical conservatism of most British women for much of the twentieth century may be surprising, but for much of that time the Left had a very poor record on women's rights. During the First World War, for example, the trade unions resisted the introduction of women into male-dominated workplaces, and struck a deal with the government to eject these women as soon as the guns fell silent. As with trade union agitation against immigrants, this was not just about job security or the undercutting of wages: the historian Gail Braybon claims that 'women were not simply resented because they were unskilled or semi-skilled workers, but because they were *women*, a class apart, who were encroaching upon men's work'. Women in the workplace were still resented even if they were unionised, on equal pay, and with a guarantee that returning soldiers would have their old jobs back. Furthermore, most of the labour movement, despite being 'a relatively radical group of people, concerned with workers' oppression and women's legal and political rights, nevertheless accepted the inevitability of women's domestic role, and did not take the matter of their employment very seriously'.[2]

At the start of the twentieth century, William Beveridge – who would go on to chair the committee that drafted the post-1945 welfare state – wrote that 'the ideal unit is the household of man, wife and children maintained by the earnings of the first alone'. Beveridge considered 'married women' or 'housewives' – the terms were used interchangeably in his report – as a particular class of 'worker', and suggested they should receive a cash sum on marriage to furnish the home, and he also insisted that men's welfare payments should include enough to support a wife. Nonetheless he argued that women should opt out of his proposed national insurance system if they took up paid work, as it was 'in the national interest' that women not be wage-earners, for 'housewives as mothers have vital work to do in ensuring the adequate continuance of the British race'.[3]

Interestingly, in the inter-war era, it was local Labour parties in coalfield seats, with the fewest women members, who pursued the most progressive policies on feminist issues such as reproductive rights. The UK's first-ever birth-control clinic was set up in 1925 in the Welsh town of Abertillery after pressure from the local miners' agent.[4] Yet this concern for maternal welfare – often linked to concerns over the health of the British 'race' – did not translate into a view of women as fundamentally equal to men. In 1950 even Michael Foot, who was one of the more advanced Labour men in terms of women's rights, defended the exclusion of equal pay proposals from Labour's manifesto on the grounds that it would cost too much.[5]

Today, aside from mainstream conservatism, there are a number of prominent women involved with the national populist movements that have emerged over the past decade. In total, more than half a dozen right-wing populist parties in Europe are led by women, from Alice Weidel of the *Alternative für Deutschland* (AfD) to Giorgia Meloni of the Brothers of Italy. Ebba Hermansson, who at twenty-two became the youngest MP in the Swedish parliament, is also the gender equality spokeswoman for the anti-immigrant Sweden Democrats. In Italy in particular, the far-Right has had notable success in winning over women who previously voted for parties of the Left.

Furthermore, the resurgence in far-Right and ethnonationalist politics across Europe owes a debt not merely to female activists, but also to a warped and cynical use of 'feminism': the AfD's Nicole Höchst, for example, claims her party are 'the only party in Germany who is really fighting for women's rights'. Nor do these women usually support traditional gender roles à la Phyllis Schlafly or Margaret Thatcher: Höchst is a single mother of four, France's Marine Le Pen is twice divorced, and Alice Weidel is a lesbian, raising two children with her female partner.[6]

The political scientist Caroline Marie Lancaster divides far-Right voters into three broad camps: 'conservative nativists', who have demographics more typical of such voters (think aging white men with beer bellies); 'moderate nativists', whose politics are closer to mainstream right-wing parties; and 'sexually modern nativists', who are younger, often well-educated, more likely to be women, and supportive of feminist and pro-LGBT positions. Back in 2004, the vast majority of the far-Right was either moderate or conservative and only 12 per cent were sexually modern. By 2016, however, fully 45 per cent – almost half – could be categorised as such.[7] (This makes sense, as women generally, whatever their political views, tend to be more supportive of gay rights. In the US, for example, 73 per cent of white women support legislation against anti-LGBT discrimination, up from 64 per cent of white men, and seven in ten black women compared to six in ten black men.[8]) Yet being a woman – and, as we shall see in the next chapter, being gay – is by no means inimical to anti-migrant or far-Right politics.

The identity myth that assumes women are left-wing or necessarily more supportive of minorities is confounded by the varied politics of women themselves. So too with feminism: it is not just that few women claim to be feminists, but also that many women who do call themselves feminists bitterly contest what feminism means. This is not just a continuation of disputes between different 'waves', or even between liberal, socialist or radical feminists, but a more fundamental contestation.

The vitriolic sexist abuse faced by female politicians emanates not merely from bitter and angry men, but from fellow women. As Caroline Criado Perez argues, both men and women view female politicians with contempt, anger and disgust.[9] Glenda Jackson, despite saying Margaret Thatcher was unworthy of the appellation 'woman', nonetheless confirms that 'all women experience sexism in parliament. All the time. Regardless of your political affiliations.'[10]

At the same time, it is expected that women in public life will either be feminists or at least have something to say about feminism, a standard that is never applied to men. As the author L. S. Hilton notes, 'no one asks Lee Child whether Jack Reacher is a profound meditation on masculinity', and that the actions of female authors are 'policed and politicised. As women not every single thing we do needs to be empowering, it can not be too.'[11]

While feminist messages have become more diffused among younger women, some would argue that this popularity, or the embrace of these issues by a broader audience, dilutes their significance. It doesn't make the issue itself less important, but it risks becoming a soothing platitude, more about a statement and less about taking actions to improve women's equality. Something which starts out focusing on the most oppressed ends up as a cultural trend, open to anyone, and devoid of meaning. For example, the singer Lizzo criticises the notion of 'body positivity' for becoming too commercialised and 'cool', with the people the term was coined for no longer benefitting from it: 'Girls with back fat, girls with bellies that hang, girls with thighs that aren't separated, that overlap . . . Girls with stretch marks. You know, girls who are in the 18-plus club.' She argues that the mainstreaming of body positivity should have benefitted these women by recasting beauty standards, but instead, as 'with everything that goes mainstream', it is the scope of body positivity that has changed.[12]

While the identity myths would enlist all the world's women into the fight against the 'Roll Call' of -isms and -phobias, the fight against sexist discrimination and male violence against women is itself being undermined by the strange notion that being a woman is somehow a privileged position. Or at least, if you are 'only' a woman, rather than, say, a poor woman, a black woman, a gay woman or a trans woman. Clearly, if you are in one or more of the latter categories, you might well be in a worse position than if you are 'only' a woman. It is not as though sexism against white, middle-class heterosexual women has been abolished. Nonetheless, there is a trend in contemporary feminism that acts as though this is the case, and many long-time feminist activists are understandably furious, as a rigid obsession with a 'hierarchy' of victimhood, although apparently concerned with intersectionality or inserting more diverse voices into feminist discourses, can end up allowing people to hate women as long as they're white. This is worse for left-wing women, as conservative women can at least take comfort in their politics, but left-wing white women have to believe, or genuinely do, that they are privileged, and guilty, and they should apologise, even as their livelihoods and mental health collapse. What's worse, if they complain about this, or even think about complaining, they feel guilty as well.

The idea that women are privileged unless they are 'women plus-something' (gay, black, trans, etc.) finds its purest expression in the 'Karen' meme. As explained by Helen Lewis in the *Atlantic*, Karens are 'the policewomen of all human behavior. Karens have short hair. Karens are selfish. Confusingly, Karens are both the kind of petty enforcers who patrol other people's failures at social distancing, and the kind of entitled women who refuse to wear a mask because it's a "muzzle".[13] Like much of the more faux and ill-thought-out examples of intersectionality discussed in this book, the Karen meme has noble origins, as a satire by black Americans against their officious and patronising treatment by jobsworth white women – and it was of necessity about women, for similar interactions with white men, without or without a badge, tended to go down a different route. Unfortunately, 'Karen' has become yet another example of the NeoOrientalist fetishisation of African-American culture detached from its original context. When utilised by white people, devoid of its original emancipatory intent, it is merely sexist.

According to Robin Abcarian of the *Los Angeles Times*, 'Because Karen is white, she faces few meaningful repercussions. Embarrassing videos posted on social media is usually as bad as it gets for Karen.'[14] Yet if you think that 'video shaming' is the worst thing that happens to white women, you are clearly living in some future utopia, not the early twenty-first century. As Catherine MacKinnon wrote thirty years ago of this kind of 'white woman': 'This creature is not poor, not battered, not raped (not really), not molested as a child, not pregnant as a teenager, not prostituted, not coerced into pornography, not a welfare mother, and not economically exploited.'[15] Aside from the very obvious fact that even the most privileged women still face specific issues related to being women, the assumption that white and middle-class women are inherently privileged and shouldn't complain can take a toll on their mental health. In Anne Helen Petersen's book *Can't Even*, she quotes Meredith, 'a self-described "over-educated white lady"' who says that she feels bad 'for feeling burnout over #richwhiteladyproblems because they are so trivial compared to other people's problems.'[16] Some women are so fearful of being called a Karen that they are willing to put their lives at risk: one woman wrote into the *Atlantic*'s 'Ask Dr Hamblin' column, which offers advice on healthcare and medical issues, to say that she was a sixty-five-year-old with non-Hodgkin's lymphoma and rheumatoid arthritis, who nonetheless said she was fearful to ask the young lady in her pharmacy to wear a mask as she did not want 'to be considered a Karen'.[17]

Despite the victories of feminism, there still are – it barely needs saying – numerous inequities and injustices visited upon women, and this includes white women. Women are nearly always paid less than men, even for the same work. This is true across many industries and even across ethnic groups. For example, the black actor Mo'Nique complained that she earned much less from Netflix for her special than the white comedian Amy Schumer, but both Mo'Nique and Schumer earned less than the (black) comedians Chris Rock and Dave Chappelle.[18]

Aside from the paydays of female celebrities, the threat of rape, kidnap and murder is as real for white and middle-class women as it is for poor women of colour. In fact, the susceptibility of women to violence is a key reason why even the most radical socialist and feminist women are sceptical of calls to abolish the police. Rahila Gupta, of the black British feminist group Southall Black Sisters, warns that while a community-based system of public safety sounds attractive, this might further imperil women if the particular community is 'riddled' with 'conservative, patriarchal and religious values'. She knows whereof she speaks, for her organisation serves as a last resort for women whose plight has not been remedied by their family, community or elders, but often worsened.[19]

In the coverage of male violence against women – which in white-majority societies is overwhelmingly perpetrated by white men – sometimes race can take precedence over gender. In the American city of Kenosha in the summer of 2020, a man named Jacob Blake was shot in the back seven times by a police officer, giving fresh impetus to Black Lives Matter protests in the United States and elsewhere. The first thing to say is that irrespective of the crimes allegedly committed by Blake, nothing warrants being shot seven times in the back. As an opponent of capital punishment, I don't believe that the state should kill criminals even if they have been convicted of the most heinous crimes, much less for attempting to enter a car where their children are sitting.

Nonetheless, the police in the Blake incident were responding to a report by his former partner that he had been harassing her for almost ten years, had broken into her home, forced his fingers inside her, and then stolen her car keys and attempted to take their children – something more or less absent from the coverage of the incident, which focused only on the police violence against Blake, rather than his own attacks on his former partner.

As the feminist campaigner Louise Perry notes, there have historically been horrendous abuses perpetrated against African Americans by doctors, yet no one talks of defunding medicine.[20] It is easy to be against police violence because so few of us, especially outside America, are complicit in it. It is much harder to take a stand against male violence and hatred of women. Furthermore, given that most murderers and rapists are white men, defunding the police will disproportionately benefit white male criminals. (There is also a huge contradiction between abolitionists and their support for trans rights, given the risk that transwomen of colour face from male violence.)

In Australia in 2020, a teenage girl with learning difficulties, Kimberly, was sexually assaulted at school several times by two of her classmates. One of the students, who was later convicted of over twenty sexual assault charges involving four children, including Kimberly, was expelled from the school. However, while the other perpetrator was suspended for thirty days, he later returned to the school, and saw Kimberly on a daily basis. When she complained, teachers told her to 'stop dwelling', 'move on' and 'get over it'. Eventually, as a way of settling the matter, the school arranged a 'forgiveness ritual'.[21] These 'forgiveness rituals' are the kind of thing proffered by a small but growing section of people who presumably think they are standing up for women's rights.

Increasingly, the idea of 'feminism' is developing as an identity in and of itself, detached from feminist theory or practice. This is sometimes made explicit, as when a female freelance journalist wrote on Twitter that in order to 'help the lads in my mentions', they should 'check this lad out for people who think that institutions like the police have nothing to do with upholding capitalist structures'; the journalist posted this alongside a photo of a book by Louis Althusser, apparently oblivious that Althusser murdered his wife.

Identity struggles over the definition of feminism are defined by a paradox: while the concept and appellation of feminism are increasingly adopted by celebrities, politicians of all stripes, corporations and so on, very few women are prepared to say that they are 'feminists'. A poll for Hope Not Hate found that one in four women agreed that 'feminism is to blame for making some men feel marginalised and demonised in society'. Two-thirds of all people told a Sky News poll that feminism had either gone too far or as far as it should. Some of the most successful and prominent women across a range of fields decline to describe themselves as feminists. The British athlete Ama Agbeze tells Helen Lewis that she refuses to say she is a feminist as 'she shies away from labels', although she wants 'everything to be equal and everything should be fair and everyone should have an equal opportunity'.[22]

And yet, senior Conservative politicians such as Theresa May, Amber Rudd and Nadine Dorries all proudly aver that they are feminists, and that their possession of values traditionally associated with the political Right – in terms of markets, limited taxation and a reduced state – does not impede their feminism. Conservative women in the last two decades have projected an abstract version of feminism that helped them construct their own identity; both through distancing themselves from it during Thatcher's era, and co-opting it in the time of David Cameron and Theresa May. Thatcher herself said she 'owe[d] nothing to women's lib', and made it clear she was 'not a feminist'.[23] According to her former aide Paul Johnson, she claimed to 'hate feminism', which she described as 'poison'.[24] Before she became prime minister, Thatcher even left the women's section of the Conservative Party as she did not find it 'to her taste'.[25]

While several elements of modern Conservative thought are compatible with elements of 'feminism', the adoption of feminist language by women of the Right generally owes more to expediency than conviction.[26] The hypocrisy of this has been pointed out by academics such as Angela McRobbie and Catherine Rottenberg, the latter of whom has written on the growth of 'neoliberal feminism', as personified by high-flying business executives Ann-Marie Slaughter and Sheryl Sandberg. It is also nicely encapsulated by supposed feminist heroines such as Beyoncé and Katy Perry. Perry collected $25 million for her role as a judge on *American Idol*, making her one of the highest-paid judges on the show, behind high-waistband enthusiast Simon Cowell, who reportedly made $45 million. Not that Perry felt upset: she told a US radio station that she is 'really proud that as a woman, I got paid. I got paid more than any guy that's ever been on the show.'

Sex work is one of the most highly contentious issues among contemporary feminists. As with the division over transgender women, male misogynists are the main beneficiary of this intra-feminist infighting. Women (and self-professed male feminists) accusing those who should be their natural allies of being 'whorephobic' is ludicrous, and the passionate defence of sex work by feminists only serves to benefit men who pay women for sex. Of course, just because something pleases these men doesn't mean it is wrong. The political scientist Cas Mudde describes the so-called 'Nordic Model', which would criminalise men who pay for sex, as 'a return to the darkest periods of left-wing paternalism, in which self-professed progressives fight for middle class utopias at the expense of the socially weak'. Mudde claims that the key sticking point for progressives in opposing the selling of sex, rather than any other product, is 'that sexuality is something "personal," which is intrinsically linked to (strong) emotions' and that 'it is the selling woman who is harmed, not the buying man, reflecting a long-standing gendered notion of sexuality, in which female sexuality is inherently problematized'.[27]

While it is an important issue based on meaningful disagreements within the practice and theory of feminism, divides over sex work can often take on an identitarian dimension that apparently has little to do with helping women. The stridency of divisions on this issue is particularly ill-warranted given the divisions among sex workers themselves. Writing on Twitter, one woman highlights the 'whorephobia within sex work', from people who earned money from 'webcam work' or stripping towards 'full service sex work[ers]' or escorts: 'the amount of lateral and whorephobia within the adult industry is grim, it's not ok for you to shit on full service sex workers including street sex workers just to make yourself feel better . . . you aren't on a moral high ground [because] you don't fuck your clients'.

The intra-feminist dispute over sex work shows how dangerous divisions can emerge from the abstracting of feminism to an ideology which can be claimed by all. Since being a feminist is a crucial shibboleth for being on the modern Left, these issues, rather than being debated in good faith with the seriousness they deserve, can often serve as ciphers for ideological battles within feminism. That so many self-professed left-wing men believe that they can call women 'SWERF [sex worker-exclusionary radical feminist] bitches' and the like simply because they disagree over how the state treats sex work, while still claiming to be feminists, makes this all too clear.

The emergence of 'feminism' as an identity distinct from ideology and practice means that it can be claimed by all kinds of unlikely figures to defend all manner of activities. Kim Kardashian is frequently framed as 'some sort of deliciously twisted empowerment icon', but as Jia Tolentino argues, 'for some women, it is difficult and indeed dangerous to live as themselves in the world, but for other women, like Kim and her sisters, it's not just easy but extraordinarily profitable', and that to claim any criticism of women's appearance as misogynistic is a mirror image of the misogynistic argument that 'a woman's appearance is of paramount value'.[28] There is an assumption in this kind of feminist celebrity analysis that 'the freedom we grant famous women will trickle down to us', and that criticism of women in the public view is always anti-feminist.

Tolentino writes of how when a 'woman is criticized for something related to her being a woman; her continued existence is interpreted as politically meaningful'. This is so ridiculously loose that 'almost anything can fit' it. (And, of course, the same can be said of gay people, black people and so on.) She criticises the pop-feminist reflex of honouring women for 'achieving visibility and power, no matter how they did so'. For example, former CIA operative Gina Haspel oversaw torture at black sites in Thailand and then subsequently destroyed the evidence. When she was later appointed by Donald Trump to head the CIA in 2018, conservatives claimed that anyone who criticised Haspel's appointment and claimed to be a feminist was a hypocrite. Tolentino gives this as just one example of the 'feminist cultural reflex to protect women from criticism in any way'. Similarly, she adds, the key Trump lieutenants Kellyanne Conway and Hope Hicks knew that they would be defended in 'feminist' terms, whatever they did, because they are women. Again, the same applies to black conservatives, gays and so on, who have a kind of 'identity armour' that makes criticism of them seem illegitimate.[29]

A focus on the 'identity' of being a woman invites conflict – are transwomen 'real' women? Can women be conservative? What is and isn't 'feminist'? – and is ultimately counter-productive. To help women, in developed and underdeveloped economies, a focus on certain policies – better public transport, better streetlighting, better treatment of unpaid carers, a stronger welfare state, better-funded sex education lessons – would be much more productive than worrying about identity.

Chapter 9

LGBT

From the perspective of the early 2020s, it is easy to forget just how recently profound homophobia was common sense for most people. There are plenty of statistics around opposition to same-sex relationships in the UK in the late 1980s, but perhaps the most depressing is that a 1987 public health survey found that 60 per cent of men and 49 per cent of women felt those suffering from AIDS deserved 'no sympathy at all'.

These bigotries were widespread across the population, irrespective of class, but as with racism, they had a special performative role in working-class masculinity. The 2014 film *Pride* tells the inspiring story of Gays and Lesbians Support the Miners, but it downplays the reality of homophobia in such communities. A 1991 social attitudes survey conducted by Health Promotion Wales – a few years after the events depicted in *Pride* – found that over 70 per cent of men and 60 per cent of women felt homosexual relations were wrong, a higher number than the British average.[1] Historians such as Matt Houlbrook and Helen Smith have uncovered same-sex relationships in 'traditional' working-class communities, but the existence of these did not translate into broader acceptance of homosexuality.[2]

Not so long ago, Pride marches were denied permits or confronted by thugs or the police, and while this risk remains in some countries – in 2019 a LGBT rights march in Białystok, Poland, was viciously attacked – the main complaint about Pride marches today is their over-commercialisation and the cynical appropriation of LGBT rights by pink-washing companies or governments (in 2015, the CIA even set up a recruiting office at the Miami Beach Pride). Given the sea-change from the virulent homophobia of the 1980s to a world of same-sex marriage, legislation against homophobic discrimination, and gay people in prominent positions in virtually every walk of life (in some countries at least), it is unsurprising that there has been a growth in LGBT people with lifestyles or politics or relationships that might once have been considered 'heteronormative'.

Writing of the 2018 French film *120 Beats Per Minute*, Caspar Salmon argues that 'the new gay theme is one of acceptance of homo-sexual people by their straight families . . . we are seeing a more emol-lient culture, one aimed at happy and accepted gay people who are sick of anguished depictions of suffering victims. But we need to rekindle some of our abrasiveness'. Salmon concludes the article with a call for a 'queerness [that is] open and generous – turning outwards rather than in on itself, to other marginalised communities, in empathy, solidarity and riotous communion'. The problem with this view is that while there are plenty of LGBT people who agree with Salmon politically, there are loads of gay people who don't want to be abrasive and instead want boring, conventional lifestyles and politics, and 'heteronormative' relationships and families. Furthermore, what about LGBT Tories, and all the gay people who have no idea what a 'riotous communion' might involve but suspect very much that it's not for them? Are they somehow less gay? This insinuation that being LGBT should involve a measure of political radicalism implies that sexuality is less fact of birth and more a form of identity.[3]

Pursuant to this, one of the main problems with the designation 'queer' is that it can be claimed by anyone. As with the ever-increasing additional letters affixed to what currently stands at LGBTQIA+, it allows straight people to claim a sort of shared identity with gay people.

For example, 'asexuals' or even 'kink-y' people need not be gay, and exactly what kind of oppression or discrimination is suffered by asexual people? As the lesbian journalist Sophie Wilkinson notes, 'I don't think anyone walks down the street and gets "Oh, you fucking asexual." '[4] In fact, the penalty for claiming that someone is not a member of a group (e.g. asexuals and LGBTs) may be greater than those pretending to be a member of that group, as it is impossible to 'prove' whether someone is asexual, or nonbinary, or whether their kinkiness is just a mere sexual fetish or is quantitatively or qualitatively substantial enough to be a protected characteristic. Therefore, for the Rachel Dolezals of the LGBT world there is no risk of exposure, as there is no need for fake tan and a perm: your word alone is good enough.

The slur that someone is merely 'seeking attention' needs to be used only carefully, but with some celebrities and prominent couples it is difficult to believe the sincerity of their 'queer' claims. For example, the actor Nico Tortorella has been in what looks like a heterosexual relationship with the 'lifestyle entrepreneur and LGBTQ activist' Bethany Meyers for the past fourteen years, and they married in a ceremony in 2018. Yet Tortorella identifies as non-binary and Meyers identifies as a lesbian. Therefore, despite having an apparently heterosexual relationship and heteronormative marriage, they are referred to as a 'queer couple'.

There is now a special Pride flag for people into 'Pup Play', which I believe is where people roleplay as dogs. Should these kinds of sexual preferences be understood as victimised identities? The historic and continuing discriminations faced by gay people were not extended to straight people who roleplayed as dogs, or to straight people into 'kinky' sex, so why should people who are interested in such things claim such an inheritance? We do not regard goths as a persecuted and protected identity, even though people have been killed for being goths. I am pretty sure that no one has ever been killed for dressing up as a dog.

* * *

I remember the first gay Tory I met. Well, at least the first *openly* gay Tory I met – there may have been others who were closet Conservatives. I was in the Angel pub in Bermondsey, south London, with a gay friend of mine, then a hard-drinking researcher for the Labour Party, now a teetotal Labour MP. We got into conversation with a couple of men in the bar, and were discussing politics when one announced that he was gay, and a Tory. My friend was shocked. 'You can't be gay and a Tory', he argued, probably mentioning Section 28 or similar. In the years since, gay conservatives have become more prominent, in the media and in politics, but there remains a persistent feeling among some on the Left that there is a contradiction in there somewhere.

Graeme Archer, a former Conservative speech writer, wrote a blistering article on this subject in the aftermath of the 2019 general election. Attacking Labour, he described his apolitical husband Keith, 'a working-class Plymothian, an electrician, but with a capable brain and a heart every bit as large' as the higher ups in the Labour Party. Graeme is an example of the types of figures usually absent from political and media discourse, and not just because they are gay Tories, but rather because of the type of gays (square and heteronormative rather than chem-sex-sauna habitués) and the type of Tories (staid Scrutonian types rather than freewheeling libertarians).

While the past few years have seen an increasing focus on working-class Tories, there is still little space given to conservative, 'heteronormative' gays, much less to working-class, heteronormative gays who are also conservatives. But they are out there, in their thousands, and may well grow in number in the coming years as a consequence of the increase in gay marriage and parenthood, both of which tend to make people more conservative. (Although the extent to which this is causation rather than correlation is debated; it might just be that more conservative people are more likely to get married.) Furthermore, it is a bad idea for sections of the Left to give the impression that gay people 'should' vote Labour, or worse that there is a certain kind of way that gay people 'should' act, things they should believe, etc. As Archer writes to the Labour Party, 'men and women like Keith' notice when Labour claims 'that only socialists like you *care* about people' and 'he understands that you think he's either ignorant, or wicked, for not being Labour'.[5]

Across the Atlantic, a *New York Times* article ahead of the 2020 presidential election profiled Chris, a fifty-year-old lesbian in Manhattan, who despite being a registered Democrat and former Bernie Sanders supporter, ended up voting for Donald Trump in 2016. She didn't want the newspaper to use her last name because of the hostility that would arise among her co-workers – she is a store manager – if they knew she were a Trump supporter. Her main reason for planning to vote Republican at the 2020 election was the economy and her own personal finances, but when pressed by the journalist Bret Stephens, she opined various conservative bromides on everything from national security to welfare policy.

When asked what she thought about Trump's infamous 'grab them by the pussy' comments, Chris confided that they 'didn't bother [her] at all. For every cad out there, there's equally a gold digger who will let you do it'.[6] I thought this was an interesting comment, as it reflects a broader generational and political divide between women who see sexual harassment as par for the course for a woman in the workplace, and those who refuse to tolerate it. It brought home to me the obvious fact that lesbians are not a particular kind of people – they are just as likely to be conservative lower-middle-class women like Chris as anyone else. It also contains a warning for the Left about the limits – should they still need to be warned about this – of the appeal of a politics based on a criticism of systemic inequality. People like me might respond to Chris's comments about 'gold diggers' by asking her why some women needed men for financial support, or why there were so many men who were able to trade wealth for affection, but so many people – lesbians living in Manhattan as much as anyone else

– simply don't believe in or care about the significance of structural disadvantage to our economy and society.

It is not surprising that, given the 'rehabilitation' of homosexuality on the Right and the potential of LGBT rights to harness anti-immigrant politics, there are now many gays and lesbians in prominent positions in conservative and far-Right parties. In Israel, the minister of public security, Amir Ohana, is a rising star of the Likud party and their first openly gay member to serve in the Knesset. Politically, he's about as right-wing as a fish knife, and at the time of writing in February 2021 is trying to prevent prisoners from receiving a COVID-19 vaccine.

In Europe, many of the leaders of nationalist-populist and anti-immigrant parties are gay. Pim Fortuyn, the anti-Islam hardliner assassinated in Amsterdam in 2002, was a pioneer in this regard. Since Fortuyn, there have been more prominent gays rising to the top of the alt-Right. As mentioned earlier, the leader of the AfD, Alice Weidel, is a lesbian, while Siv Jensen – leader of the Norwegian anti-immigrant Progress Party, who complains about the 'sneaking Islamisation' of Norwegian society – was honoured with a 'gay best friend' prize at a Norwegian LGBT award ceremony.[7] Florian Philippot – until 2017 the most senior male politician in the French *Rassemblement national* (RN; formerly the *Front national*) – is gay, and it appears that the RN has reasonable levels of support among French gays: a survey of 3200 gay French men by the dating app Hornet found that one in five were planning to vote for its leader Marine Le Pen in the 2017 presidential election. This support for the far-Right reflects differences among gay people in France, it being highest among whites and especially among married couples; exit polls after the 2015 regional elections indicated that the FN was more popular among married gay men than among the French population as a whole.

As we might expect, this support for the far-Right is not uniform across all French LGBT people. When the BBC spoke to a black

Muslim Frenchman, the DJ Kiddy Smiles, he asked if the gay RN supporters they had previously spoken to were white, and added that he was 'not surprised' to find out that they were: 'I don't want to say this, but I feel like a lot of LGBT people are very selfish. They feel like they're not targets for the FN any more so they think it's OK to vote for them.'[8] Smiles's argument is persuasive: there is absolutely no reason why LGBT people shouldn't be dispersed evenly across the political spectrum, and the reason for so few openly gay people in prominent positions in conservative politics is probably the same reason for the lack of openly gay people in virtually any field until recently.

Certainly, there is plenty of prejudice and bigotry among LGBT people themselves. The sociologist Eleanor Formby has found that LGBT people discriminate against other based on their 'age, body, disability, ethnicity, faith, HIV status, or perceived social class'. Implicit racism among gays can cause difficulties for gay men whose sexual proclivities don't match up to their ethnic stereotype. When the gay dating app Grindr asked a white man and an Asian man to let each other run their Grindr profile for twenty-four hours, messaging men and receiving pictures and propositions via the app, the Asian man's profile was on the receiving end of racist remarks and racial stereotypes, while the white man's was soon full of naked photos and suggestions to meet up. Formby even counsels against using the phrase 'LGBT community' as it 'implies that LGBT people somehow automatically belong to a ready made community' and this 'is simply not the case'. It is, says Formby, similar to talking of a 'brown-eyed community' or a 'blonde community'.[9]

Therefore, if parties formerly opposed to LGBT rights drop their homophobia, there is no reason why their number of 'out' gay supporters should not increase. Yet some would argue that these people are somehow 'traitors' or that their politics is in some way inconsistent with their sexuality. This is a process already underway in relation to people with conservative instincts or politics who are not white, and we can expect to see this develop with LGBT people in the coming decades. No one will deny their sexual orientation per se, but will instead argue that being gay isn't in reality about same-sex attraction, but rather about a lifestyle and political culture.

As with many things, there is an increasingly sharp division opening up between the extremely online self-appointed activists of specific communities, who dominate social media and the airwaves, and the larger hinterland of the community on behalf of whom they claim to act. The comedian Joe Lycett believes that the 'LGBT community has a problem with the way it communicates online'. Specifically, he tells the BBC, there are ever more complex and varied 'demands' made of non-LGBT people to understand the increasingly 'academic' language and terminology. People 'need to have it explained to them in a way that's compassionate, and is understanding that there's quite a lot to take in', says Lycett. 'Because lots of LGBTQ people are really smart, and there's so much really interesting reading that can be done, and so much academic writing that's been done about it, people can end up getting quite academic about it.'[10]

Lycett focuses on the impact of queer theory and post-structural understandings of gender identity in causing friction between gays and non-gays, but this is also occurring *among* gay people, particularly in terms of generation, class and culture. The attention given to semantics, theory and gender identity is almost unique to a certain kind of young person and is met with indifference or hostility by many other gay people. There may also be a sense of frustration among older gays, who had to live through infinitely more oppressive and perilous circumstances, that a section of the younger generation is making ever more niche and esoteric claims.

There is a relative lack of explicitly anti-trans sentiment from mainstream politicians in the UK; probably due to the lack of political capital to be gained from such sentiments. The Conservative Party under David Cameron considered legislating for self-identification (through which people can change their legal gender without undergoing medical transitioning), and many younger Tory MPs, including those elected to socially conservative Red Wall seats, are eager to do so during Boris Johnson's premiership.

On the issue of self-ID, and whether people should be able legally to change their gender without medical intervention, I'm staying well clear. Personally, I have no skin in the game, and I accept that there are strongly and genuinely held views on both sides. However, there are plenty of grifters on both sides of this issue who misuse it for their own ends, as trans people are an ideal constituency for identity myth-making. Despite – or because of – the relatively small number of trans, intersex and non-binary people, the issue has a prominent place in debates across the political spectrum, which is often divorced from the lives of actual trans people. As Jia Tolentino notes, the adulation given to Caitlyn Jenner – *Vanity Fair* cover, TV show, airing of political opinions – all happened while states were simultaneously passing bathroom bills banning transgender people from using the toilets of the gender with which they identify. What 'is often presented as evidence for Caitlyn Jenner's bravery', writes Tolentino, should 'at least as often be framed as proof of the distance between celebrity narratives and ordinary life'.[11]

Anyone familiar with trans-activist discourse will note the frequency of the suffix '-folks', something that has been increasing in recent years. A Google Ngram search for the frequency of the word 'trans' in the years 2000–19 reveals a graph that looks more or less like a horizontal line. There has been a slight increase in the use of the word trans over the past twenty years, but it has been slow and steady. In contrast, the Ngram for 'trans folks' shows a flat line until around 2010, whereupon it begins to increase, and then from 2014 it really takes off. For some reason, even though there has not been a commensurate increase in the use of the word trans, there has been a rapid increase in the use of the phrase 'trans folks' in the past ten years or so.

The ubiquity of the pairing 'trans folks' among non-American English speakers is evidence of the significance of American culture, linguistics and mores to debates around gender identity, but it also indicates the relatively privileged class position of many of the loudest online voices in support of trans rights. Of the 'folk' in the title of *Souls of Black Folk*, Gilroy argues that the word invokes a 'highly specific but also highly mystical and organic conception of community'.[12] I believe the reason for the frequency of 'trans folks' is not so much that it makes the issue itself seem more 'folks-y' and mundane, but that it confers this same impression about the person using the phrase. Barack Obama and Boris Johnson are big fans of the 'F' word in general, and possibly for the same reason: to give their rhetoric a more earthy element, sort of 'Harvard meets Hicksville' or 'Balliol meets Bolsover'.

While a few prominent media figures trade in transphobic slurs, much of what is said to be transphobic commentary is usually feminist criticism of self-ID. In this sense it is unusual, as much of the 'conservative' criticism of trans rights comes from a group who are themselves used to being attacked by the Right. In the United States, Donald Trump banned trans people from serving in the US military – an executive action promptly overturned by Joe Biden during his first days in office – but generally trans rights do not serve as a fault line in the US culture wars in the same way as abortion rights or immigration. For the Right, trans people can serve as a kind of useful bogeymen, reduced to their sexual characteristics and implied to be predators. This stereotyping finds its mirror image on the pro-trans Left – as with other minority groups, trans people are assumed by the Left to be inherently radical, intersectional, socialist and so on, which positions the trans person as an object, to be used in smashing patriarchy/racism/heteronormativity/etc., rather than a living, breathing subject whose gender identity might be the least interesting thing about them. This also detracts from the important material threats and disadvantages faced by trans people, such as vulnerability to violence and harassment, and difficulty in finding employment.

Some of the claims made by trans-rights activists might also intersect with other disadvantaged groups in unintended ways. For example, language such as 'individuals with a cervix' is less accessible to people with a lower level of education, while as Rosa Freedman, a human-rights lawyer and Orthodox Jew, notes, many religiously observant women, including Jews, Muslims and other religious minorities, believe that they cannot use spaces that feature the intermingling of sexes. There is a broad level of support for trans rights in the UK: according to a YouGov poll, as of February 2021, 28 per cent and 23 per cent of people respectively 'somewhat agree' or 'agree strongly' with the phrase 'a transgender man/woman is a man/woman', with 18 per cent 'somewhat' disagreeing and only 17 per cent 'strongly' disagreeing. Meanwhile, 50 per cent to 27 per cent of Britons believe that people should be allowed to self-identify as a gender different to the one they were assigned at birth.[13]

However, many people do not believe that trans people are of the 'sex' with which they identity. A paper in the *Journal of Personal and Social Relationships* asked participants whether they were men or women; cis or trans; and gay, straight or bisexual. They were then asked which groups they would consider as sexual partners. Only 12.5 per cent of people included trans people at all, and almost half of those that did matched their orientations to trans people's sex at birth rather than gender identity (so for example, heterosexual men who said that they would consider dating trans men but not trans women).[14] This is one thing that trans people have in common with the inept or unfortunate-looking men discussed in an earlier chapter, and indicates another way that focusing on common problems faced by disparate groups – in this case finding love and physical intimacy – is more productive than siloing people according to 'identity'.

A common concern among so-called 'gender-critical' feminists, which I think is warranted, is that after decades of feminist arguments for gender to be understood as a social construct, trans advocacy reasserts gender as a fixed and defined category, and instead casts biological sex as a construct. The British Association for Counselling Practitioners defines being a woman as 'adhering to social norms of femininity, such as being nurturing, caring, social, emotional, vulnerable, and concerned with appearance'. In contrast, it defines men as people who are 'competitive, ambitious, independent, rational, tough, sexual, confident, dominant, taking risks, and caring about their work'. This seems to countermand decades of feminist practice: on the one hand, we are rightly telling kids that not all firefighters or physicists are men, but at the same time telling them that if you are interested in being a firefighter or a physicist, you are probably a boy.

Many radical feminists, used to facing opprobrium from the tabloids and the political Right, now find themselves under attack from erstwhile comrades due to their refusal to recognise that trans-women are women in the same sense as biological women. Branded as TERFS – trans-exclusionary radical feminists – these women have been outflanked by a (usually) younger generation of feminists, who denounce them as bigots. Yet very few of these young feminists are transgender themselves. They are generally young women – or men – at university or recently graduated, and from relatively privileged backgrounds. Talking about her experiences in Liverpool in the 1970s, the artist Jayne Casey recalls:

> We were well prepared to have a fight because we'd all grown up fighting. We weren't soft kids, we came from heavy working class backgrounds and we knew how to fight. Peter Burns was a fantastic fighter. We'd shock them; the scallies would come for us and we'd

batter them! We attracted violence, every night, which was good; we hated the world and expected the world to hate us.[15]

For Casey and Burns, pioneering gender fluidity while growing up among rigidly conformist communities, life was hard. But they were of the communities they came from, so they were hard too. They knew they had to expect ridicule at the least and violence often, and were prepared to dish it out as well as receive. They had to fight to survive.

Today, the suffering of some trans people across the world is glibly used by non-trans people as a way of adding force to their political points. A particular kind of online activist refers to violence against trans people or their suicides in the same way they might note that 'Scousers Never Read the *Sun*' or that plenty of middle-class people voted for Brexit. As one of many instances of people's lives being used as bricks in the identity construction of other people it is objection-able in itself, but it is particularly irresponsible of these people to stress suicide rates – hearing that you are particularly at risk of suicide is itself one of the risk factors for suicide. Furthermore, much of the violence perpetrated against trans people is done by their own part-ners – which is not to say that it is in some way acceptable, nor that romantic relationships preclude hatred and violence – but surely it does mean that partners of trans people are not 'transphobic' in the usual sense it is meant. According to Stonewall, 19 per cent of trans people in the UK say they have experienced domestic abuse from a partner in the past year – higher than the recorded rate of domestic abuse among the wider population, which is 7.9 per cent of women and 4.2 per cent of men, according to the Office for National Statistics (although they admit that these figures probably understate the extent of domestic abuse).[16]

Evidence of the potency of 'trans' as an identity for non-trans people can be seen in the violent threats people make against one another in its name. One gay man on Twitter, who is critical of attempts to centre gender rather than sex, points out the irony of the online abuse he faces: on one day he was called 'an inbred faggot, a fascist, a supremacist' and accused of incest, 'by straight men who think they're fighting the good fight for a better world'. While violent language cannot be justified or excused, it is perhaps more understandable coming from trans people, who may have been themselves victims of abuse and prejudice, than from non-trans allies, who surely have no excuse. The sort of people who assault trans women (or trans men, for that matter) do not do so because of editorials they read in broadsheet newspapers or current affairs magazines.

Outside the usual roll call, there is a particular effort to link trans rights with anti-racism. There is one reason why this can be justified, as the majority of trans people who fall victim to violence are indeed people of colour. However, it does not then follow that criticism of trans activism is 'rooted in white supremacy'.[17] One of the most obvious repudiations of this is the anti-trans hostility of many black people, as can readily be seen by a quick perusal of the African-American women's internet forum Lipstick Ally. And while plenty of transphobes are also racists, and many racists are transphobic, any linkage between the two issues can easily confuse cause and effect. That most of the trans people murdered and raped are black or brown is not due to racism against them, but rather due to their exposure to violence in the first place – something which is affected by racism, but more than anything else is affected by class, in that they are exposed to violence, abuse and discrimination through lack of material resources.

While violence against trans people is probably under-recorded, academic research suggests that transgender people as a whole do not face a higher risk of being murdered than non-trans people, but that young transgender women of colour certainly do face a higher chance of being murdered.[18] According to transgender advocacy groups, there are roughly around 300 to 400 trans people murdered each year, the majority of whom are killed in Central and South American nations. Trans Murder Monitoring found that at least 258 trans or gender-diverse people were murdered in Latin America in the period October 2018 to September 2019. Of these, 130 were killed in Brazil, 63 in Mexico, and 14 and 13 in Colombia and Argentina respectively.

In contrast, there are usually between twenty and thirty trans people killed in the United States each year, according to reports by Trans Respect, and around one person per year in the UK. Of the American victims, the overwhelming majority are black or Hispanic. Outside Latin America, one of the next most dangerous countries is Pakistan. In September 2020, the well-known Pakistani transgender activist Gul Panra was shot dead and another trans woman wounded in an attack in Peshawar. At least sixty-nine trans people have been killed in the Khyber Pakhtunkhwa province alone in the past five years.[19] As the Twitter account 'NonBinaryMarcus' argues, Transgender Day of Remembrance 'is when middle class American and British trans activists pretend they face the same dangerous lives' as transgender street prostitutes; 'it is a shameless fraud'. Middle-class, white trans people in the UK are in no way at the same risk of physical violence; people who commemorate the Holocaust on 27 January or fallen soldiers on 11 November pay respect without claiming or implying that they themselves are at the same physical risk, even if they are Jewish or in the military.

It is obscene for university students in the UK and US – statistically the safest places in the world for trans people – to claim they are at risk of physical harm or made to feel unsafe. This is of a piece with claiming that the real threat to trans people is not those who actually harm them – their partners, johns, violent men on the streets, in pubs and on public transport – but actually feminists, academics and people on the internet, who by definition cannot physically harm anyone. It is an invocation of the very real threat faced by trans street walkers or people on their own on late-night trains and buses to attack views you don't like. Like critics of Chimamanda Ngozi Adichie encouraging people to take up machetes against her because they equated words she had written or spoken with actual physical violence. If you are a trans person in Nigeria you are indeed very much at risk of physical violence, but you should focus your ire on people who would actually harm you, rather than someone who has supported and nurtured you.

There are some issues that affect all LGBT people (homophobic violence), and those that affect some but not others (HIV/AIDs), but these are import material issues; a gay or queer 'identity' applies to only a very specific group of LGBT people, and it tends to be those who already have the most cultural resources, the greatest access to media representation, the loudest voices on social media and in popular culture, and most likely to have influence in politics and on the boards of businesses and public bodies.

When it comes to issues of sex and identity, it is vital that the identity doesn't obscure the reality; issues around 'toxic masculinity' or the apparent feminisation of society are ultimately a distraction from the real problems facing men and women. Similarly, a focus on 'woman' and 'feminism' as identities rather than on specific structural problems obscures issues faced by all women such as domestic and sexual violence, and allows all manner of charlatans glibly to claim the mantle of feminism or to deploy feminism as a cover to justify their behaviour. Finally, a focus on gay identity or transness as an identity needlessly divides people and distracts from real problems. If LGBT people are bullied, made fun of, can't find partners, can't get a job and are harassed in the streets, this is a real problem that no amount of language policing or celebrating identity will overcome.

Part IV

Youth

Part IV

Chapter 10

Generation

Almost half of the world's population is under thirty years old.[1] There is tremendous heterogeneity among these billions of children, teenagers and twenty-somethings, and there is no single experience of 'being young'. But the imperatives of identity myths would nonetheless conscript youth and youthfulness for their own nefarious purposes.

When it comes to 'young people', the list of complaints levelled by conservative commentators and politicians is so hackneyed you can probably reel it off without thinking too hard: they are lazy, entitled, easily offended, and prefer wasting their money on fripperies than saving for a better future. For the Left, the clichés are more positive, but no less inaccurate. The young are liberal, progressive, anti-racist, pro-LGBT, environmentally conscious and so scarred by the 2008 financial crash and resultant increase in inequality that they will sooner or later power a fundamental change in the politics and economics of the developed world. In reality, there is a tremendous variety of living standards, politics and lifestyles among young people today, moulded by geography, class and culture, and important generational differences are emerging between millennials and Generation Z.

What does it even mean when we say someone is 'young'? Technically, it is just a designation for juvenescence, which could be applied to any living thing, such as an animal or tree – or even imma-terial things, such as ideas or concepts – as much as to humans. Yet in reality, to say that someone is young means more than to say they are under a certain age. It is not just a biological or chronological appel-lation, but has social, cultural and political connotations. When we hear or read the word 'millennial', for instance, it does not merely conjure images of someone born within a certain date range, but brings with it various assumptions: we might assume that it refers to someone who is computer literate and an avid user of social media; that their politics are left-liberal, with a pronounced concern for the changing climate, an ease with different sexual orientations, and a scepticism about gender binaries.

Clearly, such assumptions are based upon unwieldy generalisa-tions: even among the generation in the Global North to whom it is meant to refer, there are many millennials who are technologically inept, averse to social media, unconcerned about the environment and have traditional or conservative views on sex and gender. But aside from culturally specific designations of generation such as millennial, on a global level the boundaries of being 'young' are unfixed and impermanent: there is no universally agreed age for when someone is 'young' and when they cease to be such.

Is the twelve-year-old child soldier, who may have raped and killed, seen his family murdered and home destroyed, still 'young' in anything but a biological sense? Conversely, while nations in the Global North have traditionally seen eighteen or twenty-one as the end of youth, recent developments pushing back the average age of marriage, parenthood and homeownership have seen millions of twenty- and thirty-somethings living the kind of lives that not so long ago would have been associated with childhood.

While it is difficult to find reliable global statistics on leaving home – not least because of the culturally specific nature of the term – in Europe there is a ten-year discrepancy between the likes of Sweden,

Denmark and Finland, where most people leave home by the time they are twenty-one; and Malta, Croatia and Slovakia, where this occurs a decade later on average.[2] There are similar discrepancies across the globe for marriage and parenthood (with the latter coming a year or two after the former more or less universally): in Afghanistan, Chad and Niger, the average age of marriage is around nineteen; in Chile, the Dominican Republican and Sweden it is about thirty-five.[3]

Likewise with education – among countries where higher education is commonplace, the median age of graduation from first university degrees ranges from twenty-two in the United Kingdom and Belgium to over twenty-seven in Iceland and Israel.[4] Yet we cannot infer a clear idea as to when youth ends in different countries from these statistics alone, not least because leaving home, having children and getting a job do not always correlate: Sweden has both the youngest average age for leaving home and the oldest average age for having children; while although Israelis have the oldest average age for university graduation, their average age for marriage and children is in the middle of the international spread, at twenty-six for women and twenty-eight for men.

The advanced age for graduation among Israelis can be explained by the compulsory three years' military service for both men and women (and the ubiquitous post-military time spent travelling that is effectively obligatory for all but the poorest of secular Jewish Israelis). But Iceland, which has the same average age of first-time graduates, does not even have a standing army, let alone conscription. What we can say is that the parameters of youth vary hugely across the world, affected by issues such as violence and conflict, migration, the nature of work, living arrangements, and the prevalence of higher education and compulsory military service.

Even within the UK, there are important and broadening distinctions between the attitudes of millennials and Generation Z. A *Vice* article exploring the feelings of Gen Z-ers towards millennials reveals

plenty of antagonism, with a prominent disdain for the older generation's understanding of the internet and new technology. 'They're old
people trying to use social media,' says one. 'They try to fit in with the
younger generation but they're not really the younger generation any
more. They try to use all the hashtags and gifs, but they're not very
good at it,' says another. A common complaint concerns the millennial 'mindfulness' habit of concentrating on small successes in life:
'they really get caught up in really simple, everyday stuff . . . They
grow a basic thing, like a fruit or vegetable, and they're like, "wow, I
didn't kill it". They'll spend the whole day fantasising about that fruit
or vegetable. My sister grew beetroot and she's really happy about it
– I don't really understand it.'

Perhaps most notable was the accusation of self-obsession: 'I think
they're self-obsessed. Millennials are the ones who invented selfies
and those travel Instagram pages and stuff that revolves around their
lives. They think that's what everyone else is catching on. They're
obsessed with their image', whereas in contrast, this respondent felt
that Gen Z-ers 'don't care about what we post on social media', and
were less likely to attempt to curate their lives through that medium.
This difference may owe something to the younger generation being
'born into' social media, whereas for many millennials the likes of
Facebook, and certainly Instagram, emerged after they had spent
many different years as children and young adults, without the agency
and control over their image provided by social media.

Another theme was the apparent lack of business-savvy and entre-
preneurship among millennials, whom one respondent describes as
'moan[ing] a lot and [not doing] anything. You find 16–17 year olds
on TikTok selling their creativity, whereas I feel millennials are
obsessed with a traditional nine to five job because that's the only way
to get job security. They're *obsessed* with job security. They're always
annoyed at the fact they knew they're going to be renting forever,
whereas Gen Zs know we're just not going to be able to buy a house.'

A final respondent notes that the public perception of millennials is very much class- and ethnicity-specific: 'People of colour who are millennials aren't really brought into this conversation . . . For a long time, Instagram was very white, so the media represented millennial culture as those fruit bowls and travel pages. Middle-class whiteness just became branded with millennials.'[5]

Even on racial justice, although there is a clear correlation between age and views on these issues, there are some areas of divergence between the views of millennials and the younger generation. In the United States, totemic (no pun intended) issues such as the rebranding of racially insensitive sports team names, nicknames or mascots divide, rather than unite, people under thirty. In 2020, the NFL side the Washington Redskins yielded to years of pressure and changed their name to the Washington Football Team, yet the move had a plurality of support only among Generation Z, of whom 45 per cent supported the change, while 23 per cent were opposed and 32 per cent had no opinion. Perhaps surprisingly, among millennials, fully 47 per cent opposed the move and only 31 per cent supported, with 22 per cent having no opinion.[6]

One of the most common stereotypes about young people in the West is that they are inherently individualistic, lacking the community spirit found among older generations. There is plenty of statistical and anecdotal evidence to suggest that is the case, although it may well be that the nature of what it means to be community-minded is changing. In a column for the London *Evening Standard*, millennial writer Phoebe Luckhurst describes having to meet the neighbours as 'a Londoner's worst nightmare'; discovering that her ceiling was leaking, she realised that she 'was going to have to talk to my upstairs neighbour. The dread pooled in my ears; my heart thumped in triple time.' Despite living in the same place for six months she hadn't met another resident of the building: 'As a stereotypical millennial nomad, I am used to piggybacking between leases when landlords sell up, or up the rent – not to bonding with the neighbours. Moreover, as a millennial, I am pathologically neurotic: too wimpy to make a phone call, let alone introduce myself to a neighbour.' After putting it off for a while, she eventually summoned up the courage to write a note and push it under the neighbour's door, and then 'literally ran downstairs' to her own flat.[7]

Luckhurst is not alone in her fear of meeting neighbours or talking on the phone – a viral Twitter post from May 2019 highlighted how many millennials refuse to respond to their doorbell ringing or a knock at the door unless they are expecting someone. This aversion to unmediated 'real life' contact is of a piece with the millennial social media preference for selfies taken and selected by themselves, with the most flattering filters applied, over photographs taken and uploaded by others, over which they have no control.

Along with their reluctance to answer the door and talk on the phone, younger people show a preference for the automated checkouts in supermarkets. This surely cannot be for the sake of convenience – anyone who has used these machines knows they can be anything but convenient – and I suspect it is due to a desire to avoid the perils of unscripted, spontaneous human interaction.

This trend may not be a harmless product of technological advance. Professor Adrian Beck, a criminologist at the University of Leicester, argues that self-service checkouts encourage theft not only through making it easier to steal, but also by undermining empathy between customers and shopworkers. Similarly, while the rise of automation and the decline in face-to-face interactions have been a great boon to some people, not least those with autistic spectrum condition or even old-fashioned misanthropes, this lack of human interaction can have negative mental health implications for other people.[8] Tolentino describes a snake of people 'texting, shuffling, eyes-down', while queueing up to be served in the US chain Sweetgreen (which I believe is like a version of the British chain Pret a Manger). Tolentino notes that since Sweetgreen is 'a marvel of optimisation', the queue can be processed in ten minutes, 'as customer after customer orders a kale Caesar with chicken without even looking at the other, darker-skinned, hairnet-wearing line of people'.[9] This process nicely encap-sulates the lifestyles of many overworked young people in big cities, without the time to eat properly or even look at people. At the same time, the ordinary human interaction between employee and customer that used to take place in such situations is increasingly too awkward for millennials to manage, further undermining any sense of generational solidarity between those who buy the food and those who serve it.

This apparent decline in solidarity and communality may have important political ramifications, which is especially relevant as the identity myth-making around young people applies most signifi-cantly in terms of their politics. There is an assumption for many on the Left that the young will ride to the rescue of the world, and so to be young is not just an age, nor even a politico-cultural designation, but rather a mantle to wear and an obligation to bear.

In many ways this is quite a Western-centric understanding of youth. For example, the Bharatiya Janata Yuva Morcha – the youth wing of India's BJP – claims tens of millions of members, substantially more than the combined membership of all of the youth movements of liberal and socialist parties throughout the West. These young people are committed to a nationalistic, often anti-Muslim politics that would be anathema to many of their counterparts elsewhere in the world. A recent survey found that nearly a quarter (24 per cent) of Indians between the ages of fifteen and thirty-four are 'extremely patriarchal' in their outlook. Nearly half, girls included, disapprove of women wearing jeans. One in three women disapproved of women working – that is, working outside the home and earning an inde-pendent income – after marriage; 53 per cent disapprove of dating and 45 per cent disapprove of interfaith marriages.[10]

The current correlation between age and political allegiance in the UK is also a recent phenomenon. The British Election Study (BES) reveals that there was little difference between the voting habits of under twenty-fives and pensioners between 1964 and 2001. At the 2005 general election a 6-point gap emerged between the young and the old, which increased to 40 points at the 2017 and 2019 polls.

Despite this, the image of enthused youngsters clamouring for a better world does not translate into greater engagement with politics, and there has been a notable decline in trust in democracy among young people. According to Dr Roberto Foa of the University of Cambridge, 'this is the first generation in living memory to have a global majority who are dissatisfied with the way democracy works while in their twenties and thirties'. For members of Generation X (defined in Foa's study as born between 1965 and 1980), satisfaction with democracy peaked at 62 per cent in the 1990s and 2000s, but for millennials today, it has sunk to just 48 per cent. Although Foa is at pains to stress that this dissatisfaction with democracy does not reflect an attraction to authoritarianism, but rather discontent with the material conditions of the modern world, these statistics complicate the image of engaged, politically active millennials.[11] Even elections that appeared to inspire a wave of youthful enthusiasm, such as the 2014 Scottish independence referendum, often failed to do so: despite the franchise being extended to sixteen- and seventeen-year-olds, turnout among voters under twenty-four was just 54 per cent.[12]

Furthermore, the youthful radicalism of right-wing nightmares, despite the impression given by social media, is largely reserved for politically engaged students in the rarefied atmosphere of university campuses. Recalling his undergraduate days at Cambridge ten years ago, Tobias Phibbs lists a litany of absurd and clichéd attempts by privileged, overwhelmingly white radicals to police their environment: 'The organiser of a gay night was denounced for playing a song by Katy Perry because another song of hers was deemed problematic.

A rare working class boy had his Union Jack flag stolen and set on fire during a commemoration for the Queen, while students (many of whom from one elite international school in Geneva) denounced him as a racist. We queued round the block for Judith Butler and we tried, sometimes successfully, to get others blocked from public platforms altogether.'[13]

Yet these students were not representative of their contemporaries at Cambridge, much less of a whole generation. Despite their hand-wringing over their own privilege, many of Phibbs's peers went on to elite careers in law, media, politics or finance, just like their parents and grandparents. Meanwhile, as anyone who has taught at a university can attest, the depiction of students as being uniformly politically engaged and radicalised, whether in the dreams of left-wing firebrands or the nightmares of tabloid hacks, is a fantasy. YouGov's 'Profiles' series polls hundreds of thousands of people across various age groups, and one question asks respondents to describe themselves on a seven-point scale from 'very Left-wing' to 'very Right-wing'. Between the ages of eighteen and forty, around 30 to 40 per cent of people claim that they don't have a strong political identity, with no clear age-based correlation within that group. Intriguingly, the views of eighteen-year-olds do not meaningfully diverge from those of forty-year-olds, suggesting that while millennials are more left-wing than Generation X-ers, the Generation Z-ers are actually more conservative.

This is supported by the British Election Study, which in 2015 had eighteen-year-olds as the most left-wing, but this was no longer the case by 2020, when twenty-two-year-olds were more radical than eighteen-year-olds. According to the BES, a typical eighteen-year-old in 2015 had a 73 per cent chance of voting for a Left party, whereas an eighteen-year-old in 2019 had only a 67 per cent chance of doing so.[14] The political scientist Eric Kaufmann theorises that this is due to a fading of the 'Brexit shock', when young people woke up to see that their futures had been irreversibly changed, without their consent or even involvement (it's estimated that only 36 per cent of eighteen- to twenty-four-year-olds voted in the referendum).[15]

It could also owe something to a typical adolescent defiance of the prevailing orthodoxy of the time: the 'Profiles' database also suggests that support for 'political correctness' is 5 to 10 points lower among eighteen- and nineteen-year-olds compared to those aged twenty-two to twenty-nine. This divergence is particularly marked among men between eighteen and nineteen years old, who are typically 10 to 15 points more opposed to political correctness than in favour of it – compared to women from the same generation, who are between 30 and 40 points more in favour than against.[16] A similar study in the US found that 74 per cent of people aged twenty-four to twenty-nine, and 79 per cent of under twenty-four-year-olds agreed that 'political correctness is a problem in our country'.[17] There is also a risk that the policing of language might backfire in unexpected ways, even among demographics that are more supportive. In one of my wife's supervision classes at the University of Cambridge, featuring two black girls, one from an underprivileged background, and one white girl from an elite public school, they were all highly intelligent and committed feminists. However, when tasked to come up with 'manifestos' of their ideas for a better world, they were extremely hesitant, as they were each so worried they would say one wrong thing and thus be 'cancelled' among their peers.

Disturbingly, there is a positive correlation between youth and homo- and transphobic hate crime. Although the targets of such crimes are more or less evenly spread among under sixties, with twenty- to twenty-nine-year-olds the most likely to become victims, there is a clear correlation between age and the likelihood of abusing or assaulting someone because of their sexuality or gender identity. People in their twenties are accused of homophobic hate crimes more often than any other age group, and suspects in transgender hate crimes are most likely to be teenagers or children.[18]

In Europe too, the politics of the young are diverse and often coun-terintuitive. In the 2017 French presidential elections, while only 27 per cent of over sixty-fives backed Marine Le Pen, this rose to 34 per cent among eighteen- to twenty-four-year-olds. In Italy, 46 per cent of under forty-fives would vote to remain in the EU if they had a referendum on the issue, while 51 per cent would leave. In contrast, 68 per cent of over forty-fives would vote to remain, and only 26 per cent to leave. These unexpected political trends among youngsters also intersect with race, further complicating the NeoOrientalist view of non-white political radicalism. In the US, for example, young black voters aren't as negative about Donald Trump as older black Americans: according to *FiveThirtyEight*, Trump's support among young black voters aged eighteen to forty-four doubled from around 10 per cent in 2016 to 21 per cent in 2020. A July 2020 poll for the African American Research Collaborative found that in key swing states 35 per cent of eighteen- to twenty-nine-year-old black people agreed that 'although they didn't always like Trump's policies, they liked his strong demeanour and defiance of the establishment'. In contrast, only 10 per cent of blacks older than sixty said the same.[19]

More than any other subculture, the figure of the hipster has come to stand for the best and worst of the values of the millennial generation. Broadly despised – even by people who are, objectively, hipsters them-selves – there have nonetheless been attempts by some on the Left, particularly those associated with the Exonerators school, to rescue the image of the hipster. In *Authentocrats*, Kennedy refers to the hipster as 'a latter-day folk devil in a way notably similar to the place occupied by provincial, old-fashioned Conservatives in the collective comic consciousness of the Major years'.[20] The source of this oppro-brium may be that, in the same way that the shire Tory of the 1990s, with their warm beer and village greens, seemed a relic of backward age, so too the hipster, with their combination of the live-and-let-live ethos of the sixties and the 'I'm-alright-Jack' attitude of the eighties, leaves them open to attacks from all sides. As Jeffrey Boakye has it, 'the problem is that hipsterism doesn't have a cause. It's only vaguely countercultural and it's hopelessly tied into commercialism.'[21]

This is the argument put forward by Melina Cooper in *Between Neoliberalism and the New Social Conservatism*, which argues that the 'Third Way' of Bill Clinton and Tony Blair in the 1990s was effectively an accommodation between neoliberalism and the cultural politics of the 1960s, paid for by access to cheap credit and ballooning personal debt, to give the masses financial empowerment – or at least the illusion of it – at the expense of political power. The emergence of hipster capitalism – and its younger step-sibling 'woke capitalism' – has elicited a plethora of comment over the past few years. From the infamous Kendall Jenner Pepsi commercial in 2017 to a tone-deaf Gillette advert in 2019 featuring brawling, predatory men and the lament 'Is this the best a man can get?', plenty of people from across the political spectrum have complained about the appropriation of formerly radical or unpopular causes by multinational behemoths. The corporate sponsorship of Pride events, which in the 2020s have an entirely different aesthetic to that of even a decade earlier, is one of the most visually obvious examples. Large companies, aware that millennials value personal identity above all else, have attempted to 'pink-wash' their brands, often in extremely incongruous ways: back in 2014, the company behind the Keystone XL pipeline (a highly controversial project to bring tar sands oil to the United States through Indigenous land) tried to sell itself as a gay-friendly alternative to the Arab-nation dominated OPEC, with a website called OPEChatesgays.com.[22]

The unique intersection between consumerism and countercultural values within hipsterdom is not the only reason for antipathy towards hipsters. Reminiscing about the New Romantics of the 1980s, Andrew O'Hagan writes that during that era, 'suddenly kids with nothing else going for them could be the entitled ones' and that 'snotty narcissism' is at least an 'equal opportunity sport'.[23] I think this hits on the core reason for hostility to hipsters: they can be people who have no obvious talent – either for music, sport, acting, writing or even natural good looks – who have nonetheless decided that they won't let any of that stop them from living a certain lifestyle, which can be obtained through basing their identity on what they consume. The hipster ideal – of consumption as identity and the curated lifestyle – has become increasingly commonplace among millennials and Gen Z-ers, for whom the outward expression of identity often has more meaning than their actual lifestyle, and where all sorts of personal issues, from healthcare to sex, have become consumption goods.

The politico-cultural identity of many young people – at least in the West – is based upon an admirable and instinctive lack of judgement towards people's nationality, ethnicity, religion, sexuality or gender identity. 'You do you', goes the refrain. Yet the other side of this ideal, which privileges individual identity above all else, is a tendency to regard communal, collectivist ideas as irrelevant and passé. Dolly Alderton, who formerly wrote a column on relationship advice for the *Sunday Times* and now co-hosts a successful podcast, writes in her recent memoirs that 'if you're still getting drunk and flirting with other people in front of your boyfriend, there's something wrong with your relationship. Or more likely, with you.'[24] While the advice itself might be solid enough, I was instantly struck by the similarity between this and the Ayn Randian bromides of Gene Simmons, the long-tongued lead singer of execrable American rock band Kiss, now in the self-help business: 'Get rid of all your loser friends', advises Simmons. 'You know the ones – they drink too much, they get high. And like vampires they will suck the life blood out of you. That may not leave you with very many friends, but . . . in business your friends will not be much help. You're too young and not rich enough to take vacations.'[25]

Reviewing Alderton's book alongside those of other millennial memoirists, Maggie Doherty notes how their self-worth 'seems to be measured out in acceptance letters' to prestigious colleges and in high-powered professional careers. Likewise, there is an instinctive belief in the righteousness of meritocracy, personified in the career of Barack Obama: 'Obama's biography seems to validate what they had been told at school', writes Doherty, 'trust in meritocracy; adapt to new conditions.'[26] As far back as 2001, the American journalist David Brooks wrote of his surprise at the difference between the students of his day and those he encountered on twenty-first-century campuses: instead of rebels, 'they were résumé builders', accomplishment collectors 'distinguished by their serenity, their faux-adult professionalism [and] their politesse'.[27] Were he to visit a university campus today, he would likely find the same focus on careers and professional development, but increasingly combined with an identitarian and performative leftism. Given the spiralling costs of higher education and the dwindling number of secure, professional careers, a focus on hard work and attainment is understandable. The young writer Brandon J. Graham reports that on his university campus there was a rivalry between students to appear the most exhausted, and to be calm and well-rested was to be a failure.[28] In these circumstances, many fall back on identities – campus radical, entrepreneurial Girl Boss, hipster – as succour, but it provides only the illusion of relief.

On the ten-year anniversary of the 2010 student protests, Tobias Phibbs lamented that the politics of many of the students he marched with in 2010 are now characterised less by collectivism but more by the performative leftism typical of social media, 'an ideology which every power we claimed to be protesting against' – from big business to the United States government and the CIA – 'has embraced wholesale.'[29] Your view on all this may well depend on your broader politics, but there are reasons to believe that this combination of cultural radicalism and free market spirit is harming the mental health of young people.

The economic climate of the 2020s currently does not bode well for young people, and especially for the neoliberal hipster. The pressures of having to keep up with the advancing frontier of politico-cultural values (especially hard for white, middle-class, heterosexual hipsters, whose lack of demographic armour means they must work especially hard), while at the same time aspiring to a job in competitive and ever-shrinking sectors such as media, academia and journalism, all the while carefully cultivating and maintaining an online image, are beginning to take their toll.

Revisiting his old university in 2020, the *New York Times* columnist Ross Douthat notes the 'most striking difference' between now and his college days twenty years earlier 'is the disappearance of serenity, the evaporation of contentment, the spread of anxiety and mental illness [and] the reputed scale of antidepressant use'.[30] Tolentino writes of her 'sense of my own ethical brokenness', after 'seven years of flogging my own selfhood on the internet [just] to get to a place where I could comfortably afford to stop using Amazon to save fifteen minutes and five dollars at a time'.[31] Hipsters demonstrate that people can be both entitled and narcissistic and disadvantaged by the economy, and serve as an important warning for economically left-wing movements that structural and material disadvantage does not necessarily translate into support for collectivist or redistributive politics.

William Deresiewicz, an author based in Portland, Oregon – one of the homes of American hipsterdom – laments that modern youth culture lacks the radical dissent or rebellion inherent in previous generations. There are some data that support this. According to a Reason-Rupe poll from 2014, 55 per cent of millennials claim they would like to own their own business. An earlier poll from the Kauffman Foundation found that 54 per cent of American millennials had entrepreneurial ambitions, with higher levels among Latinos (64 per cent) and blacks (63 per cent); 65 per cent of them argued that making it easier to start a business should be a priority for Congress.[32]

Writing in the UK's *Guardian* newspaper, whose pages are not exactly a hostile place for hipsters, a columnist described a visit to a barbershop in which:

> the thirtysomething owner 'crafted' each haircut as a 'unique experience' . . . faux 'hunting lodge' panelling was lit by wireless mood lighting; customers sat on 're-engineered' 1920s barbering chairs; hidden state-of-the-art speakers played tech-house from what appeared to be a vintage iPhone dock.

When asked how they described themselves, the owner and one customer, who owned a tattoo parlour across the road, both claimed to be 'socialists', before quickly adding that they were not looking 'to build empires' but just to 'make a living'. They had both left safe jobs working for the state and local government respectively.[33] This last sentence is particularly revealing: people who had 'steady jobs' in the public sector leaving for more exciting roles as entrepreneurs with greater room for self-expression could be a metaphor for the changes to the Western Left over the past few decades.

All of this – the decline in economic security, rapid technological and ecological change, and the even more rapidly evolving political mores – might all have an effect on the wellbeing of young people. And this issue provides fertile grounds for identity myths, and the mental health of young people is possibly politicised more than any other aspect of the generation.

There is a debate around whether or not there is a mental health crisis among young people in the first place, with voices from across the political spectrum supporting the idea, but other dissident voices claiming this as hyperbole. Prominent among the latter is the science writer Tom Chivers, who insists that the statistics do not support the tale of declining mental health among young people, and borrows from the 'nothing new under the sun school' popular among historians, which instinctively plays down the novelty of any trend. Furthermore, there are predictable divisions over the cause of any deterioration in mental health, with right-wingers pointing the finger at technology, social media and millennial culture, and the Left citing inequality, climate change and racism.

Some commentators, such as Phibbs, speculate that emphasising the significance of their poor mental health allows privileged young people 'to see themselves not as the guilty children of the elite, but as subjects of a politics of anti-oppression in their own right'. Recalling his time as an undergraduate, he describes 'one of my more sordid memories is of person after person taking turns at a public assembly to declare themselves "disabled", presumably by nature of their mental disorder, and therefore oppressed'.[34] Certainly, there appears to be a connection between left-wing politics and depression: a 2020 study found that 'individuals vulnerable to depression are less likely to identify with mainstream conservative parties, to vote for them, and to place themselves on the right side of the political spectrum'.[35]

When we consider the entire population irrespective of generation, the number of people with reported mental health problems is actually pretty stable, at least in the UK, where the MIND charity estimates that one in four people has a diagnosable mental illness. Although this may seem worryingly high, according to the National Health Service's septennial Adult Morbidity Survey, it is about the same as in 1993, 2000, 2007 and 2014. Nonetheless, people are more likely to *report* mental health struggles, whether as a result of attempts to 'destigmatise' mental illness or for other reasons. In the UK, the percentage of people receiving treatment for common mental disorders rose from 25 per cent to 40 per cent between 2007 and 2014. It may also be that journalists, academics and political activists are more likely to suffer from poor mental health – or, more probably, be more open to talking about it – which increases the public salience of the issue.

While it is a good thing that more people feel comfortable to report mental illness, and that more are able to access treatment, this does not mean there has been a concomitant increase in government expenditure on mental health services. In fact, according to the *British Journal of General Practice*, there are fewer mental health beds in Britain today than there were in 1998.[36] Yet the lack of mental health provision receives less attention on social and conventional media than the plethora of celebrities talking about their own issues, the importance of destigmatisation, and encouraging everyone to come forward and declare their own struggles.

Fortunately, suicide in general is declining, including among young people. In 1998, 6.1 out of every 100,000 teenagers in England and Wales killed themselves, by 2004 this had fallen to 4.7, and in 2010 it was 3.1. Among ten- to twenty-nine-year-olds, there were more or less consistently around 15 suicide deaths per 100,000 people from the late 1980s to the early 2000s; for some reason this fell to about 9 per 100,000 around 2004, and has remained more of less constant ever since.[37] Clearly this is still too high, and there is no single factor we can attribute this to, but one thing we can be certain of is that it is not due to lavishly funded mental health services.

It is often argued that the 'mental health crisis' is particularly acute among students. According to UK statistics, 33,000 students were recorded as having a mental health condition, however defined, in the academic year 2014/15; by 2018/19, this had risen to 82,000, a 150 per cent increase. During the same period, the number of students rose by only 5 per cent. Students also report increased anxiety year-on-year, and in the academic year 2019/20 only one in six students said their level of anxiety was 'low'. There was some variation according to ethnicity, with white students most likely to report feeling anxious, and a clear gender discrepancy, with female students constituting more than 70 per cent of those reporting mental health struggles.[38] Since 1985, incoming undergraduates at the American university

UCLA have been asked whether they 'felt overwhelmed by all [they] had to do' in the previous year (i.e., their last year of school, before they started at university). In 1985, 18 per cent said they did. Twenty-five years later that number had increased to 29 per cent, and by 2016 it had leapt up to 41 per cent.

The US has also witnessed a doubling of hospital admissions for suicidal teenagers in the decade to 2017, with hospitalisations spiking during the autumnal return to school.[39] Stephanie Eken, a psychiatrist who oversees teenage-anxiety programmes across the US, is emphatic that social media is the most common cause of anxiety for today's youth, who are 'relentlessly comparing themselves with their peers', with 'almost uniformly distressing' results. Although teenage anxiety and fears that they compare unfavourably with their peers are nothing new, the internet habits of today's youth – constantly responding to texts, posting to social media, and obsessively following the exploits of others – most certainly are. It would be beyond foolish not to believe that this would have *some* effect on the mental health of adolescents. Kevin Ashworth, the clinical director of NW Anxiety Institute in Portland, worries that many teens 'have lost the ability to tolerate distress and uncertainty'.[40]

We can speculate as to the various technological, societal and cultural factors that impact on the mental health of today's young people, but it would be foolish to discount the importance of economic pressures. In the modern economy, it is increasingly difficult for young people to 'settle down', with a decline in secure employment, the rise of the gig economy, a lack of affordable housing in big cities, and a later age of marriage and children. There is also evidence that inequality specifically, rather than just poverty, can hamper mental health. In June 2019, the United Nations' special rapporteur on health, Dr Dainius Puras, argued that confronting excessive inequality was likely to prove much more beneficial to mental health than any amount of therapy or medication, and yet so much of the discourse around mental health is focused on individuals: individual victims, individual remedies, individual identity.

Yet economics cannot explain everything, as plenty of materially disadvantaged people have both better mental health and longer lives than average. Perhaps one of the problems is that many of the possible remedies for loneliness and poor mental health, such as marriage, family, living in the same place, and religious belief, are associated with conservative values. As Noreen Hertz writes in *The Lonely Century*, ultra-orthodox Jewish people in Israel are disproportionately poor, overweight and sedentary, yet live notably longer than secular Israelis. In the UK, there are lower rates of common mental health issues among black and Asian Britons, who are more likely than white Brits to live near their extended family and have religious faith.[41] Conversely, many of the remedies popular among younger people might be less effective, or even counter-productive. A meta-survey of fifty-five journal articles by Miguel Farias of Coventry University finds that one in twelve people attempting meditation or mindfulness activities experiences a *worsening* of their symptoms, or even the onset of new mental health issues – from milder conditions such as depression and anxiety through to psychosis and even suicide. Farias also warns that this may be an underestimate, as many studies of meditation record only serious negative effects or don't record them at all.[42]

According to the Children's Society's *Good Childhood Report*, overall childhood happiness in the UK peaked in 2009 and has been falling ever since, yet children say they are happier at school and with schoolwork than in the past, which suggests that increased academic pressure is not to blame. Perhaps most surprisingly, girls are reporting being happier with their appearance than in previous years. There are also notable and unexplained variations along lines of class and ethnicity; the report indicates that poor white girls are especially unhappy and rich black boys are particularly happy.

Perhaps it is important to make children and teenagers understand that unhappiness is normal, a part of life, and an entirely healthy and appropriate response to some situations and events, so that by normalising unhappiness we can make them better prepared for the vagaries of life.[43]

Irrespective of whether or not numbers are increasing, poor mental health among those young people who do suffer from it is very real, very serious, and caused by a range of complicated factors that defy any single easy explanation. It appears to be particularly bad for young women, and perhaps especially so for people from apparently 'privileged' backgrounds or in elite institutions. At Oxford and Cambridge universities, the dreaming spires of the colleges are closed during the exam term to prevent students from throwing themselves off. I remember from my student days the women with scarred arms and legs, many of whom had devastating and heart-wrenching stories, despite, or maybe because of, their ostensible academic success.

For most humans, social interaction is critical to their health and wellbeing; hence why loneliness can be so destructive, and the solitary confinement of prisoners can be a kind of torture. Yet as we have become more likely to live apart from our family and friends, and technology has stepped in to connect people over great distances, many people have become dependent on the internet, and particularly social media, for keeping in touch. This increasing dependency has negative side effects, as communicating through the prism of social media can undermine mental health, yet at the same time people feel compelled to do so, and attempts to quit social media can themselves lead to deteriorating mental health. This has led to a cruel paradox whereby social media can undermine mental health, even as it offers ways of connecting and overcoming loneliness. With people whose mental health issues make it difficult to leave their home, it can seem to offer a way out, yet may increase their suffering.

Furthermore, the irresistible impulse to use social media to curate your life and define yourself as an individual, alongside broader political and cultural trends to focus on your 'identity', means that people suffering from poor mental health manifest this in ways inimical to the kind of joint action needed to break down these conditions. As the writer Louise Perry puts it, 'those "snowflake" young people on Twitter are telling the truth when they write about their profound unhappiness. It's just that they're using these feelings as evidence of their special, oppressed status, rather than seeing themselves as part of a lonely generation in need of better company.'[44]

There is a tendency by some to view any complaints about technology as inherently reactionary. They roll their eyes and point out the similar language that was used around the advent of the telegraph, telephones, automobiles, cinema, radio, television and so on. In fact, there is a whole Twitter account – Pessimists Archive – dedicated to historical news reports about how one or another kind of new-fangled technology meant that the end was nigh.

The benefits of smartphones and their like are politicised by both the neoliberal Right, who stress their transformation of knowledge acquisition and personal leisure, and by some on the Left, who see criticism of modernity and progress – especially an aspect of modernity beloved by youth – as inherently conservative.

One of the most nefarious effects of social media is the way it brings the inequalities of the world into stark contrast. The Oxford philosopher James Williams notes that in the past, 'all the world's moral transgressions weren't competing for our attention every day' – according to a study in the US and Canada, less than 5 per cent of the population will ever experience a truly moral misdeed themselves. Thanks to smartphones, however, 'if anyone experiences a misdeed, then everyone potentially experiences it'.[45] Inequality is nothing new, but now through Instagram and Twitter we can see people who apparently have enviable and unattainable lives, or at least can create a realistic facsimile of such a life. The 'availability heuristic' – the idea that we hate what we can see and hear about – means that social media allows us to find out about all kinds of things to which we would have earlier remained oblivious, and this increases our potential for anger, envy and resentment.

In 2018, the British academic and journalist Will Hutton wrote that you can 'turn on the TV or visit a middle-class shopping mall and a very different and unattainable world presents itself', which leads to people thinking that they 'are valueless', so that they 'resort to drugs, antidepressants and booze . . . eat junk food and watch [their] ill-treated body balloon'. Hutton concluded that 'it is not just poverty, but growing relative poverty in an era of rising inequality, with all its psychological side-effects, that is the killer'.[46] Even at the time, this seemed like a charmingly naive understanding of technology and capitalism; you do not need to turn on the TV, or go anywhere, to have this inequity thrust in your face: nearly everyone has small rectangles in their pockets, which many people look at obsessively from the first thing in the morning to the last thing at night, broadcasting this inequality more or less every waking minute, including when walking down the street, lying in bed or sitting on the toilet.

As Roger McNamee – a long-time silicon valley investor and former mentor to Facebook founder Mark Zuckerberg – has it, when it was confined to computers, the 'persuasive technology' used by social media companies was no more harmful than it was on television; however, smartphones 'changed everything' and user count and usage 'exploded'.[47] After reading about a thirteen-year-old girl in North Texas who woke to the smell of something burning and found that her phone had overheated and melted into the sheets, the psychology professor Jean M. Twenge wondered why anyone would sleep with their phone next to them. The next day she asked her undergraduates:

Their answers were a profile in obsession. Nearly all slept with their phone, putting it under their pillow, on the mattress, or at the very least within arm's reach of the bed. They checked social media right before they went to sleep, and reached for their phone as soon as they woke up in the morning . . . if they woke in the middle of the night, they often ended up looking at their phone.[48]

Today, the number of people who check their phone within five minutes of waking ranges from one-fifth of people in France to two-thirds in South Korea.[49]

There is a certain amount of scepticism about the amount of damage smartphones can cause. Chief among these sceptics is Tom Chivers, who stresses that data on the impact of smartphones, social media and technology on mental health are often unreliable. Furthermore, there are many benefits to the use of mobile phones, such as allowing otherwise lonely or unpopular kids to connect with others from across the world. Many of the bullied and lonely teenage goths or gays from pre-smartphone days could today find comfort in being part of a much larger online community of like-minded souls. And there are many benefits to child physical and mental health from these changes: today's kids are less likely to be kidnapped, hurt in car crashes, smoke, drink or become pregnant. But at the same time, this heightened connectivity cuts both ways, as excluded kids can find out about and see all the fun parties other kids are having.

Ultimately it is difficult, if not impossible, to quantify the effect that smartphones have on kids' development and emotional wellbeing, but the lack of conclusive data does not mean we should share Chivers's Panglossian attitude. The tech tycoons themselves, interestingly, are less sanguine, and there is a whole litany of quotes from tech entrepreneurs denouncing smartphones and social media. When asked what his daughters felt about the iPad, the late Steve Jobs replied that 'they've never seen one', while Bill Gates forbade his kids from having mobile phones until they entered high school. The former Facebook executive assistant Athena Chavarria has said that 'the Devil lives in our phones', while Chamath Palihapitiya, a former senior executive for the company, warns that tech capitalists have 'created tools that are ripping apart the social fabric of how society works', and insists that his children 'aren't allowed to use that shit'. Jonathan Rosenstein, one of the creators of the 'Like' button, has deleted his own Facebook account.[50]

Naturally, this attitude is easier if you are blessed with plenty of time to supervise your kids and provide other distractions, or can pay for someone else to do this; among the London super-rich, it is common to require nannies to sign 'no phone' contracts, pledging to prevent their charges from using phones, or from using their own in front of them. South Hampstead High School, an elite private school in London, asks parents to ban phones from the table during mealtimes and insist that they are charged outside bedrooms during the night.[51]

In recent years Facebook has received growing criticism from a host of different people and organisations, and there is a developing subgenre of books that condemn the social media giant. In *Zucked*, his 2019 account of the rise of the social media giant, McNamee paints a sympathetic portrait of Zuckerberg as conscientious and idealistic, but argues that this idealism is 'unbuffered by realism or empathy'. Significantly, according to McNamee, Zuckerberg 'assumed that everyone would view and use Facebook the way he did'.[52]

This hits on one of the key issues with many social media platforms: the (invariably) men who founded them tend to be very different from the majority of users. Zuckerberg, for example, hails from a comfortable middle-class family, won a place at Harvard, and left to become a billionaire in his twenties. He met his wife while at university, and they have remained together, apparently happily, ever since. This kind of professional success and personal fulfilment is not, to put it mildly, characteristic of problematic social media users – those who use the platforms to abuse others, agitate for extreme politics, spread conspiracy theories or suffer from poor mental health due to their use of the platforms.

The difference between the mindset of tech engineers and ordinary users is nicely encapsulated by the adoption of 'blue ticks' in Facebook Messenger and WhatsApp to indicate when a recipient has read a message. For a happily married man like Zuckerberg, this was a useful and harmless innovation – why wouldn't you want to know when someone has read your message? But millions of lovelorn teens and twenty-somethings (and possibly many much older people) can testify to the emotional impact of seeing those blue ticks appearing on a message that is not returned. These unintended misjudgements of the consequences of their innovations are the least of the crimes on social media platforms' charge sheet. The most serious misdeeds stem from their fundamental purpose: to keep users scrolling, no matter what.

As McNamee argues, social media platforms 'prey on weaknesses in human psychology, using ideas from propaganda, public relations, and slot machines to create habits, then addiction'. Anyone who has ever found themselves compulsively scrolling through their phone while brushing their teeth, urinating or even during sex – as one in ten Americans reportedly do – can testify to the addictive nature of social media. And, as with all addictions, knowledge of the harm it is doing does not by itself allow people to stop using. Plenty of people know full well how sad they feel after looking at perfect bodies on Instagram, or how angry the nonsense on Twitter makes them, and yet they keep coming back for more. This sort of response has been noted in lab rats, who will stop pressing a lever if it dispenses food regularly or not at all – but if they are rewarded rarely but irregularly, they will never stop pressing.[53]

In trying to resist the allure of social media, the individual is fighting against the arrayed forces of capitalism and Silicon Valley. As the philosopher James Williams notes, 'thousands of the world's brightest psychologists, statisticians, and designers are now spending the majority of their waking lives figuring out how to tear down your willpower', so to suggest that people should simply have more will-power doesn't really cut it.[54] This addiction is not only harmful to individuals, but has broader effects on civil society. The spread of social media has allowed more than two billion people (and count-ing) to curate their own reality and sort themselves into groups where they don't hear alternative views, and has promoted digital interac-tion as an alternative to real life.[55]

Just as technology permitted social media platforms to extend their control over their users, now the reality distortion of the socials is being taken up by technology companies. Millennial writer Emily Bootle notes that 'photo editing apps and Instagram filters have allowed millions of women to make themselves more Kardashian-like as their picture is taken, increasing the "Instagram vs reality" divide that causes body image and self-esteem problems for many women, especially young women, online.'[56] The headphone manufac-turers Bose now sells a product called Hearphones, which allow users to focus only on a desired source and block out all other sound. The product tagline on its website boasts that it will allow you to 'focus on the voices you want to hear – and filter out the noises you don't – so you can comfortably hear every word. From now on, how you hear is up to you.'[57] As with much of the other technology and phenomena discussed in this chapter, this is not an entirely original innovation – thirty years ago Iain Chambers wrote of how the Sony Walkman allows for 'imposing your soundscape on the surrounding aural envi-ronment and thereby domesticating the external world' – but it repre-sents a marked innovation in the technology and escalation of the pervasiveness of the phenomenon.[58]

The adverse effects of Facebook on individual mental health and the health of civil society are not the greatest crimes of the medium,

which can be used for violent and even genocidal aims. As the journalist Arwa Mahdawi wrote in the *Guardian*, Facebook was instru-
mental in atrocities committed against the Rohingya people in
Myanmar in 2018, and the company later hired a PR firm to discredit
its critics by claiming, disturbingly, that they were agents of George
Soros – a folk devil of the alt-Right and common target of antisemitic
conspiracy theories.[59]

Social media platforms are not the only elements of smartphones
with negative effects for young people; many other apps also have
notably deleterious effects, not least popular dating apps such as
Tinder and Grindr. A study of 1300 students by the American
Psychological Association asked participants to rate how they felt
about aspects of their body image and self-esteem, with questions
such as 'how satisfied are you with your appearance?' and 'how likely
are you to make physical comparisons to others?', with the final question asking the participants whether or not they used Tinder. The
researchers found that Tinder users had lower levels of self-worth,
were less satisfied with their faces and looks, and more ashamed of
their bodies. They were also more likely to compare themselves to
others and to constantly monitor how they looked.[60] In a 2018 poll of
over 200,000 iPhone users, Tinder was ranked ninth among the apps
that made people feel most unhappy, and the gay dating app Grindr
was in first place, with 77 per cent of users claiming it made them feel
miserable. In addition to these mental health implications, dating
apps also make it even easier to stalk and abuse people online, and
through a medium where they are already exposed and vulnerable;
according to a Pew Research Center survey, 28 per cent of people
using online dating sites or apps have been made to feel uncomfortable or harassed.[61]

Even mindfulness and wellbeing apps are problematic; in most
cases their profit depends on selling data about their users to other
companies. While such data is meant to be anonymised, there is

something distasteful about smartphone apps profiting from the mental health issues brought on, at least for some people, by other apps.[62] The suspicion that criticising smartphones or social media is somehow conservative correlates with how closely the app in question is associated with young people. Many on the Left are happy to criticise Facebook due to its apparent influence on the Brexit vote and the rise of Donald Trump, and will similarly blame Twitter for allowing the latter to lambast his enemies and curate his connection with his base. But Instagram is not viewed as political in this sense, and given its predominant use by young people, there is a sense not only that it is good, but also somehow important. The British literary and political magazine the *New Statesman* has several journalists apparently dedicated to reporting the goings-on of social media, and a weekly newsletter driven by the same.

This is despite the adverse impact of Instagram on mental health, in particular through quantifying popularity and increasing narcissism; a study from Swansea University found that people who repeatedly took selfies suffered from a 25 per cent increase in narcissistic tendencies.[63] Tom Chivers argues that platforms such as Instagram are no worse than traditional media such as celebrity or fitness magazines, which also offer a plethora of unrealistic body and beauty standards, but this fails to take account of two important differences. Firstly, the sheer numbers: it is impossible to quantify the seemingly endless numbers of people hawking their appearance on Instagram, in contrast to the decidedly finite number of people in a magazine. Secondly, there is the ostensible 'everyman' nature of most of the men and women of Instagram: a few years ago, looking at an actor or model, most women would have concluded, *Well, these are some of the most beautiful women in the world, very few people look like that, so it's no shame that I don't,* and instead compared themselves to women they knew from real life (which in itself was painful enough for some). Likewise, a man contemplating the abs of a meathead in

Men's Health would have understood that this was an exceptional specimen who worked out for a living. Today, there are not only endless numbers of such women and men on social media, but they are apparently 'ordinary', and the implication is that anyone could look like that if they could only eat and exercise properly, or afford the surgery.

As expressed by Tolentino, the particular problem with Instagram is that it has created a culture where 'ordinary faces are routinely photographed for quantified approval' and 'it is politically important to designate everyone as beautiful'.[64] Furthermore, the 'Like' function of most social media platforms means that things that might have been subjective are now quantified; people who might have thought that they were less attractive or popular than their friend now have this confirmed by numbers. Again, while the effect of this – unlike online popularity – is difficult to quantify, there is some evidence we can draw on. Dr Max Malik, a cosmetic surgeon based in London, states that 'there is a hugely prevalent trend with young girls asking for bigger lips and contoured cheeks in a bid to emulate their filtered selfies on social media', something made more concerning since children as young as thirteen can access these filters. Melissa Atkinson, a psychologist at the University of Bath, warns that 'particularly in Western society, the appearance ideals that are promoted to us reflect such a narrow ideal of beauty that, for most people, it's unachievable', and that people who become used to seeing their face through a filter can become 'dependent' on the distorting lens of social media.[65] Nor is this the preserve of Western countries: as of 2021, South Korea has the highest proportion of young women undergoing cosmetic surgery.

Fears around social media, and Instagram in particular, extend to people whose career has benefitted from the medium. The American popstar Selina Gomez, at one point the most followed profile on the app, feels compelled to frequently delete and reopen her account due to trolls making her feel depressed: 'It's like they want to cut to your soul. Imagine all the insecurities that you already feel about yourself and having someone write a paragraph pointing out every little thing – even if it's just physical.' Gomez says she is particularly worried about the impact it is having on people from her generation without her clout and celebrity, especially young girls.[66]

The father of Molly Russell, a British teen who took her own life in 2017, specifically blames the scrapbook site Pinterest for contributing to her death, through allowing users to upload images of self-harm and suicide. This demonstrates a clear innovation of the internet and social media; while there are records of humans killing themselves since antiquity, until around ten or twenty years ago, they would not have been able instantly to access a whole community of like-minded people who could swap tips and give encouragement. Specifically, Ian Russell blames social media, as the only media his daughter had access to while in her room came through her phone or iPad. This is another key difference between social and traditional media: it was much easier to hide, remove or prevent access to books, magazines and videotapes; given their centrality to the lives of today's teenagers, it is impossible to do this with phones.

When journalists at the *Sunday Times* created a fake account for a child aged fourteen, the Pinterest algorithm immediately started to suggest pictures relating to suicide, 'including a fist holding white pills and images of blood and cuts'. On Instagram, despite more than twenty complaints made by the paper about images promoting suicide, the company claimed that the images were suitable to be viewed by children over thirteen.[67] A survey of fifty thousand UK schoolchildren by the Headmasters' and Headmistresses' Conference has also found a growth in the trend of 'sadfishing', whereby people make 'exaggerated claims about their emotional problems to generate sympathy', which left young people with genuine mental health problems 'facing unfair and distressing criticism'.[68]

Facebook argues that passive consumption of social media can increase mental health risks, but active consumption can counter them.[69] That may well be the case – certainly people aimlessly scrolling through these apps, drinking in the endless feed of idiocy, confrontation and cosmetic-surgery-brochure countenances might be less unhappy than someone who is actively posting their own profundities and carefully curated lifestyle pics. However, there are clear risks involved with increased participation: every post you make increases the chance of you being ridiculed, abused, piled-on or, worst of all, becoming one of those people whose social media faux pas is so great that they reach the highest levels of internet infamy.

As Richard Seymour notes, social media provides us with 'snippets of information, appearing within microseconds of one another', which all manage to 'set the wheels whirring, triggering mental and emotional work that often goes on throughout the day'.[70] Here's a political opinion that you disagree with and makes you angry; here's an acquaintance and their perfect new house; here's an obnoxious celebrity apparently famous for no reason – this constant bombardment of stimuli has a discombobulating effect. The confluence of capitalism and social media is a key theme in the writing of Tolentino, who argues that 'the underlying idea between twenty-first century technology and culture' is that 'ordinary personhood would seamlessly readjust itself around whatever within it would sell'.[71] The social media companies were founded by a particular kind of entrepreneur, and their apps teach users to think of themselves as would-be entrepreneurs, if they could only get enough likes and shares. This idea is personified in the rise of the 'influencer', an individual who can monetise their social media following – itself often based on their appearance – to fund a career of sorts.

In his book *The Twittering Machine*, Seymour describes social media as a 'stock market of status' where users engage in a 'competitive like-hunt, status-hungry and celebrity-obsessed'. While this has benefitted some people who do not have or could not have such status in the offline world, this benefit does not make up for the extension of competition into yet another area of life: for all of the 'ordinary' people who have become rich or famous through the internet, there are a great many more people who are angered and aggrieved by the medium.[72] As he points out, the only people online who are 'genuinely liberated' from the constraints of identity are trolls, as their anonymity means they can enact 'the utopian promise of the internet' by saying and doing whatever they want without concern for how it makes them look.[73] This has myriad negative consequences for people's self-esteem, reputation and financial solvency. That anyone can reply to Twitter posts has also fundamentally altered political statements – they now hew closer to the settled opinion of whichever group the poster is a member of, the better to draw on reinforcements.

A meta-analysis of over fifty different studies has found that social media use is linked with increased narcissism. Other studies have concluded that social media pressure has led to more young people undergoing cosmetic surgery, and found that the pursuit of fame is the main value espoused by today's children's television shows.[74] It is difficult for people who are not young to appreciate the power and currency of fame for younger people, even as it is increasingly divorced from financial success. In the early 2000s, the British television character Alan Partridge complained that he wanted to be famous, not infamous; the eponymous star of the cult film *Withnail & I* (1987) lamented that the only programme he was likely to get on was the fucking news; today, many young people would be happy with either.

The significance of the internet and social media in particular is one important aspect of what it means to be young that is near universal, especially due to the increase in smartphone use by young people across the Global South in the past decade. It is often observed of the business model of social media companies that they are selling us to the advertisers; we are not the consumers, but the product. One of the by-products of this is that being young in today's world means selling yourself constantly; the concentration and focus that might once have been required only while filling out an application form or at a job interview are now required all the time, through your social media profiles.

While downward mobility is a feature of life for a specific type of young person in the Global North, and is not universal, there is a real and increasing disparity between the lifestyles young people aspire to and the ability of the twenty-first century economy to provide such lifestyles. This aspiration combines with a lack of opportunities to lead many young people to sell themselves online, both figuratively in the sense of flogging their identity or literally in terms of the burgeoning online sex industry. Sadly, pornography, modelling and Instagram influencing are the only careers in which women regularly out-earn men.

Nor is this consequence of the internet and social media limited to the Global North. In 2012, a group of British Conservative MPs produced a pamphlet, *Britannia Unchanged*, in which they claimed that 'whereas Indian children aspire to be doctors or businessmen, the British are more interested in football and pop music', which displayed an ignorance of the millions of Indian children who do indeed dream, however improbably, of being the next Sachin Tendulkar or Aishwarya Rai.[75]

The psychologist Tess Brigham reckons there are several reasons why millennials hate their jobs, but important ones are unrealistic expectations, impatience and frustration with the pace of their career advancement, and 'social media overload, which can create a distorted reality where everyone else seems to have an amazing life'.[76] Aside from the possible mental health problems engendered in young women and men by these influencers, they often suffer tremendously themselves, from the barbs of trolls and the pressure of having to maintain an impossibly curated image, or from even more tragic consequences: in 2018, an Australian model and influencer was found dead on a billionaire's yacht off the coast of Mexico, and there have been several suicides of people associated with the British TV show *Love Island*.[77]

The superficiality of this world was revealed through the shenanigans of Anna Sorokin, aka Anna Delvey, who, on pure chutzpah alone, conned the New York social scene into believing she was a millionaire heiress. As her lawyer told the jury during her fraud trial, 'in her world, this is what her social circle did. Everyone's life was perfectly curated for social media. People were fake. People were phoney. And money was made on hype alone.' These kinds of swindlers and confidence tricksters are nothing new, but their actions are now facilitated and made easier by social media. The psychologist Maria Konnikova, whose book *The Confidence Game* analyses con artists, argues that due to social media, 'the barrier of entry is so much lower', as perfectly ordinary people can curate their lives to give a misleading impression that would have been impossible ten years ago.[78]

Members of the Kardashian family, described by Piers Morgan as 'vacuous, talentless ... the most shameless, grasping family in America' – and on this issue he knows whereof he speaks – are viewed by some ostensibly left-wing writers as somehow inspirational, and criticism of them is depicted as somehow conservative.[79] When Barack Obama upbraided Kim Kardashian in 2013, a writer for *Vice* – the house bible of hipsterdom – advised him to 'look past the relatively harmless world of reality-television materialism and examine his administration'. This writer noted that 'Kanye West grew up with a single mother in urban Chicago, toiled at the mall for years while tirelessly writing beats, and eventually became a superstar, creating some of the decades most loved and iconic albums in the process. And like me, Kim is the descendent of survivors of the Armenian genocide.'[80]

This quote nicely encapsulates a certain kind of left-liberal response to critiques of celebrity, which replicates traditional conservative defences of privilege. Kanye West may well have grown up with a single mother, but came from a notably more middle-class background than most rappers, as acknowledged in his music, while Kardashian is indeed descended from genocide survivors, but nonetheless grew up enjoying a luxurious lifestyle vastly removed from that of most Americans – never mind most Armenians.

Way back in 2012 – the equivalent of the Palaeolithic age in internet years – a British head teacher called Helen Wright prophesied that Kardashian represented 'the decline of Western civilisation'. Wright's argument was that the success of someone apparently so vapid, 'famous for being famous', was a direct break with the tradition whereby people were celebrated for their achievements. Responding to these comments at the time, Dr Angie Hobbs, professor in the public understanding of philosophy at the UK's University of Warwick, concurred with Wright, arguing that although human beings had desired status since at least Plato's time, 'when a society starts divorcing status from doing honourable things and awards it for materialistic things, that's when you are in trouble. You have to look very carefully at why people want to be famous, what they are lacking. And at why people who don't want to be famous themselves want to follow famous people, what they are lacking.' Nonetheless she was still optimistic:

Already it is impossible for anyone to be as famous as the Beatles, for example, because already the media conversation is so diverse. You can be famous in one chunk but unknown in another. No matter how many videos and blogs you put up, no one will be watching. So celebrity itself will implode ... Perhaps that's why Kardashian herself is exploiting every moment of her already extended 15 minutes of fame.[81]

Unfortunately, these comments did not prove prophetic. Rather than implode, celebrity has expanded and morphed; rather than prove the exception, Kardashian proved a harbinger of a future where celebrities would achieve success through selling their identities, rather than their talents. As Tolentino notes, the two most prominent families in American politics and culture today – the Trumps and the Kardashians – rose to the top because they understood 'how little substance is required to package the self as an endlessly monetizable asset'.[82] By itself, this is not necessarily a problem, but the rise of the Kardashians suggested to hundreds of thousands – if not millions – of impressionable minds that they too could have such success if they were willing to sell themselves in the same manner, resulting in severe consequences for some young people. A reality TV producer, explaining to Tolentino why she has no shortage of applicants to appear on her shows, despite the risk of public humiliation and online abuse, says that 'everyone thinks they could be a better Kardashian than the Kardashians . . . everyone likes to have an audience. Everyone thinks they deserve one.'[83]

The internet has also hyper-charged 'fandom', as it is referred to, whereby children and teenagers obsessively follow and support certain celebrities. Rather than a politically neutral cultural trend, this has been depicted by many on the Left as politically significant and generally good and important, as when fans of the Korean pop band BTS registered for tickets at Donald Trump's ill-fated Oklahoma rally in June 2020, contributing to the myriad unfilled seats in the BOK Center.

Yet there are reasons to believe that 'fandom' can be harmful. Ruth Sims, a social psychologist, argues that fandom attracts by 'filling a need if someone has something missing in their life . . . Learning everything you can about a particular person can help give a focus, and might give you a lifestyle, skills, knowledge that you can aspire to . . . or they might enable you to "live vicariously" through their own adventures.'[84]

Similar to hipsters, who refuse to let their lack of talent stand in the way of their lifestyle aspirations, fandom could allow mediocre or unhappy people to be part of something bigger than themselves. While this can clearly be beneficial to some, it also has its downsides. Dr Sims warns that sharing an opinion which unexpectedly jars with the rest of the fandom community can lead to people being ostracised or bullied, with kids at risk of being summarily and brutally rejected by the very people closest to them. And I say kids, because really this is something that should be restricted to kids. If you are an adult who 'stans' a celebrity or group in this way, you have to ask yourself why you need to rely on someone else for your own sense of identity.

There are clearly many benefits of social media for children, not least that it facilitates communication for those with various disabilities, such as Down's syndrome or autistic spectrum condition. It could well be that it is not the medium itself that is the problem but rather how it is used. One of the key issues with social media is that it deprives human communication of several aspects – such as body language and tone – that are key to its success. Devoid of these markers, communication on social media can easily descend into misunderstanding and acrimony. This may be good for people who struggle with traditional, face-to-face communication, but it can be difficult for everyone else. Yet a key argument for the outpatient treatment of people with learning difficulties and mental health problems was the negative effects of institutionalisation and the importance of them having 'real life' contact with other people, even if this might cause distress in the short term. It is ironic then, that people who would presumably oppose the institutionalisation of people with learning difficulties or mental illnesses would also vigorously defend social media, which has a similar institutionalising effect.

Moaning about social media is not another example of reactionary Luddites railing at a world they don't understand, and nor is social media an obvious asset to progressive politics. James Williams is clear that we must reject the related temptation to say, 'Oh well, perhaps the next generation will be better adjusted to this attentional warfare by virtue of having been born into it.'[85] Young people themselves, incidentally, appreciate this more than the Panglossian political and cultural commentators of older generations. Many prominent millennials and Gen Z-ers have spoken out against socials and the effect they have on individuals and the broader community. The writer and actor Michaela Coel notes sadly that social media is 'the only place we feel like we have power and where justice might be done', and that young people use it as a way of 'fulfilling a fantasy of trial and retribution and justice there because it doesn't really exist in the real world'.[86]

When it comes to social media and mental health it appears that we are heading towards an iceberg, and it is not alarmist or reactionary to say so. In response to the myriad of voices crying out 'There's an iceberg!', to say: 'Hmmm, well the sonar doesn't show anything, and I think I'll trust the science over subjective and fallible human eyesight, thank-you-very-much' is a clear mistake. Aside from the mental health implications, social media has had a profoundly negative impact on politics. Without wishing to revisit the same ground as my previous book, *A Left for Itself: Left-wing Hobbyists and Performative Radicalism*, the internet encourages political hobbyism, whereby we engage in a facsimile of political action without actually achieving anything. Memes, tropes and phrases associated with the online Left such as 'the ratio', 'wallet inspectors', etc., are not quite the sigh of an oppressed creature, but maybe the smarm of a dispossessed creature; they don't have much, but they have this. People of all kinds of political persuasions engage in harmful behaviour online, furiously lashing out while knowing that counterattacks will follow, in a very modern form of self-harm. They cannot bear to leave, and even when they do, feel obliged to tell people that they are leaving.

With social media and mental health, we must resist the temptation to say 'there is nothing new under the sun' or depict any claims about the novelty of current developments as inherently alarmist or reactionary. We should also resist seeing everything associated with youth as inherently significant or meaningful. The politics of young people are diffuse and sometimes contradictory – exactly as we would expect. Both the nightmares of tabloid hacks and the wide-eyed admiration of left-wing activists are wide of the mark. Yes, as young people age we can expect those in the West to maintain their progressive values, but there is no guarantee that they will do so in terms of economics, much less party politics.

Young people, like the other groups discussed in this book, are not a homogenous bloc to be appropriated and used for various ends, but complicated human beings, containing disparate multitudes and prone to contradiction and change. It is essential for any political project that wants to capture their allegiance in the future to be aware of this. This goes for political projects of the Left as well as those of the Right. Today the youth seem to be for the Left – there is no guarantee that this will remain the case.

Conclusion

Few of the examples of identity myth-making discussed in this book are entirely novel. Twenty years ago Paul Gilroy wrote of the trend within African-American academia that held that their fellow blacks were on the wrong road, 'and it is the intellectual's job to give them a new direction' by 'donating the racial awareness that the masses seem to lack'.[1] But the development of the internet and of social media in particular has created the ideal conditions for the growing dominance and pervasiveness of these myths.

Rather than making people better-informed about and more sympathetic towards others, this technology seems to fuel ignorance and anger; possibly because the internet encourages us to emphasise and exaggerate aspects of our identities, so that we see each other both more narrowly and particularly. The disconnect between the 'base' of people's lives and the 'superstructure' of their perceived and projected identity has never been greater.

In many ways a focus on identity is a way of compensating for a lack of agency and resources; given the inability of the modern economy and society to provide status, people turn to their identities instead. You may have noticed the recent rise in the frequency of possessive pronouns: do you want *your* receipt? How is *your* meal? It is of a piece with the substitution of 'based' for 'lives', as in he is 'based' in London, suggesting that individuals have some kind of corporate identity greater than themselves. In America, this trend has traditionally expressed itself through names: even the most wretched and dispossessed has control over their own name. 'I want my name!' screams Eddie Carbone at the end of Arthur Miller's *A View from the Bridge*, and for Americans this desire to have control over their own name – in a literal sense – is very important, hence their use of middle names and initials and regnal-number and fastidiousness around titles.

If identity myths provide compensation for material dispossession, it is thin gruel. Those who are theoretically advantaged by modern society – men, white people, heterosexuals, the rich and middle class – do not consider themselves particularly privileged. Many of those who fall back on identity for a sense of self-esteem are suffering indeed: even those well-paid, ostensibly professionals are unhappy. In the US, most workers say they would take an 8 per cent pay cut to maintain the ability to work from home two or three days a week.[2]

This, again, is a problem of perceptions. White, heterosexual men very rarely see threats or abuse against people unlike themselves, and so they assume it has disappeared. They do see Pride festivals, the prominence of fabulous gay men in popular culture, and people mocking straight white men on social media. The rise in 'soft' anti-semitism, or at very least the perception that Jews aren't really under threat, is another notable consequence of this disconnect between perceptions and reality. If you think that Jews stopped having anything to worry about seventy years ago, and that, say, Muslims are the main victims now, then you will have a very hard time understanding concerns about antisemitism and why some otherwise left-liberal Jewish people are ardent Zionists.

That appeals to identity are starkly limited as mobilising tactics for achieving social justice is a key lesson of this book, especially since people's perceptions of disadvantage are hopelessly subjective. 'Educate yourself' goes the online refrain encouraging individuals to avail themselves of the plentiful literature on particular identity issues and improve their own attitudes accordingly. But any political project dependent on people having a certain level of education is doomed to fail. Imagine if the Thatcher and Reagan strategists predicated their success on a decent chunk of the population suddenly reading Milton Friedman and Friedrich Hayek.

A friend of mine volunteers for a charity trying to rehabilitate sex offenders who have been released from prison. One of these men has decidedly right-wing views and spends a lot of time ranting about Brexit and immigrants and '*Guardian*-reading academics'. His malice towards that latter constituency strikes me as strange, as while there are plenty of people with apparently paradoxical politics, I have never encountered someone with such spite towards the very people standing between himself and chemical castration. My friend wants to ask him what people like him think should be done with people like him. It is a useful reminder that people's politics relate to their personal situation in unpredictable ways. You might think that a sex offender, whose release and state-funded rehabilitation is dependent on the progress of a particular kind of political liberalism, might extend to other unpopular minority groups some of the compassion extended to him.

Likewise, many women, black and brown people, gay people, trans people and so on do not let their experiences of prejudice or humiliation or worse translate into a broad, 'rainbow politics' of friendship to all. The Indian politician Bal Thackeray, founder of the Hindu nationalist Shiv Sena party, railed against migrants into his state of Maharashtra despite the fact that his own parents were migrants. In particular, he attacked south Indians, whom he accused of being better-educated and taking the better jobs, with slogans including *Pungi bajao aur lungi hatao* (Blow the horn, remove the lungi), a call for physical violence against those who wear the lungi sarong common in south Indian dress – despite the fact that Thackeray *himself* wore lungis.[3]

We should not expect that because people have been victimised or disadvantaged due to an aspect of their identity, they will feel empathy with or sympathy for other people with similar identities, never mind vastly dissimilar identities. As Wesley Yang writes of the experience of himself and the other academically gifted children at his high school, 'being bullied during our school days made us not lovers of humanity but victimizers of others the moment we had the numbers on our side'.[4] This book has covered a working-class city demonising residents of a particular estate, who themselves look down on a segregated block within their own community; plenty of black and brown people across the world holding an equal variety of political views; gay and female far-Right leaders; and conservative young people. Anyone who wants to understand politics in the twenty-first century needs to start from a position that these identities are more complex than we suppose and manifest in complicated ways, rather than being surprised when that is the case.

This book has tried to focus on elements of identity myth-making from across the political spectrum. Usually, the Left is merely ignorant while the Right is disingenuous, but I have focused more on the Left as I have an interest in seeing the Left improve how it deals with matters around identity so that it can fare better at the polls. When it comes to specific groups, while the Left might talk about material reality – housing, education, mental health – the Right is able to counter by talking about chimerical 'progress' for those identities that nonetheless make them feel threatened. It points to advances made by different identities and says: 'Look, you've got all this, what more do you want?' The Right would do that anyway, even without the excesses of left-wing identity myths; but the latter makes its strategy more effective. Those on the Left should focus on commonalities that cut across 'identity' divisions.

For example, Wesley Yang notes that American Asians don't pick up the implicit knowledge about social norms and propriety transmitted by those who already have it, despite their storied academic achievements.[5] The means many Asians apply to achieve academic success, with its narrow emphasis on rote memorisation and test preparation, 'could not be more out of step with the attitudes and practices of the socially liberal elite that Asians aspire to join'.[6] This is like many working-class kids in the UK, who can achieve academic success but, shorn of intangible cultural assets, don't necessarily bank the rewards they were led to believe such success entailed. There are all kinds of such commonalities analysed in this book that cut across identities, from access to quality housing, steady employment, fresh air and good quality public transport, to robust mental health provision.

The slow disappearance of class from our discourse and our understanding of the world has fanned the flames of this gap between perceptions and reality. If you class all white, straight men as the same, whether billionaires, politicians or media moguls, then it is harder for poor white men to perceive their privilege. Further, it makes them more likely to identify with Tory toffs, because they're constantly being told they're one and the same. But ultimately, any politics that relies upon the privileged seeing themselves as privileged – or indeed the underprivileged seeing themselves as victims – is bound to fail.

One way to end the increasing dominance of the identity myths over our lives is a clear break with the political economy of the past four decades. At the time of writing, it appears that Joe Biden has come to this realisation: for many years the centrists' centrist, the consummate Washington insider who played a prominent role in the Democratic Party's accommodation with neoliberalism, he seems to have realised late in life that the only way to stop his country tearing itself apart is to turn on the tap of federal munificence. Would the army of online trolls be so great if they had jobs that gave them happy and rewarding lives? Surely the volume of hate online would be lessened by an increased supply of jobs in academia and media, and greater funding of mental health provision. Biden thinks he can end identitarian strife not through concessions to the claims of identity, but rather through child benefit, parental leave, expanded health and unemployment insurance, well-paying jobs and infrastructural investment. I think and hope he is right.

Acknowledgements

I'd like to thank my agent Matthew Hamilton and my publisher Andreas Campomar for their encouragement and assistance in bringing this book from conception to publication. I would also like to thank Howard Watson for his fastidious copyediting. There is a prohibitively long list of academics, politicians, journalists and online personalities, too long to include here, to whom I owe a debt, but suffice to say if you have helped me in any way over the years, I am very grateful.

I would also like to thank all my friends and family and, in particular, my wife, Michal Huss, who puts up with my ways and is a perpetual font of insightful guidance, particularly in terms of persuading me that angry slights at various enemies don't contribute to the overall text.

This book was written entirely during the 2020–2021 Covid-19 pandemic and, while it would be inappropriate to 'thank' the virus for causing the successive lockdowns which facilitated the writing, it certainly did help. The pandemic also made starkly apparent the distance between those who know such a crisis will likely leave them fundamentally unscathed, and those for whom it poses an existential risk, and so I suppose I am thankful I'm in the former category.

Notes

Part I: Class

Chapter 1

1   Deborah Ross, 'Got a kettle and a dog? Have a ticket to Britain', *The Times*, 18 July 2020.

2   Claire Ainsley, *The New Working Class* (Bristol: Policy Press, 2018), p. 27.

3   https://www.bsa.natcen.ac.uk/latest-report/british-social-attitudes-33/social-class.aspx.

4   Sam Friedman, Dave O'Brien and Ian McDonald, 'Deflecting Privilege: Class Identity and the Intergenerational Self', *Sociology*, vol. 55, no. 4 (2021).

5   Sam Friedman, 'Why do so many professional, middle-class Brits insist they're working class?', *Guardian*, 18 January 2021.

6   As recalled by Linda Ali at 'What is this "black" in "black" History and Culture?: Interdisciplinary Reflections upon Blackness and Racial Categories', Black History Month seminar, University of York, 26 October 2010.

7   Stephen Bush, 'Marvel's *Black Panther* and the politics of diverse superheroes', *New Statesman*, 16 February 2018.

8   James Baldwin, *Notes of a Native Son* (Boston: Beacon Press, 2012), pp. 147–8.

9   Paul Gilroy, *The Black Atlantic* (London: Verso, 1999), p. 184.

10 Darren McGarvey, *Poverty Safari: Understanding the Anger of Britain's Underclass* (London: Picador, 2018), p. 28.

11 Ainsley, *New Working Class*, p. 17.

12 Ibid., p. 129.

13 Kerry Hudson, *Lowborn: Growing Up, Getting Away and Returning to Britain's Poorest Towns* (London: Chatto & Windus, 2019), p. 230.

14 Deborah Mattinson, *Beyond the Red Wall: Why Labour Lost, How the Conservatives Won and What Will Happen Next?* (London: Biteback, 2020), p. 252.

15 Ainsley, *New Working Class*, pp. 68–9 and 129.

16 Ibid., p. 25.

17 Ibid., p. 2.

18 'Average household income, UK: financial year ending 2019', Office for National Statistics, 2019.

19 Ainsley, *New Working Class*, p. 25.

20 Lisa McKenzie, *Getting By: Estates, Class and Culture in Austerity Britain* (Bristol: Policy Press, 2015), p. 74.

21 Ibid., p. 86.

22 Ibid., p. 156.

23 Ainsley, *New Working Class*, p. 60.

24 Ibid., p. 81.

25 Geoffrey Evans and James Tilley, *The New Politics of Class* (Oxford: Oxford University Press, 2017), p. 205.

26 McKenzie, *Getting By*, p. 41.

27 Evans and Tilley, *New Politics of Class*, pp. 123 and 127.

28 Ainsley, *New Working Class*, p. 141.

29 Evans and Tilley, *New Politics of Class*, p. 132.

30 Ibid., p. 163.

31 Steve Rayson, *The Fall of the Red Wall* (self-published, 2020), p. 41.

32 Evans and Tilley, *New Politics of Class*, pp. 147 and 159.

33 Édouard Louis, *Who Killed My Father* (New York: Harvill Secker, 2018), pp. 3–4.

34 Evans and Tilley, *New Politics of Class*, p. 192.

35 Ainsley, *New Working Class*, p. 63.

36 Ibid., p. 136.

37 Nick Cohen, *Pretty Straight Guys* (London: Faber & Faber, 2003), pp. 227–8.

38 Malakaï Sargeant, 'I Watched the Neighbourhood I Grew Up in Get Gentrified', *Vice*, 12 July 2019. Emphasis added.

39 Joe Kennedy, *Authentocrats: Culture, Politics and the New Seriousness* (London: Repeater, 2018), pp. 226–7.

40 Maria Sobolewska and Robert Ford, *Brexitland: Identity, Diversity and the Reshaping of British Politics* (Cambridge: Cambridge University Press, 2020), pp. 24–6.

41 Jonathan Wolff, 'Doctor, doctor . . . we're suffering a glut of PhDs who can't find academic jobs', *Guardian*, 21 April 2015.

42 Robert Crampton, 'Don't write off my son just because he decided not to study A levels', *The Times*, 22 January 2013.

43 https://assets.publishing.service.gov.uk/government/uploads/system/uploads/attachment_data/file/635103/SFR39-2017-MainText.pdf.

44 Stephen Gibbons and Anna Vignoles, 'Geography, choice and participation in higher education in England', *Regional Science and Urban Economics*, vol. 42, nos 1–2 (2012), pp. 98–113.

45 Peter White, 'Geographic and Socio-Economic Inequalities and Access to Higher Education: Is the Proximity of Higher Education Institutions Associated with the Probability of University Attendance for Young People in England?', MA thesis, University of Oxford, 2016.

46 https://www.centrefortowns.org/reports/the-coming-crisis-access-to-health-services-in-our-towns/download.

47 https://www.newstatesman.com/spotlight/devolution/2019/02/why-northern-powerhouse-tale-too-few-cities

48 Lisa Nandy, 'Why the Northern Powerhouse is a tale of too few cities', *New Statesman*, 23 February 2019.

49 https://www.mentalhealth.org.uk/a-to-z/b/black-asian-and-minority-ethnic-bame-communities.

50 https://www.centrefortowns.org/reports/launch-briefing/download.

51 Mattinson, *Beyond the Red Wall*, p. 66.

52 Rayson, *Fall of the Red Wall*, p. 85.

Chapter 2

1 Valerie Wright, '"I know he's trying": gender, deindustrialisation and unemployment in Ferguslie Park, Paisley', paper given at the Working Class Studies Association Conference, University of Kent, September 2019.

2 Brian Reade, *44 Years with the Same Bird* (London: Pan Books, 2009), p. 89.

3 Brian Reade, 'Bible Belt Feels the Wrath of God', *Daily Mirror*, 5 January 2006.

4 Hudson, *Lowborn*, p. 213.

5 Stuart Maconie, *Pies and Prejudice: in Search of the North* (London: Ebury, 2008), pp. 12, 43, 62, 143 and 214.

6 David Langrish, 'Conscription, Tribunals and Sacrifice: The papers of the Middlesex Service Appeals Tribunal', paper given at 'Labour and the First World War' conference at Anglia Ruskin University, 3 May 2014.

7 Trevor Griffiths, *The Lancashire Working Classes c.1880–1930* (Oxford: Clarendon Press, 2001), p. 209.

8 Jon Lawrence, *Me, Me, Me: The Search for Community in Post-war England* (Cambridge: Cambridge University Press, 2019), p. 35.

9 Ibid., p. 40.

10 Ibid., p. 143.

11 Ibid., p. 186.

12 Ibid., p. 188.

13 Ibid., p. 112.

14 Mattinson, *Beyond the Red Wall*, pp. 104 and 195.

15 Lawrence, *Me, Me, Me*, p. 205.

16 Megan Nolan, 'Class, justice and media frenzy: humanising the boys who killed James Bulger', *New Statesman*, 23 January 2019.

17 Hudson, *Lowborn*, p. 156.

18 Ilyas Nagdee, 'Half-Truth Histories . . .', in Shukla and Jones, *Rife*, p. 198.

19 Lawrence, *Me, Me, Me*, pp. 148–9.

20 Mattinson, *Beyond the Red Wall*, p. 46.

21 Ibid., pp. 88–9.

22 Kennedy, *Authentocrats*, p. 98.

23 Sobolewska and Ford, *Brexitland*, p. 180.

24 Kennedy, *Authentocrats*, p. 103.

25 'Twiggy squares up to Sainsbury's in the avocado wars', *Scotsman*, 23 May 2009.

26 McGarvey, *Poverty Safari*, p. 118.

27 Nicholas Preston, 'Dumping the Green Belt', in Shukla and Jones, *Rife*, p. 313.

28 Sargeant, 'I Watched the Neighbourhood I Grew Up in Get Gentrified'.

29 Hudson, *Lowborn*, p. 86.

30 Ibid., p. 88.

31 Suli Breaks, 'Why it is important for young black men to floss (not their teeth)', in Derek Owusu (ed.), *Safe: On Black British Men Reclaiming Space* (London: Orion Books, 2019), p. 28.

32 Ibid., pp. 30–2.

33 Keith Gildart, *Images of England through Popular Music: Class, Youth and Rock 'n' Roll 1955–1976* (Basingstoke: Palgrave Macmillan, 2013), pp. 32–3.

34 Ibid., p. 98.

35 Ibid., p. 85.

36 Mattinson, *Beyond the Red Wall*, p. 38.

37 Ibid., p. 125.

38 Ibid., pp. 128–9.

39 Kennedy, *Authentocrats*, p. 200.

40 Ibid., pp. 184 and 221.

41 Cited in F. O. Shyllon, *Black Slaves in Britain* (London: Oxford University Press for the Institute of Race Relations, 1974), p. x.

42 David Holland, 'The Social Networks of South Asian Migrants in the Sheffield Area During the Early Twentieth Century', *Past & Present*, vol. 236, no. 1 (2017), pp. 249 and 272.

43 Amrit Wilson, *Finding a Voice* (London: Virago, 1978), pp. 18–19.

44 Ibid., p. 136.

45 Akala, *Natives: Race and Class in the Ruins of Empire* (London: Two Roads, 2018), p. 5.

46 Ibid., p. 8.

47 Ibid., pp. 10–11.

48 Jess Bernard, 'Treddin' on Thin Ice', in Owusu, *Safe*, p. 73.

49 Aniefiok Ekpoudom, 'The Sticks', in Owusu, *Safe*, p. 114.

50 Fred Lindop, 'Racism and the working class: strikes in support of Enoch Powell in 1968', *Labour History Review*, vol. 66 (2001), p. 82.

51 Amy Whipple, 'Revisiting the "Rivers of Blood" Controversy. Letters to Enoch Powell', *Journal of British Studies*, vol. 48, no. 3 (2009), pp. 726–8.

52 Sobolewska and Ford, *Brexitland*, p. 99.

53 Ibid., pp. 90–1.

54 Glenn Jordan and Chris Weedon, 'When the subalterns speak, what do they say?', in Paul Gilroy, Laurence Grossberg and Angela McRobbie (eds), *Without Guarantees: In Honour of Stuart Hall* (London: Verso, 2000), pp. 174–5.

55 Hudson, *Lowborn*, p. 66.

56 Ibid., p. 13.

57 McGarvey, *Poverty Safari*, pp. 129–30.

58 Ibid., pp. 147–8.

59 Simon Kuper, 'The revenge of the middle-class anti-elitist', *Financial Times*, 13 February 2020.

60 http://natcen.ac.uk/media/1319222/natcen_brexplanations-report-final-web2.pdf and https://www.ipsos.com/ipsos-mori/en-uk/how-britain-voted-2016-eu-referendum.

61 Matthew Goodwin, 'Populism isn't about class', *UnHerd*, 21 February 2020.

62 Kuper, 'Revenge of the middle-class anti-elitist'.

63 McGarvey, *Poverty Safari*, pp. 129–30.

64 Sobolewska and Ford, *Brexitland*, pp. 61–2.

65 Ibid., p. 82.

66 Ibid., p. 7.

67 Mattinson, *Beyond the Red Wall*, pp. 25–6.

68 Ibid., p. 32.

69 Ibid., p. 256.

70 Lawrence, *Me, Me, Me*, p. 18.

71 Sobolewska and Ford, *Brexitland*, p. 150.

72 Mattinson, *Beyond the Red Wall*, p. 197.

73 Sobolewska and Ford, *Brexitland*, p. 316.

74 Rayson, *Fall of the Red Wall*, p. 13.

75 Reni Eddo-Lodge, *Why I'm No Longer Talking to White People about Race* (London: Bloomsbury, 2018), p. 14.

76 Anne Witchard, 'The Chinese Connection', in Jennifer Craig-Norton, Christhard Hoffmann and Tony Kushner (eds), *Migrant Britain: Histories and Historiographies: Essays in Honour of Colin Holmes* (Abingdon: Routledge, 2018).

77 Vera Chock, 'Yellow', in Nikesh Shukla (ed.), *The Good Immigrant* (London: Unbound, 2016), pp. 42–3.

78 Dave Hill, *Out of His Skin: The John Barnes Story* (Beckenham: WSC Books, 2001), p. 30.

79 Kennedy, *Authentocrats*, p. 92.

80 'Dark Side of the Mersey: The Scallies Rally to Pink Floyd', *The Face Magazine*, January 1989.

81 Hudson, *Lowborn*, p. 155.

82 Lawrence, *Me, Me, Me*, p. 33.

83 'Joe Anderson is first elected Liverpool Mayor after runaway vote success', *Liverpool Echo*, 4 May 2012.

84 Lawrence, *Me, Me, Me*, p. 119.

85 Mattinson, *Beyond the Red Wall*, p. 138.

86 Lawrence, *Me, Me, Me*, p. 18.

87 Ibid., p. 40.

88 Mattinson, *Beyond the Red Wall*, p. 23.

89 Lawrence, *Me, Me, Me*, p. 138.

90 McGarvey, *Poverty Safari*, p. xxii.

91 Ibid., p. 33.

92 Alison Baskerville, 'The Womanly Face of War', paper delivered at 'The war veteran in culture and society: historical and contemporary perspectives' symposium at the University of Leeds, 21 May 2019.

93 Afua Hirsch, *Brit(ish): On Race, Identity and Belonging* (London: Jonathan Cape, 2018), pp. 4–6.

94 Lawrence, *Me, Me, Me*, p. 208.

95 Ibid., p. 47.

96 Evans and Tilly, *New Politics of Class*, p. 165.

97 McGarvey, *Poverty Safari*, p. 90.

98 Ibid., p. 125.

99 Daniel Dylan Wray, 'Home Coming: Driffield, a Small Market Town in East Yorkshire', *Vice*, 21 August 2020.

100 Ibid., pp. 182, 185 and 191–2.

101 McKenzie, *Getting By*, p. 2.

102 Sobolewska and Ford, *Brexitland*, pp. 73–4.

103 Ibid., p. 244.

104 Cosmo Landesman, 'Is snobbery as bad as racism?', *UnHerd*, 18 August 2020.

105 McKenzie, *Getting By*, p. 51.

106 Ibid., p. 86.

107 Ibid., p. 157.

108 Grace Gausden, ' "I now advise winners": One of the UK's first lottery millionaires reveals how she's lived off her £2.7m win – here's 25 top Lotto facts on its anniversary', ThisIsMoney.co.uk, 14 November 2019.

109 Lawrence, *Me, Me, Me*, p. 110.

110 McKenzie, *Getting By*, p. 168.

111 Pierre Bourdieu and Loïc Wacquant, *An Invitation to Reflexive Sociology* (Chicago: University of Chicago Press, 1992), p. 167.

112 Beverley Skeggs, *Formations of Class & Gender* (London: Sage, 1997), p. 82.

113 Landesman, 'Is snobbery as bad as racism?'.

114 Angela Nagle, 'Goodbye, Pepe', *Baffler*, 15 August 2017.

115 Nick Srnicek and Alex Williams, *Inventing the Future: Postcapitalism and a World Without Work* (London: Verso, 2015), p. 14.

116 Rajini Vaidyanathan, 'Confessions of a call-centre scammer', *BBC News*, 8 March 2020.

Part II: Race

1 Frantz Fanon, *Black Skin, White Masks* (New York: Grove Press, 1967), p. 10.

2 Jeffrey Boakye, *Black, Listed* (London: Little Brown, 2019), p. 285.

3 Edward Said, *Orientalism* (London: Penguin Classics, 2019), p. 11.

4 Ibid., p. 270.

5 Ibid., p. 273.

6 Ibid., p. 39.

7 Dorothy L. Hodgson, ' "Once Intrepid Warriors": Modernity and the Production of Maasai Masculinities', *Ethnology*, vol. 38, no. 2 (1999), p. 134.

8 Jessica Hatcher, 'The Masai Mara: "It will not be long before it's gone"', *Guardian*, 23 August 2013.

9 Said, *Orientalism*, pp. 150, 234 and 247.

10 Hodgson, '"Once Intrepid Warriors"', pp. 136 and 142.

11 Ibid., p. 122.

12 Ibid., p. 134.

13 Asef Bayat, 'Revolution without Movement, Movement without Revolution: Comparing Islamic Activism in Iran and Egypt', *Comparative Studies in Society and History*, vol. 40, no. 1 (1998), pp. 136–69.

14 Vera Chok, 'Yellow', in Shukla, *Good Immigrant*, p. 90.

15 Eric Kaufmann, *Whiteshift* (London: Allen Lane, 2018), p. 445.

16 Rakesh Kochhar and Anthony Cilluffo, 'Key findings on the rise in income inequality within America's racial and ethnic groups', Pew Research Center, 12 July 2018.

17 'Racial Economic Inequality', Inequality.org, https://inequality.org/facts/racial-inequality/#racial-wealth-divide.

18 Thomas Chatterton Williams, *Self-Portrait in Black and White: Unlearning Race* (New York and London: W. W. Norton, 2019), p. 75.

19 Cherry Wilson, 'Why 14 black male Cambridge students posed for this photo', *BBC News*, 3 May 2017.

20 MappingPoliceViolence.org.

21 Williams, *Self-Portrait*, p. 146.

22 Ibid., p. 108.

23 David Cortez, 'Latinxs in La Migra: Why They Join and Why It Matters', *Political Research Quarterly*, vol. 74, no. 3 (2020).

24 Todd Richmond, 'Officer accused in Floyd's death opened fire on 2 people', Associated Press, 29 May 2020.

25 Sabrina Tavernise, 'They Fled Asia as Refugees. Now They Are Caught in the Middle of Minneapolis', *New York Times*, 1 July 2020.

26 Kaufmann, *Whiteshift*, p. 323.

Chapter 3

1 Said, *Orientalism*, p. 276.

2 Ibid., p. 278.

3 Eric Kaufmann, *Whiteshift*, pp. 82–6.

4 Ibid., p. 350.

5 Ibid., p. 507.

6 Geraldo Cadava, 'Op-Ed: Is the Republican Party poised for a comeback with Latinos?', *Los Angeles Times*, 25 May 2020.

7 Ian Haney López and Tony Gavito, 'This Is How Biden Should Approach the Latino Vote', *New York Times*, 18 September 2020.

8 Jennifer Medina, 'The Macho Appeal of Donald Trump', *New York Times*, 14 October 2020.

9 'National and Five State Survey of the 2020 Latino Electorate', UnidosUS and Latino Decisions, 5 August 2019.

10 Jennifer Medina, 'The Macho Appeal of Donald Trump', *New York Times*, 14 October 2020.

11 Isvett Verde, 'Some Latinos Voted for Trump. Get Over It', *New York Times*, 5 November 2020.

12 Paul Gilroy, 'The Sugar You Stir', in Gilroy, Grossberg and McRobbie, *Without Guarantees*, p. 130.

13 Tasha S. Philpot, *Conservative But Not Republican: The Paradox of Party Identification and Ideology Among African Americans* (Cambridge: Cambridge University Press, 2017); Chryl N. Laird and Ismail K. White, *Steadfast Democrats: How Social Forces Shape Black Political Behavior* (Princeton: Princeton University Press, 2020).

14 Noah Y. Kim, 'How Andrew Yang Quieted the Asian American Right', *Atlantic*, 3 February 2020.

15 Cecilia Hyunjung Mo, 'Why Asian Americans don't vote Republican', *Conversation*, 2 November 2015.

16 Akala, *Natives*, p. 14.

17 'Perceptions and Reality', Ipsos MORI.

18 Omar Khan and Debbie Weekes-Bernard, 'This is Still About Us: Why Ethnic Minorities See Immigration Differently', Runnymede Report on Race and Immigration, 2015.

19 Nazia Parveen, 'Why do some ethnic minority voters want to leave the EU?', *Guardian*, 1 July 2016.

20 Khan and Weekes-Bernard, 'This is Still About Us'.

21 Ben Judah, *This Is London* (London: Picador, 2016), pp. 274–5 and 285.

22 Paul Bickley and Nathan Mladin, 'Religious London: Faith in a global city', Report by the Theos think tank, 2020.

23 Wilson, *Finding a Voice*, p. 32.

24 Azadeh Moaveni, 'The Garment of Terrorism', *London Review of Books*, 30 August 2018.

25 Alison Shaw, 'Kinship, cultural preference and immigration', *Journal of Royal Anthropological Institute*, vol. 7, no. 2 (2001), pp. 315–34.

26 Vron Ware, *Who Cares About Britishness? A Global View of the National Identity Debate* (London: Arcadia Books, 2007).

27 Chris Gourlay, 'UK Muslims are Europe's most patriotic', *Sunday Times*, 13 December 2009.

28 'Boycotting France is ignoring the reality of its ideals: the appeal of Muslim intellectuals to "concord and union"', *Le Monde*, 31 October 2020.

29 Maya Rao, 'Some Minneapolis black leaders speak out against City Council's moves to defund police', *Star Tribune*, 2 July 2020.

30 YouGov/Renie Anjeh Survey Results, 2020.

31 Paul Gilroy, *There Ain't No Black in the Union Jack* (London: Routledge, 2010), pp. 60–1.

32 Gargi Bhattacharyya, 'Racial Neoliberal Britain?', in Nisha Kapoor, Virinder S.

Kalra and James Rhodes (eds), *The State of Race* (Basingstoke: Palgrave Macmillan, 2013), pp. 44–6.

33 Paul Gilroy, *Small Acts: Thoughts on the Politics of Black Cultures* (London: Serpent's Tail, 1993), p. 230.

34 Akala, *Natives*, pp. 14–17.

35 Ibid., p. 43.

36 Rob Waters, *Thinking Black* (Oakland: University of California Press, 2019), p. 187.

37 Interview with Louis Theroux, BBC Radio 4, 15 August 2020.

38 Lawrence, *Me, Me, Me*, p. 153.

39 Hudson, *Lowborn*, p. 216.

40 Ekpoudom, 'The Sticks'.

41 E. Alex Jung, 'RuPaul on His First Emmy Nomination, Donald Trump, and Hillary Clinton', *Vulture*, 12 August 2016.

42 Donovan X. Ramsey, 'The Political Education of Killer Mike', *GQ*, 8 July 2020.

43 'Spanish-speaking Taco Bell worker fired for refusing English-speaker', *BBC News*, 15 September 2018.

44 Ashni Lakhani, 'I'm Bengali, my boyfriend was black – and my mum freaked out', *BBC News*, 20 October 2019.

45 'Twitter users falsely claim #BLM protesters trashed Gujarati restaurant in London', *Barfi Culture*, 15 June 2020.

46 Waters, *Thinking Black*, p. 78.

47 Owen Jones, 'Muslims and LGBTQ people should stand together, not fight each other', *Guardian*, 11 April 2019.

48 'Actress exits musical over anti-gay post', *BBC News*, 22 March 2019.

49 'Over a third of British Asians say same-sex relationships "unacceptable" ', *Gay Star News*, 13 August 2018.

50 'Junior Flemmings: Phoenix Rising midfielder gets six-game ban for homophobic slur', *BBC News*, 6 October 2020.

51 'Black Trans Lives Matter: "We're tired of having to pick sides" ', BBC Three, 15 June 2020.

52 Wilson, *Finding a Voice*, p. 20.

53 Waters, *Thinking Black*, p. 76.

54 Andrew Liu, 'Blaming China for coronavirus isn't just dangerous. It misses the point', *Guardian*, 10 April 2020.

55 'Coronavirus: Oprah warns black Americans about outbreak', *BBC News*, 13 April 2020.

56 Sobolewska and Ford, *Brexitland*, pp. 70 and 62.

57 Ibid., p. 7.

58 Ibid., pp. 40 and 45–6.

59 Ibid., p. 236.

60 Ibid., p. 214.

Chapter 4

1 Boakye, *Black, Listed*, pp. 169–72.

2 Martin Barker, *The New Racism: Conservatives and the Ideology of the Tribe* (London: Junction Books, 1981).

3 Quoted in Dick Hebdige, *Subculture: the meaning of style* (London: Routledge, 1991), p. 56.

4 Akala, *Natives*, p. 168.

5 Paul Gilroy, *Against Race: Imagining Political Culture Beyond the Color Line* (Cambridge, MA: Harvard University Press, 2001), p. 23.

6 Zygmunt Bauman, *Life in Fragments* (Cambridge: Polity Press, 1995), p. 119.

7 Gilroy, *Against Race*, p. 185.

8 Ta-Nehisi Coates, 'I'm Not Black – I'm Kanye', *Atlantic*, 7 May 2018.

9 Musab Younis, 'Bitch Nation', *London Review of Books*, 7 February 2019.

10 Ibid.

11 Salena Godden, 'Shade', in Shukla, *Good Immigrant*, p. 199.

12 Dominic Cadogan, '"I Can't Breathe" Beauty Looks Are the Last Thing We Need Right Now', *Dazed*, 2 June 2020.

13 Boakye, *Black, Listed*, p. 11.

14 Josh Hall, 'Does BBC Radio Still Have a Diversity Problem?', *Vice*, 29 January 2014.

15 Briana Younger, 'From Prince to Whitney to Nicki: The Plight of the Black Pop Star', *Vice*, 21 October 2020.

16 Akala, *Natives*, pp. 154–5.

17 Gilroy, *Against Race*, p. 180.

18 Ibid., pp. 253–5.

19 Kelefa Sanneh, 'How Post Malone Became Pop's King of Heartbreak', *GQ*, 2 March 2020.

20 'X Factor's Alexandra Burke reveals music industry racism', *BBC News*, 20 June 2020.

21 Lola Young, 'Unfixing the Singular black (Female) Subject', in Gilroy, Grossberg and McRobbie, *Without Guarantees*, p. 419.

22 Gilroy, *Black Atlantic*, p. 107.

23 Ibid., p. 186.

24 Boakye, *Black, Listed*, p. 172.

25 Ibid., p. 159.

26 Kim Knott, 'Hinduism, colonialism, and modernity', in Kim Knott (ed.), *Hinduism: A Very Short Introduction* (Oxford: Oxford University Press, 2016), p. 71.

27 Aoife McElwain, 'Halloween: Forget pumpkins – carved turnips are truly frightening', *Irish Times*, 27 October 2018.

28 David Agren, 'Mexico City's James Bond-inspired Day of the Dead parade gets mixed reviews', *Guardian*, 30 October 2016.

29 'The *Guardian* view of *Dad's Army*: it was wonderful but we must now move on', *Guardian*, 29 July 2018.

30 Ibid., p. 180.

31 Iain Chambers, 'Modernities, Music and the Journey of Identity', in Gilroy, Grossberg and McRobbie, *Without Guarantees*, p. 75.

32 Reza Zia-Ebrahimi, 'Self-Orientalization and Dislocation: The Uses and Abuses of the "Aryan" Discourse in Iran', *Iranian Studies*, vol. 44, no. 4 (2011), pp. 445–72.

33 Neil MacGregor, 'From gardens to pop music, how the world sees Britain', *The Times*, 4 January 2019.

34 Gilroy, *Black Atlantic*, p. 199.

35 Ibid., p. 27.

36 'The Sohofication of Restaurants', *Vittles*, 6 September 2020.

37 Joanna Fuertes, 'The Bourdainification of Food Travel', *Vittles*, 4 November 2020.

38 George Reynolds, 'Great white shark: George Reynolds takes a bite out of Bourdain', *Civilian*, 12 February 2017.

39 Gilroy, *Black Atlantic*, pp. 220–1.

40 Ibid., pp. 250–1.

41 Quoted in Gilroy, *Black Atlantic*, p. 219; Williams, *Self-Portrait*, p. 18.

Chapter 5

1 Pankaj Mishra, 'Flailing States', *London Review of Books*, 16 July 2020.

2 Chenchen Zhang, 'The curious rise of "the white left" as a Chinese internet insult', OpenDemocracy.net, 11 May 2017.

3 Gideon Rachman, 'The US and China's dangerous blame game will do no good', *Financial Times*, 4 May 2020.

4 Aris Roussinos, 'The irresistible rise of the civilisation-state', *UnHerd*, 6 August 2020.

5 Zheng Wang, *Never Forget National Humiliation: Historical Memory in Chinese Politics and Foreign Relations* (New York: Columbia University Press, 2012).

6 Shadi Hamid, 'China Is Avoiding Blame by Trolling the World', *Atlantic,* 19 March 2020.

7 Lily Kuo, 'Trump sparks anger by calling coronavirus the "Chinese virus" ', *Guardian*, 17 March 2020.

8 Selam Gebrekidan, Matt Apuzzo, Amy Qin and Javier C. Hernández, 'In Hunt for Source, W.H.O. Let China Take Charge', *New York Times*, 3 November 2020.

9 Jason Horowitz, Emma Bubola and Elisabetta Povoledo, 'Italy, Pandemic's New Epicenter, Has Lessons for the World', *New York Times*, 21 March 2020.

10 Ware, *Who Cares About Britishness?*, pp. 120–1.

11 Slavoj Žižek, 'Why Donald Trump is wrong about American history and liberals are wrong about the West', *Independent*, 5 September 2017.

12 Caitlin Moran, 'Caitlin Moran's Celebrity Watch: Ben Bradley too busy with merch to worry about meals', *The Times*, 29 October 2020.

13 Vasuki Shastry, 'When I moved from India to the US, I believed in the American dream. Now I realize how terrifyingly similar both countries are', *Independent*, 5 June 2020.

14 MacGregor, 'From gardens to pop music'.

15 Riz Ahmed, 'Airports and Auditions', in Shukla, *Good Immigrant*, p. 162.

16 Akala, *Natives*, p. 87.

17 Baldwin, *Notes of a Native Son*, pp. 168–9.

18 Gilroy, *Black Atlantic*, p. 16.

19 Williams, *Self-Portrait*, p. 27.

20 Akala, *Natives*, p. 283.

21 Aris Roussinos, 'Britain should stay out of Cold War II', *UnHerd*, 8 June 2020.

22 Roussinos, 'Irresistible rise of the civilisation-state'.

23 Emily Cousens, 'I Teach at Oxford, But I Don't Want It to Win the Coronavirus Vaccine Race', *Huffington Post*, 24 April 2020.

24 Oliver Wiseman, 'Letter from Washington: Nancy Pelosi and the coming vaccine wars', *Critic*, 10 October 2020.

25 Inua Ellams, 'Cutting Through', in Shukla, *Good Immigrant*, p. 135.

26 Kennetta Hammond Perry, *London Is the Place for Me* (Oxford: Oxford University Press, 2015), p. 8.

27 Cited in Waters, *Thinking Black*, p. 11.

28 Judah, *This Is London*, p. 385.

29 Ibid., p. 66.

30 Stephen Bush, 'Why the British empire alone cannot explain the politics of the present', *New Statesman*, 10 February 2021.

31 Anna Sauerbrey, 'A Turkish-German Couple May Save Us from the Virus. So Why Is Germany Uneasy?', *New York Times*, 2 December 2020.

32 Bim Adewunmi, 'The everyday microaggressions I experience as a black woman in Berlin', *Guardian*, 8 December 2013.

33 Ed West, 'Everything you know about Europe is wrong', *UnHerd*, 22 January 2020.

34 Williams, *Self-Portrait*, p. 63.

35 Annie Zaidi, *Bread, Cement, Cactus: A Memoir of Belonging and Dislocation* (Cambridge: Cambridge University Press, 2020), pp. 17–18.

36 Kumar Uttam, 'BJP youth wing plans drive for "NaMo 2019"', *Hindustan Times*, 19 December 2018.

37 Rahul V. Pisharody, 'Telangana: Upset over Trump contracting Covid, his ardent fan dies of cardiac arrest', *Indian Express*, 12 October 2020.

38 Kunwar Khuldune Shahid, 'A third of Muslim voters backed Trump. Why?', *Spectator*, 11 November 2020.

39 Judah, *This Is London*, p. 310.

40 Ibid., p. 345.

41 Ibid., p. 392.

42 Akala, *Natives*, p. 160.

43 kihana miraya ross, 'Call It What It Is: Anti-blackness', *New York Times*, 4 June 2020.

44 Ellen E. Jones, 'Why do light-skinned women dominate the pop charts?', *Guardian*, 13 July 2019.

45 'Miss Algeria beauty queen Khadija Ben Hamou hits back at racist abuse', *BBC News*, 9 January 2019.

46 'China McDonald's apologises for Guangzhou ban on black people', *BBC News*, 14 April 2020.

47 'Esha Gupta: Has Instagram exposed everyday racism in India?', *BBC News*, 1 February 2019.

48 Judah, *This Is London*, p. 66.

49 Megha Mohan, 'Blasian love: The day we introduced our black and Asian families', *BBC News*, 11 March 2020.

Chapter 6

1 James Jordan, '"The Most Varied, Colourful, Confusing Hubub in the World": The East End, television and the documentary imagination, July 1939', in Craig-Norton, Hoffman and Kushner, *Migrant Britain*, p. 255.

2 Nissim Mizrachim, 'Beyond the Garden and the Jungle: On the Social Limits of Human Rights Discourse in Israel', *Ma'asei Mishpat*, no. 4 (2011), p. 52.

3 Jemele Hill, 'The Anti-Semitism We Didn't See', *Atlantic*, 13 July 2020.

4 Pankaj Mishra, *Age of Anger* (London: Allen Lane, 2017), p. 207.

5 Ibid., pp. 240–2.

6 Gilroy, *Black Atlantic*, p. 23.

7 Quoted in Mishra, *Age of Anger*, pp. 146–7.

8 Gilroy, *Black Atlantic*, p. 207.

9 Ta-Nehisi Coates, *Between the World and Me* (Melbourne: Text Publishing, 2015), p. 115.

10 Gilroy, *Black Atlantic*, p. 13.

11 Jodi Burkett, *Constructing Post-Imperial Britain* (Basingstoke: Palgrave, 2013), p. 137.

12 Jack Dromey and Graham Taylor, *Grunwick: The Workers' Story* (London: Lawrence & Wishart, 1978), p. 119.

13 Helen Lewis, *Difficult Women: A History of Feminism in 11 Fights* (London: Vintage, 2020), p. 37.

14 Noel Ignatiev, *How the Irish Became White* (London: Routledge, 2008), p. 10.

15 Ibid., p. 2.

16 Ibid., p. 16.

17 Ibid., p. 159.

18 Ibid., pp. 47–50.

19 Ibid., p. 56.

20 Ibid., p. 81.

21 Ibid., p. 102.

22 Geoffrey Wheatcroft, 'The Finchley Factor', *London Review of Books*, 13 September 2018.

23 https://twitter.com/PennyRed/status/796276848162439169.

24 https://twitter.com/OwenJones84/status/579375589410381825.

25 Gilroy, *Against Race*, p. 220.

26 Hirsch, *Brit(ish)*, pp. 140–1 and 289.

27 Gilroy, *Against Race*, p. 237.

28 Eddo-Lodge, *Why I'm No Longer Talking*, pp. 215–18.

29 Gilroy, *Against Race*, p. 221.

30 Said, *Orientalism*, p. 45.

Part III: Sex

Chapter 7

1 See for example Noreena Hertz, 'Why Loneliness Fuels Populism', *Financial Times*, 24 September 2020; Jeffrey Boakye, *Hold Tight: Black Masculinity, Millennials and the Meaning of Grime* (London: Influx Press, 2018); and Owusu, *Safe*.

2 Arwa Mahdawi, 'Men are less likely to wear masks – another sign that toxic masculinity kills', *Guardian*, 16 May 2020; and 'If women are hesitant about the vaccine, it's because the health industry hasn't earned their trust', *Guardian*, 19 December 2020.

3 Helen Smith, 'Working-class Ideas and Experiences of Sexuality in Twentieth-Century Britain: Regionalism as a Category of Analysis', *Twentieth Century British History*, vol. 29, no. 1 (2018), p. 71. See also Matt Houlbrook, *Queer London: Perils and Pleasures in the Sexual Metropolis* (Chicago: University of Chicago Press, 2005).

4 Smith, 'Working-Class Ideas and Experiences of Sexuality', pp. 72–6.

5 Jia Tolentino, *Trick Mirror: Reflections on Self-Delusion* (London: 4th Estate, 2019), p. 24.

6 Tom Chivers, *The AI Does Not Hate You* (London: Weidenfeld & Nicolson, 2019), p. 215.

7 Hugo Rifkind, 'Nothing wrong with being a pick up artist', *The Times*, 22 November 2014.

8 Diana Fleischman, 'Uncanny Vulvas', *Jacobite*, 24 April 2018.

9 Wesley Yang, *The Souls of Yellow Folk: Essays* (New York and London: W. W. Norton, 2018), p. 147.

10 Grayson Perry, *The Descent of Man* (London: Penguin, 2017).

11 Ibid., p. 54.

Chapter 8

1 Beatrix Campbell, *The Iron Ladies: Why Do Women Vote Tory?* (London: Virago, 1987), 1975.

2 Gail Braybon, *Women Workers in the First World War: The British Experience* (London: Croom Helm, 1981), pp. 72 and 226.

3 Susan Pedersen, 'One-Man Ministry', *London Review of Books*, 8 February 2018.

4 Duncan Tanner, 'Gender, Civic Culture and Politics in South Wales: Explaining Labour Municipal Policy, 1918–1939', in Matthew Worley (ed.), *Labour's Grassroots* (Farnham: Ashgate, 2005), pp. 175–6.

5 Campbell, *Iron Ladies*, p. 73.

NOTES

6 Angelique Chrisafis, Kate Connolly and Angela Giuffrida, 'From Le Pen to Alice Weidel: how the European far-right set its sights on women', *Guardian*, 29 January 2019.

7 Caroline Marie Lancaster, 'Why the radical right is no longer the exclusive domain of older, male voters', *LSE Blogs*, 24 September 2019.

8 Daniel Greenberg, Maxine Najle, Oyindamola Bola and Robert P. Jones, 'Fifty Years After Stonewall: Widespread Support for LGBT Issues – Findings from American Values Atlas 2018', *PRRI*, 26 March 2019.

9 Caroline Criado Perez, *Invisible Women: Data Bias in a World Designed for Men* (London: Chatto & Windus, 2019), p. 269.

10 Georgina Roberts, 'What I've Learned: Glenda Jackson', *The Times*, 8 August 2020.

11 Jessica Barrett, 'Maestra author L. S. Hilton: "Online porn means sex scenes have to be direct these days. No euphemisms"', *I*, 4 August 2018.

12 'Lizzo says body positivity has become too "commercialised" and "cool"', *BBC News*, 25 September 2020.

13 Helen Lewis, 'The Mythology of Karen', *Atlantic*, 19 August 2020.

14 Robin Abcarian, 'Is the "Karen" meme sexist? Maybe, but it's also apt', *Los Angeles Times*, 23 May 2020.

15 Catherine MacKinnon, 'From Practice to Theory, or What is a White Woman Anyway?', *Yale Journal of Law and Feminism*, vol. 4, no. 13 (1991).

16 Anne Helen Petersen, *Can't Even: How Millennials Became the Burnout Generation* (London: Chatto & Windus, 2021), pp. 235–6.

17 James Hamblin, 'Ask Dr Hamblin: Am I Wrong to Tell Someone to Pull Up Her Mask?', *Atlantic*, 27 January 2021.

18 'Mo'Nique takes on Amy Schumer in a row over Netflix', *BBC News*, 25 January 2018.

19 Rahila Gupta, 'Why abolishing the police and turning to the community won't protect women', *Independent*, 21 June 2020.

20 Louise Perry, 'Why defunding the police will hurt women most', *UnHerd*, 8 September 2020.

21 Janine Fitzpatrick, Jessie Davies and Benjamin Sveen, ' "Get over it": A NSW school's failure to protect students from a predator left this family broken', *ABC News*, 17 October 2020.

22 Lewis, *Difficult Women*, p. 120.

23 *Observer*, 1 December 1974, and the *Hornsey Journal*, 21 April 1978.

24 Paul Johnson, 'Failure of the Feminists', *Spectator*, 12 March 2011.

25 G. E. Maguire, *Conservative Women: A History of Women and the Conservative Party, 1874–1997* (London: Macmillan, 1998), p. 176.

26 David Swift, 'From "I'm not a feminist, but . . ." to "call me an old-fashioned feminist . . .": conservative women in parliament and "feminism", 1979–2017', *Women's History Review*, vol. 28, no. 2 (2019), pp. 317–36.

27 Cas Mudde, 'The Paternalistic Fallacy of the "Nordic Model" of Prostitution', *Huffington Post*, 4 August 2016.

28 Tolentino, *Trick Mirror*, p. 257.

29 Ibid., pp. 253–6.

Chapter 9

1 Daryl Leeworthy, 'For our common cause: Sexuality and left politics in South Wales, 1967–1985', *Contemporary British History*, vol. 30, no. 2 (2016), p. 273.

2 Smith, 'Working-Class Ideas and Experiences of Sexuality', p. 76.

3 Caspar Salmon, 'LGBT people need to rediscover their rage in this age of protest', *Guardian*, 2 April 2018.

4 Lewis, *Difficult Women*, p. 197.

5 Graeme Archer, 'Does Labour understand why it lost?', *UnHerd*, 16 December 2019.

6 Bret Stephens, 'Meet a Secret Trump Voter', *New York Times*, 28 September 2020.

7 'Norway Finance Minister Receives Gay Friends Award', *The Nordic Page*, undated.

8 Wilt Chalk, 'Why gay French men are voting far right', *BBC News*, 20 April 2017.

9 Eleanor Formby, 'Why you should think twice before you talk about "the LGBT community"', *Conversation*, 8 August 2017.

10 'Joe Lycett calls for better LGBT dialogue', *BBC News*, 26 March 2019.

11 Tolentino, *Trick Mirror*, p. 246.

12 Gilroy, *Against Race*, p. 126.

13 Matthew Smith, 'Where does the British public stand on transgender rights?', YouGov, 16 July 2020.

14 Karen L. Blair and Rhea Ashley Hoskin, 'Transgender Exclusion from the World of Dating: Patterns of Acceptance and Rejection of Hypothetical Trans Dating Partners as a Function of Sexual and Gender Identity', *Journal of Social and Personal Relationships*, vol. 36, no. 7 (2019), pp. 2074–95.

15 Dave Haslam, *Not Abba: The Real Story of the 1970s* (London: 4th Estate, 2005), pp. 132–3.

16 Chaka L. Bachmann and Becca Gooch, 'LGBT in Britain: Home and Communities', Stonewall, 2018.

17 Emily Belfiore, 'Jonathan Van Ness Says J. K. Rowling's Gender "Fears" Are "Rooted in White Supremacy"', *E! Online*, 24 June 2020.

18 R. L. Stotzer, 'Data Sources Hinder Our Understanding of Transgender Murders', *American Journal of Public Health*, vol. 107, no. 9 (2017), pp. 1362–3.

19 Falah Gulzar, 'Pakistan: Transgender activist shot dead in Peshawar, netizens demand #JusticeforGulPanra', *Gulf News*, 9 September 2020.

Part IV: Youth

Chapter 10

1 https://blog.euromonitor.com/special-report-the-worlds-youngest-populations/.

2 'When are they ready to leave the nest?', Eurostat, 14 May 2019.

3 United Nations, Department of Economic and Social Affairs, Population Division, 2013, https://www.un.org/en/development/desa/population/publications/pdf/fertility/worldFertilityReport2013.pdf.

4 'Education at a Glance 2019', OECD, 2019.

5 Diyora Shadijanova, 'What Gen Z'ers Really Think of Millennials', *Vice*, 18 June 2020.

6 Valerie Richardson, 'Only 29% of Americans want to drop "Redskins," while half want to keep it: Poll', *Washington Times*, 18 July 2020.

7 Phoebe Luckhurst, 'It's a Londoner's biggest nightmare – I've got to meet the neighbours', *Evening Standard*, 31 May 2018.

8 Libby Purves, 'The self-service revolution making us steal', *The Times*, 4 February 2019.

9 Tolentino, *Trick Mirror*, p. 66.

10 Zaidi, *Bread, Cement, Cactus*, p. 110.

11 Rhys Blakely, 'Millennials all over the world have lost faith in democracy', *The Times*, 20 October 2020.

12 Sobolewska and Ford, *Brexitland*, p. 272.

13 Tobias Phibbs, 'Confessions of a student Marxist', *UnHerd*, 17 September 2020.

14 Eric Kaufmann, 'Are young people turning to the Right?', *UnHerd*, 8 July 2020.

15 Mick Hume, *Revolting! How the Establishment are Undermining Democracy and What They're Afraid Of* (London: William Collins, 2017), p. 214.

16 Eric Kaufmann, 'Are young people turning to the Right?', *UnHerd*, 8 July 2020.

17 Yascha Mounk, 'Americans Strongly Dislike PC Culture', *Atlantic*, 10 October 2018.

18 Ben Bryant and Wesley Stephenson, 'How LGBTQ+ hate crime is committed by young people against young people', *BBC News*, 28 December 2018.

19 Geoffrey Skelley and Anna Wiederkehr, 'Trump Is Losing Ground with White Voters But Gaining Among Black And Hispanic Americans', *FiveThirtyEight*, 19 October 2020.

20 Kennedy, *Authentocrats*, p. 195.

21 Boakye, *Black, Listed*, p. 285.

22 William Davies, 'Against Responsibility', *London Review of Books*, 8 November 2018.

23 Andrew O'Hagan, 'I'm being a singer', *London Review of Books*, 8 October 2020.

24 Dolly Alderton, *Everything I Know about Love* (London: Penguin, 2018).

25 Will Smale, 'Top business tips for 2016', *BBC News*, 28 December 2015.

26 Maggie Doherty, 'Get a Brazilian', *London Review of Books*, 13 September 2018.

27 David Brooks, 'The Organization Kid', *Atlantic*, April 2001.

28 Brandon J. Graham, 'The University Myth', in Shukla and Jones, *Rife*, p. 264.

29 Tobias Phibbs, 'The Left's lost decade', *UnHerd*, 13 November 2020.

30 Ross Douthat, 'The Real White Fragility', *New York Times*, 18 July 2020.

31 Tolentino, *Trick Mirror*, p. 194.

32 Elizabeth Nolan Brown, 'Rise of the Hipster Capitalist', Reason.com, October 2014.

33 Stephen Pritchard, 'Hipsters and artists are the gentrifying foot soldiers of capitalism', *Guardian*, 13 September 2016.

34 Phibbs, 'Confessions of a student Marxist'.

35 Luca Bernardi, 'Depression and Political Predispositions: Almost Blue?', *Party Politics* (2020).

36 Polly Mackenzie, 'There is no mental illness epidemic', *UnHerd*, 20 January 2020.

37 Tom Chivers, 'Do we really have a "suicidal generation"?', *UnHerd*, 4 February 2019.

38 Cassandra Russell, 'Degrees of Mental Illness', *Critic*, July/August 2020.

39 'Children's hospitals admissions for suicidal thoughts, actions double during past decade', *AAP News*, 4 May 2017.

40 Benoit Denizet-Lewis, 'Why Are More American Teenagers than Ever Suffering from Severe Anxiety?', *New York Times*, 11 October 2017.

41 However, specific mental health problems such as psychosis appear to disproportionately affect black men, and black people are more likely than whites to be sectioned under the Mental Health Act than white people.

42 Clare Wilson, 'Mindfulness and meditation can worsen depression and anxiety', *New Scientist*, 14 August 2020.

43 David Aaronovitch, 'Getting to the heart of why girls self-harm', *The Times*, 29 August 2020.

44 'There is no student mental health crisis', *UnHerd*, 30 September 2020.

45 James Williams, *Stand Out of Our Light* (Cambridge: Cambridge University Press, 2018), p. 72.

46 Will Hutton, 'The bad news is we're dying early in Britain – and it's all down to "shit-life syndrome"', *Observer*, 19 August 2018.

47 Roger McNamee, *Zucked: Waking up to the Facebook Catastrophe* (London: HarperCollins, 2019), p. 17.

48 Jean M. Twenge, 'Have Smartphones Destroyed a Generation', *Atlantic*, September 2017.

49 Richard Seymour, *The Twittering Machine* (London: Indigo Press, 2019), p. 26.

50 Ibid., pp. 27 and 47.

51 Janice Turner, 'We've been turned into iPhone crackheads', *The Times*, 1 December 2018.

52 McNamee, *Zucked*, p. 4.

53 Tolentino, *Trick Mirror*, p. 30.

54 Williams, *Stand Out of Our Light*, p. 101.

55 McNamee, *Zucked*, pp. 84 and 203.

56 Emily Bootle, 'How the Kardashians commodified authenticity', *New Statesman*, 10 September 2020.

57 Williams, *Stand Out of Our Light*, p. 23.

58 Iain Chambers, 'A miniature history of the Walkman', *New Formations*, no. 11 (1990).

59 Arwa Mahdawi, 'Is 2019 the year you should finally quit Facebook?', *Guardian*, 21 December 2018.

60 Jessica L. Strübel and Trent A. Petrie, 'Love Me Tinder: Objectification and Psychosocial Well-Being', poster at the annual convention of the American Psychological Association, 4 August 2016.

61 Suzanne Bearne, 'Are "swipe left" dating apps bad for our mental health?', *BBC News*, 6 September 2018.

62 Rosie Collington, 'The mood apps profiting from your mental illness', *New Statesman*, 3 December 2018.

63 'Swansea University study says selfies fuel narcissism', *BBC News*, 17 November 2018.

64 Tolentino, *Trick Mirror*, p. 80.

65 Sarah Manavis, 'How Instagram's plastic surgery filters are warping the way we see our faces', *New Statesman*, 29 October 2019.

66 'Selena Gomez: Instagram "would make me depressed"', *BBC News*, 13 June 2019.

67 Sian Griffiths, Rosamund Urwin and Caroline Wheeler, 'Revealed: How Big Tech pushes teens like Molly Russell to suicide', *Sunday Times*, 27 January 2019.

68 Sean Coughlan, ' "Sadfishing" social media warning from school heads', *BBC News*, 1 October 2019.

69 Seymour, *Twittering Machine*, p. 72.

70 Ibid., p. 159.

71 Tolentino, *Trick Mirror*, p. 39.

72 Seymour, *Twittering Machine*, p. 172.

73 Ibid., p. 113.

74 Williams, *Stand Out of Our Light*, p. 59.

75 Kwasi Kwarteng et al., *Britannia Unchained: Global Lessons for Growth and Prosperity* (London: Palgrave Macmillan, 2012).

76 Tess Brigham, 'A "millennial therapist" explains why young people hate their jobs – and what to do about it', *CNBC*, 30 July 2019.

77 Anthee Carassava, 'Model Sinead McNamara left no suicide note on superyacht owned by Mexican billionaire', *The Times*, 4 September 2018.

78 Vicky Baker, 'Anna Sorokin: The trial of New York's fake heiress', *BBC News*, 26 April 2019.

79 Piers Morgan, 'My sincere, heartfelt 10-point tribute to the Kardashians – a bunch of talentless narcissistic brain-dead bimbos whose absurd antics have shown the world how NOT to behave', *Daily Mail*, 9 September 2020.

80 Emalie Marthe, 'Obama Blames Kimye, Not Corrupt Politicians, for the Death of the American Dream', *Vice*, 17 August 2013.

81 Tracy McVeigh, 'Kim Kardashian: how did she become such a threat to western civilisation?', *Guardian*, 23 June 2012.

82 Tolentino, *Trick Mirror*, p. 174.

83 Ibid., p. 44.

84 'The psychology of stanning', *BBC Bitesize*, undated.

85 Williams, *Stand Out of Our Light*, p. 101.

86 Bolu Babalola, 'Michaela Coel Looks Beyond Binaries with "I May Destroy You"', *Paper Mag*, 20 July 2020.

Conclusion

1 Gilroy, *Black Atlantic*, p. 32.

2 Jose Maria Barrero, Nicholas Bloom and Steven J. Davis, 'Why Working from Home Will Stick', BFI Working Paper, 22 April 2021.

3 Zaidi, *Bread, Cement, Cactus*, pp. 66–7.

4 Yang, *The Souls of Yellow Folk* pp. 195–6.

5 Ibid., p. 37.

6 Ibid., p. 67.

Index